Shine Brighter

CONTENTS

INTRODUCTION

While pondering how best to explain the purpose of this book, I happened to watch an episode of the Netflix series "The Crown." On this particular show, Prince Phillip–the husband of Queen Elizabeth II–was portrayed as anxiously preparing for a private conversation with the three Apollo 11 astronauts who had recently returned from the first moon landing. A skilled pilot himself, the prince was hoping that their experiences had generated some transcendent insights into the human condition and that somehow, they could help him find an answer to the existential question that had dominated his thoughts throughout the mission: "Does mankind have a destiny?" Sadly, he discovered that they had no life-changing, consciousness-raising insights that could resolve his query and bring peace to his unsettled mind. Instead, he concluded that the answer to his question can only be found individually, as each of us conducts a personal, searching, and life-long examination of mind and heart. I couldn't have said it better. That's what this book is about.

We are all saddled with the task of searching for an understanding of the "how" and "why" of our existence–especially the "why." Science, philosophy, history, and religion all have something of value to contribute to that endeavor, and I have included ideas from all four. They provide some insight into the nature of our existence and offer instructions on how we should live our lives, both individually and collectively, if we are to reach our highest and brightest potential as human beings. It is that innate desire to learn and improve that drives our efforts and shapes our eternal destinies. As twentieth century French philosopher Simone Weil put it, "At the center of the human heart is the longing for an absolute good, a longing which is always there and is never appeased by any object in this world."

The great philosophers and religious leaders throughout history understood that our existence involves much more than the brief period of time between conception and death. (As theologian Pierre Teilhard de Chardin once described our lives, "We are not human beings having a spiritual experience, we are spiritual beings having a human experience.") Each believed that materialism and individualism do not produce real happiness, but it is the degree to which our lives are in harmony with eternal truths and the quality of our relationships with others that most contribute to lasting happiness and joy. Each labored to find some additional pieces to the great Puzzle of Truth that life behooves each of us to complete. Committing to the pursuit of light and truth throughout our lives is key to accomplishing that goal. That is also what *Shine Brighter* is about. Its purpose is to assist you as you:

- **Envision your life** by defining yourself and your purpose in life from an enlightened, positive perspective.
- **Align your thoughts and actions** to be in harmony with that vision.
- **Turn your vision into reality** and achieve the most desirable outcomes for yourself, and your loved ones.

To aid in that effort, this book offers several tools that will help you to clarify your values, evaluate your choices, and select a meaningful direction for your life. It is intended to be a source of ideas and examples that stimulate you to fruitful action. So, throughout the book I will ask you not only to consider the principles it teaches, but most importantly, to act on them.

Yes, mankind has a destiny. A destiny that extends far beyond the cramped quarters of this singular speck of cosmic dust that we call home.

And as you will discover in the opening chapter of this book, the Creator has placed, just above our heads, an ever-present reminder of our options.

This destiny-determining process begins with two simple yet monumentally important endeavors:

- **Choosing** the kind of person you want to be.
- **Applying** the principles and practices that go with that choice to your roles as an individual; a spouse; a parent; and a citizen of your community, your nation, and the world.

Ultimately, the values and priorities you choose in this life will remain your values and priorities in the next. That's how your destiny is shaped. But the choice will always be yours to make. It's your life, your choice, and your destiny. Choose wisely.

CHAPTER 1 Preview

Life is short. Nevertheless, the choices we make during this paper-thin slice of time sandwiched between the endless before and the forever after will determine our fates in this life, and our destinies in the life to come. Scary thought? Probably, but not so much when we understand what those choices are and what outcomes they will produce. Then the process becomes relatively simple. Over time, making consistently good choices will produce predictably good outcomes, just as making consistently bad choices will produce predictably bad outcomes. The first step in understanding what constitutes good and bad choices is to identify the overarching choice that encompasses all the others. Let's begin that process.

3 KINDS OF PEOPLE

●●◖◖◖◖◖ ◖ ◖

"Maybe she lied," he thought angrily as he crouched under the table. "Maybe she's not coming back at all. Maybe this is some stupid grownup joke, like when Mom and Dad told me that they had eaten all of my Halloween candy."

"All I have to do is not *eat* the marshmallow," he kept reminding himself. "Easy-peasy."

He'd tried staring at it, petting it, squeezing it; he'd even gotten really close and (sniff, sniff) smelled it. That just made things worse. Now he had marshmallow smell in his nose and there was no way of getting it out.

Next, he tried singing jingles from the thousands of toothpaste, cigarette, beer, and Alka-Seltzer commercials he had seen on TV during his four short years of life. That worked for about two minutes.

Then he tried making faces in front of the giant mirror in the tiny, windowless basement room where he was confined. But he could still see the marshmallow in the mirror. Hiding under the table where he couldn't see or smell the marshmallow was his last resort.

He was beginning to doubt that he could wait any longer for the lady with the clip board to return. The smell of marshmallow was in his nose.

Images of last summer's camping trip and roasting marshmallows over the campfire filled his head. Cellular memories of the sticky-sweet taste of semi-burnt marshmallow mingled with chocolate and graham cracker were embedded in his tongue. It seemed like the whole world was conspiring against him. Maybe it was more than *any* four-year-old could resist.

"I'm gonna count to ten," he thought, "and if she isn't back when I get to ten, then...." Suddenly the door swung open and the lady with the clipboard entered the room.

"Freddie, I see you waited and didn't eat the marshmallow," she said with a smile. "Here's the second marshmallow I promised. Enjoy your treats!"

The 3 Categories

Imagine being one of the children at Stanford University's Bing Nursery School participating in this 1972 study by psychology professor Dr. Walter Mischel. The professor was testing the children's ability to delay gratification—to postpone satisfying their immediate desires in order to earn a greater reward, later. The giant mirror was a 2-way mirror that allowed the researchers to observe how the children responded to the challenge. How do you think you would have reacted at their age?

About one-third of the children ate the treat within three minutes—several, within thirty seconds. Another one-third struggled to wait and tried many of the distraction methods described above to avoid eating the spongey sweetness. Some waited longer than others, but they too eventually succumbed and ate the marshmallow before the researcher's return. The last one-third of the children managed to hold out for the full fifteen minutes, often employing many of the same tactics, and gleefully received the second treat as a reward for their self-control.

Ongoing research followed those same children for forty years after the initial study. It showed in large part, that the children's approach to the marshmallow dilemma reflected a general pattern of thinking and behavior that tended to remain consistent throughout their lives and that produced predictable results:

- Those who waited were more cooperative, worked better under pressure, and were more self-reliant and self-confident than their less-patient peers. They did better academically, in their relationships, in their career achievements, and experienced greater overall satisfaction with life.
- Those who didn't wait tended to be moodier, reacted more intensely to frustration, were more indecisive, and were more prone to jealousy and envy.

If the marshmallow study is reflective of the general population, our choices will someday place all of us into one of these three categories:

1. Those who make little or no effort to resist the temptations of life and as a result, never reach their full potential. (Or as a counseling client of mine once described them, these are people afflicted with "RFN disease"–they want what they want, and they want it "right freaking now!" Only, he used a different word.)
2. Those who may aspire to something better in life, but struggle to control their desire for immediate gratification and temporal satisfaction and as a result, miss out on a greater reward.
3. Those who successfully focus their attention on loftier goals and because of their patience and determination, receive the reward of a better life in the present, as well as in the future.

Benjamin Franklin once postulated, "All mankind is divided into three classes: those that are immovable, those that are movable, and those that move." Not only does social science and Ben Franklin's keen observations of human nature acknowledge this three-way division among people, it also appears to be a wisdom tradition that is present in many of the world's major religions.

For example, according to doctors of the Muslim religion, there are three incremental stages in the development of the human soul: Ammarah, Lawwarah, and Mutma'innah.

Tibetan Buddhism also teaches that the spiritual path to enlightenment involves progressing through three levels called "scopes," each representing progressively higher levels of understanding and altruism.

It was the Apostle Paul who described what the Christian world believes to be the three categories into which virtually all human beings will someday find themselves. When writing to fellow believers in the Greek city of Corinth about the doctrine of the resurrection of the dead, Paul taught that we will each face an appointed moment when our spirits and bodies will be reunited after death and we will stand before our Creator to account for the choices we have made in life. When that occurs, wrote Paul, our bodies will be restored to life in one of three states of heavenly glory that he compared to the glory of the sun, the moon, and the stars. When that moment arrives, our eternal destinies will be forever determined. We will either be sun people, moon people, or star people.

A Universe Within

Several philosophers and scientists have proposed a theory that the universe we inhabit is not the only one that exists. They promote the notion that multiple universes co-exist in varying dimensions of time and space, each containing different incarnations of you and me. They suggest that some of those incarnations may turn out to be better or worse versions of "you" than the one reading this book, but each will be the result of "your" choices, whichever the universe. While I am not a proponent of this theory, I am convinced of the importance of the choices we make in shaping our characters, both here and hereafter. As the apostle describes it, the Creator has given each of us a singular, me-defining opportunity to choose between good and evil. In doing so, we are each creating a template within our hearts and minds of a universe we will inherit someday and determining the role we will play in it—as a sun person, a moon person, or a star person.

Regardless of the broad array of religious and secular beliefs about what happens when we die, I feel that Paul's three-way description of the afterlife offers some practical guidance that can help us all as we make the important, everyday decisions of life. If there are going to be three kinds of people in Heaven as Paul described, it will be because there have been three kinds of people here, during our mortal lives. Understanding the attributes of these three kinds of people is essential if we are to make the choices that will produce the character traits we most desire, generate the greatest amount of happiness in our present and future lives, and potentially determine our eternal place of residence.

Let's ponder Paul's metaphors and what they might mean.

The Sun: The Greatest of Servants

Without the sun, life could not exist on Earth. We are literally dependent upon it for every breath we take because the sun makes photosynthesis possible so we have sufficient oxygen to breathe. The sun is our source of light and heat. It provides nutrition directly in the form of vitamin D, and indirectly through its essential role in the reproduction and growth of all the varieties of vegetation and microscopic organisms that serve as food for the various forms of life on this planet.

The sun's huge mass produces a gravitational field that reaches to the boundaries of the solar system and holds the planets in orbit around this superheated ball of light. Without the sun's influence, Earth would be another lifeless orb floating through the immensity of space.

But despite its superior size and power, the sun is patient. Instead of dominating the Earth, the sun's gravitational force is more like a strong and constant invitation to the planet to participate in a beneficial relationship that allows life to exist here. The sun is about giving; about contributing to the welfare of others. It exists to serve, providing light, heat, nutrition, and guidance. The sun is self-emptying, constantly expending its own resources for the benefit of others. Despite its many positive attributes, the sun is not perfect. It generates a magnetic field known as *solar wind*–a stream of electromagnetically charged particles that envelopes the whole solar system. Disruptions in the sun's magnetic field in the form of geomagnetic storms can wreak havoc on much of our magnetically influenced and electronically powered world.

But the benefits of the sun far outweigh its occasional quirks and unintended misdeeds. In human terms, the sun is a patient, hard-working, and loving contributor to our lives. It invests all its energy into fulfilling its vitally important mission of providing light, warmth, and nutrition to the inhabitants of this planet and directing its path for good.

Sun people do the same. They are vessels of light and truth in a darkening world. They offer warmth and compassion to an increasingly cold-hearted society. They provide physical, emotional, and spiritual nutrition to the famished bodies, minds, and spirits of those around them. And they consistently use their knowledge and resources to help guide others toward happiness and fulfillment. Their lives exemplify what *The New York Times* columnist and author David Brooks refers to as "eulogy virtues"–those enduring qualities of character that uplift others, make the world a better place, and that we hope people will give us credit for at our funerals.

Like most others, sun people can also enjoy the pleasures of life. They just do so in moderation. Their focus is more on joy than on pleasure. Because of that, they can wait for the better things that come from patience, sacrifice, and hard work.

Sun people give, but unlike the huge ball of fire in the afternoon sky, they never run out of resources. While scientists claim that the generous, self-emptying actions of the sun will eventually deplete it of its thermal reserves, resulting in a great, existence-ending implosion, the opposite reaction occurs with sun people. Their deep sense of gratitude for the light, truth, and virtue in their own lives, fuels their efforts to share those good things with others, which in turn generates an even greater supply of them. Their selfless service magnifies rather than depletes their levels of virtue. Instead of burning out, sun people are constantly transforming into beings with ever-increasing levels of light, power, wisdom, and goodness, as are the people they serve.

> *Sun people are vessels of light and truth in a darkening world.*

With their ever-expanding understanding, sun people also realize–as eighteenth-century Irish statesman and philosopher Edmund Burke once explained–that our Good Samaritan responsibilities as neighbors not only involves service to the living, but also to the dead, and to the unborn. That means loyalty and respect for the generations that preceded us, as well as concern for the welfare of those who will follow.

Sun people shun darkness and dishonesty. Their behavior is governed by voluntary adherence to the principles of light and truth that they carry within them rather than by restrictive rules imposed on them by others. The presence of these virtues causes other people to gravitate toward them. They sense the love, the joy, the peace, and the confidence that emanates from sun people.

According to research conducted at the HeartMath Institute in California, the human heart–like the sun–emits a measurable electromagnetic field that extends 360 degrees from the heart and radiates several feet from our bodies. This field transmits the emotional energy that each of us carries inside–positive and negative–and impacts everyone and everything around us in much the same way the sun's electromagnetic field and gravitational force reaches out and influences the planets in our solar system. Sun people project positive energy that influences others for good, inviting connection, and bringing out the best in them.

But also like the sun, sun people are not entirely perfect. But they want to be. And because of their commitment to truth and to doing what is right, they are willing to correct any flaws, faulty perceptions, and misdeeds once they become aware of them.

The Moon: Living in The Shadows

If you have ever taken an evening stroll in the moonlight, you know a full moon provides Earth with a moderate amount of nighttime illumination–light that it does not produce itself, but borrows from the sun. At its fullest, the moon is only fifty percent in the light while its other side is shrouded in darkness. As the days of the month pass, the moon seems to get smaller and smaller. Based on the changing angle from which we view it from Earth, we see less and less of the side of the moon that faces the sun. It goes through phases, providing less and less light to the Earth, gradually changing from a full circle of light to a slender crescent, and eventually, to a nearly totally darkened New Moon.

Occasionally, something occurs during a full moon called a lunar eclipse when the moon goes through these phases in a matter of minutes with the lighted area getting smaller and smaller (waning) and then gradually increasing (waxing) until it returns to a full moon minutes later. What causes this phenomenon of a suddenly less luminous and shrinking moon to occur? **Earth gets in the way**, blocking the rays of the sun from reaching the moon.

Moon people share a similar experience. They let the things of the world get in the way and increasingly block their access to greater light and truth. What light they have is primarily borrowed from the sun people they associate with, which means they have limited amounts to share with those around them. And when they face temptations, they "eat the marshmallow" too soon. And sometimes, they choke on it.

Moon people satisfy themselves with the transitory and perishable things of life while overlooking the most significant and enduring things; namely, their relationships. Their lives are focused on what David Brooks refers to as "résumé virtues"–those accomplishments or skills that will generate worldly success, fame, and fortune. They mistakenly allow temporal things to define their identity, their purpose, their values, their goals, and their happiness. Their vision is myopic (short-sighted). They focus their attention on things that are available now, right in front of them, and fail to see the greater rewards that loom in the distance. They also have a hearing problem.

As the Arabic word *kafir* describes them, moon people are among those who are choosing not to listen to God. They are the half-concerned, partially-convinced, and fractionally-committed people of the world. They might like to believe in something bigger, wiser, and grander than themselves or that life has a greater purpose than the short-term pursuit of wealth, pleasure, and entertainment. But they often allow their appetites–and sometimes their intellects–to get in the way. As British scholar and novelist C.S. Lewis once wrote, "Aim at Heaven and you will get Earth thrown in; aim at Earth and you will get neither." Moon people have their sights set too low.

Their intentions are often good, but they can be distracted by the allure of money, power, and prestige. And like the cowardly lion in the Wizard of Oz, moon people are vulnerable to fear. They fear losing the social status they have come to value so much, and what other people may think of them if they do.

In psychology professor Dr. Allen Bergin's book *Eternal Values and Personal Growth*, one of his students described this dilemma when he wrote, "I'm embarrassed to admit how often my ideal and true self is overshadowed by my actions and earthly concerns. I believe that if I can make better decisions in my actions toward others, my shaky self-esteem will improve and others' opinions will have a negligible effect upon my self-evaluations."

But moon people often choose convenience over courage. When faced with difficult decisions they may let fear determine their choices. This also makes them vulnerable to manipulation by others and increases the likelihood of them "melting like a snowflake" when confronted with life's challenges.

Moon people are ambivalent. They struggle with having to choose between the two opposing opinions exemplified in the marshmallow study: (1) should they gratify their immediate desires, appetites, and passions, or (2) should they regulate them?

William Shakespeare described the moon predicament beautifully when he wrote:

> *What win I if I gain the thing I seek?*
> *A dream, a breath, a froth of fleeting joy.*
> *Who buys a minute's mirth to wail a week?*
> *Or sells eternity to gain a toy?*

Instead of making the hard decision of choosing light over darkness, moon people mistakenly want to believe that they can combine the two; that these two opposites can somehow amiably coexist within the same person. Comfort soon becomes more important than convictions. Or they may simply be convinced that having too much light in their lives somehow reduces the amount of fun they can have.

It has been said that there is good and there is evil, and parenthetically, there is "something in-between." Moon people are caught in the middle. They live the proverbial dilemma of having an angel on one shoulder and a demon on the other, so they vacillate between the two. Their three options are:

1. Ascend toward greater light in pursuit of growth and improvement;

2. Embrace mediocrity with its diminished levels of light and truth; or
3. Slide regressively downward and deeper into darkness.

The more darkness they allow in, the more indifferent they become to the pursuit of light and truth in their lives, and in the lives of others.

For some moon people this may not always be a conscious or intentional act, but instead, one that is influenced by a lack of understanding what their options are. Their access to light and truth may have been impeded by the environment in which they were raised or in which they currently live.

But while the inaccuracy of their moon choices may not always be obvious at first, over time, more enlightened choices become more apparent. Blaming others is no longer an option to escape responsibility for their choices. Ignorance becomes less and less of an excuse.

A sincere commitment to the pursuit of light and truth will allow persistent individuals to overcome whatever barriers they may encounter along the way. Where there's a will, there's a way. Moon people lack the will, so they can easily lose their way.

While sun people are determined and valiant in the pursuit of increased levels of light and truth, moon people tend to remain lukewarm. But they will often excuse this indecisiveness and congratulate themselves on their ability to integrate truth and error by calling themselves "broad-minded." As cowboy humorist Will Rogers once said, "I reckon some folks figure it a compliment to be called broad-minded. Back home, broad-minded is just another way of saying a feller is too lazy to form an opinion."

> Where there's a will, there's a way. Moon people lack the will, so they can easily lose their way.

What radiates from the hearts of moon people are feelings of uncertainty, complacency, and contradiction. They think that a leisurely examination of the inescapable questions of life is sufficient, or they may leave those questions for others to answer entirely. They forget that we not only have a *right* to choose between good and evil, we have an *obligation* to. We cannot pass that responsibility onto others. We cannot hold onto the coattails of more valiant sun people and consider ourselves worthy to merit the same rewards.

The defining attributes of moon people can be summed up this way: (1) they focus their attention and expend their energy in the pursuit of temporal things. By definition, temporal things are temporary–they don't last. As a result, moon people may one day discover they have sacrificed things that have the greatest, enduring value for things that have the least. And (2) they believe that they have enough light and truth in their lives and lack the determination and the discipline to gain more. As a result, their lives are lived in the shadows, and if they don't correct the situation, they will inevitably be tempted to make choices that plunge them deeper into darkness. Theologian Lewis Smedes described moon people well when he wrote, "We cannot always tell where our light ends and our shadow begins, or where our shadow ends and our darkness begins."

The Stars: Delighting in Darkness

Stars are tiny specks of light in an endless sea of darkness. If you were to remove the moon and all the other stars from the night sky and leave just one, it wouldn't provide enough light to see your hand in front of your face. Similarly, star people have so little light in their own lives, they have none to share with others. In fact, they don't like light. They avoid it like vampires.

Confirmed star people are not uncertain about their options. They have experienced both good and evil and have chosen evil. And since they have chosen darkness over light, they resent sun people and all that they stand for. That's because sun people are painful reminders of what star people could become, but have chosen not to. Their moral blindness is self-imposed. As C.S. Lewis would say, "They have chosen cunning, instead of belief."

Star people look for moon people who are unsure of themselves and uncertain about their values, or who are so enamored and blinded by the things of the world they can easily be flattered into joining their under-enlightened star peers. Their weapon of choice in this contest for the hearts and minds of people is the **Lie,** and they are experts in its use. Sometimes their lies are blatantly bitter and poisonous. Other times they are dipped in honey, wrapped in shiny packaging, and presented with great pomp and fanfare to their unsuspecting victims. But the intended outcomes are the same: to deceive others and lead them into darkness.

In addition to lies, star people employ an arsenal of other offensive weapons such as discouragement, shame, derision, and fear. Violence is their favorite form of entertainment. Anger is their primary emotion. Lust and greed are sentiments they applaud. Mischief and mayhem are recreational sports at which they excel.

They see humility as a character weakness and hubris as a sign of strength. They don't share jovial laughter that uplifts people and lightens the burdens of life for those around them, like sun people do. Instead, they cackle in celebration of the misdeeds and misfortunes of others, like the demons Screwtape and Wormwood in the C.S. Lewis book *The Screwtape Letters*. The German word *schadenfreude* describes star people well: "Those who delight in the failures of others."

Star people lust for power and pleasure. They seek to indulge their appetites without limits or accountability. They may experience the temporary pleasure that comes from doing evil things, but they cannot escape the inevitable consequences that follow. The regret comes later, but it always comes. Their hearts radiate contention, hypocrisy, and immorality.

As Ernest Hemingway wrote in his novel *Death in the Afternoon*, "So far, about morals, I know only that what is moral is what you feel good after, and what is immoral is what you feel bad after." Star people may try to hide from it, but they cannot escape the sorrow that will inevitably follow their immoral behaviors and the darkness that will eventually engulf them.

An old Persian proverb states, "When it becomes dark enough, you can see the stars." If you have ever gone camping or traveled in a remote area, far away from the ambient lights of the city, you may have noticed how bright the stars become and how many more are visible in the rural night sky.

The downward path star people take plunges them deeper and deeper into darkness until one of two things typically happens. First, because their lives contain so much darkness, the faint glimmer of light left inside may begin to be more noticeable. Like an addict in the gutter who has finally hit bottom or the Prodigal Son from the parable of Jesus who "came to himself," the star person may come to understand that choosing darkness and evil will never produce lasting happiness and that it's time to consider a change of direction in life. But if they make no effort to change once they become aware of better options, then the second alternative may occur: the remaining flicker of light in the heart and soul of the star person is in danger of being extinguished and darkness is on the verge of taking full control.

Hold On. The Light Will Come

I have met several people in my life who have expressed the feeling that all of the goodness in them has been sucked out by the difficult circumstances of their lives. Too many people who betrayed their trust. Too many marshmallows that were promised but never delivered. Too much pain. Too many defeats to believe that there is anything virtuous in life worth striving for. "So," they ask, "why try?" The result is, they may adopt star behaviors as a way of coping with the pervasive fear and hopelessness that surrounds them.

But remember, we are not defined by the things that happen to us in life. We define ourselves by how we choose to respond to those events, and there are three ways of responding.

Don't make the mistake of believing that a few star behaviors are proof that you are destined to become a star person. Circumstances change, and when you become convinced of the bad results that star thinking and behaviors produce and remember that there are more enlightened alternatives, then you are able to make better choices.

What It Is and What It Isn't

The continuum of light represented by the sun, the moon, and the stars offers us all a constant reminder of the importance of the choices we make. We did not come into this world predestined to be sun, moon, or star people in life, or in eternity. Our outcomes will be determined by our choices. The purpose of this book is to help you identify sun, moon, and star beliefs and behaviors so you can exercise free will and make an informed decision about the direction you want your life to take and the ultimate destination you want to reach. Those who select enlightened goals and pursue them faithfully are those who are going to attain their highest and brightest potential. Those who wander directionless and purposeless through life, living only for the moment, typically take the path of least resistance–the downhill path that leads to error and darkness.

I firmly believe that anyone who recognizes and understands the differences between these three ways of being, has the desire to improve, is willing to exercise some faith, and is committed to making the diligent effort necessary to apply sun principles in his life, can achieve the greater happiness and peace that comes with sun living. That is the Providential promise: that the greatest happiness will be achieved when we commit to living by sun principles.

> We did not come into this world predestined to be sun, moon, or star people in life, or in eternity. Our outcomes will be determined by our choices.

You may be thinking, "But sun living is harder, requires more patience and diligence, and sun people face more opposition in life than star people." True, but those experiences are often what contribute most to their growth and eventual achievement of lasting happiness. As Charles Dickens wrote in *Great Expectations*, "Suffering has been stronger than all other teaching....I have been bent and broken, but–I hope–into a better shape."

Becoming a sun person isn't easy, but no achievement of lasting value ever is. And keep in mind that sun people do not typically conquer all their weaknesses and achieve the pinnacle of sun-hood overnight, nor are they expected to. They don't overcome all moon and star temptations the first time, the second time, or even the tenth time, but they do overcome them–*in time*. And with an occasional nudge from friends who are equally committed to the same goals, the process of sun living becomes easier. In addition, the more we do it, the greater the rewards become. That's how sun living works.

Unfortunately for the world, because sun people have been in the minority throughout human history, they need all the support and encouragement they can get. This book is especially intended to validate sun people and to encourage them in the courageous pursuit of light and truth. It is intended to assist them with the task of identifying and magnifying their strengths as well as recognizing and overcoming their weaknesses. Their examples are desperately needed. They are the watchmen on the tower; citizens of the City on the Hill; beacons of light in the darkening world in which we live.

This book also offers an invitation to moon people to change the direction of their lives and to join their sun peers in the pursuit of greater light and truth. Regardless of the marshmallow temptations that will be set before them throughout their lives with their alluring promise of immediate gratification and temporal satisfaction, moon people can improve.

Finally, it is intended as a compassionate-but-seriously-needed warning to star people about what consequences await them if they continue rejecting light and truth and keep introducing more darkness and error into their lives, and the lives of others.

But it is *not* intended as a tool to make premature or unfair judgments. We are all capable of recognizing and choosing from among sun, moon, and star beliefs and behaviors and are divinely mandated to do so. But we do not have the omniscient perspective that allows us to know, with absolute certainty, the minds and hearts of others. It is all too easy to fall into the trap of seeing others, or ourselves, as hopelessly under-enlightened moon or star people whose fates are sealed because of a series of poor life decisions. That is not the case. Remember that appearances can often be deceiving, even when looking in the mirror.

Shine Brighter

We are all here for a purpose, and that purpose is to choose a path in life. That choice will determine the quality of our lives here, and hereafter. So, choose wisely. Shine brighter. Choose the sun.

And so it goes. There are three ways of thinking; three ways of acting; three ways of being. Like the preschoolers at Bing Nursery School, the long-term outcomes of our lives are predictable based on the kinds of everyday choices we make. As a result, there will be three kinds of people in this world, and in the world to come.

In this first volume you will learn how your choices will determine the kind of person you become as an individual; a spouse; a parent; and a citizen in your community, your nation, and the world.

CHAPTER 2 Preview

In discussing the human condition, Russian novelist and political dissident Alexander Solzhenitsyn wrote:

> *The line separating good and evil passes not through states, nor between classes, nor between political parties either, but right through every human heart, and through all human hearts. This line shifts. Inside us, it oscillates with the years. And even within hearts overwhelmed by evil, one small bridgehead of good is retained. And even in the best of all hearts, there remains an unprooted small corner of evil. Since then I have come to understand the truth of all the religions of the world: they struggle with the evil inside a human being (inside every human being). It is impossible to expel evil from the world in its entirety, but it is possible to constrict it within each person.*

Achieving sunhood involves a protracted battle between the forces of good and evil that wrestle to occupy each human heart. The process of creating sun families and sun societies begins when individuals commit to learning and living by sun principles for themselves.

3 KINDS OF ME AND 3 KINDS OF YOU

● ●❙❙ ❙ ❙ ❙ ((

Philosopher-poet Ralph Waldo Emerson wrote, "Life is a succession of lessons which must be lived to be understood." According to author Dr. Cherie Carter-Scott, when we resist those lessons they will be repeated throughout our lives until learned. Each lesson will include a test that will bring either increased levels of light and truth into our lives, or darkness and error. Like most people, I can be a slow learner at times. Gratefully, I have also learned that Providence often provides us with repeated opportunities to retake the exams, correct our mistakes, and make further progress along the path of life.

> *"Life is a succession of lessons which must be lived to be understood."*
> *-Ralph Waldo Emerson*

But we must have the desire to improve and the willingness to act if we are to take advantage of those opportunities when they come along. Let me share an account of one of life's lessons that I have learned. You have likely had similar experiences and opportunities because the lessons are universal for us all.

The Baseball Glove That Refused to Be Forgotten

It has been said that the personality traits and behaviors we find least desirable in others are the same behaviors and traits we will often find in ourselves, if we are honest and brave enough to take a close look. All I knew as a fourteen-year-old high school freshman at a small Catholic boarding school in the fall of 1965 was that I didn't particularly like one of my classmates.

I considered Paul Bonhoeffer (not his real name) to be a self-absorbed show-off who had to win at everything he did. We were both competitive in sports, but it appeared to me that he had no problem bending the rules a little if it ensured victory. Of course, I was the expert at bending all of the boarding school rules about dormitory pillow fights and kitchen raids.

Living together for nine months of the year and sharing a communal lifestyle allowed me and my classmates to get to know each other very well. As a result, my disdain for Paul only seemed to increase as time went by. During the fall semester of my sophomore year, I made a decision that would affect me for the rest of my life and ultimately teach me one of life's most important lessons.

While watching an intramural flag-football game from the sidelines, I saw Paul do something that appeared to me to be an obvious violation of the rules and that resulted in a touchdown and victory for his team. The referee missed the infraction, so nothing was done to correct it.

That was it! I had taken all I could stand of Paul Bonhoeffer and I let him know it with a barrage of insults from the sidelines. It was time for Paul Bonhoeffer to be held accountable. He needed to be punished for his behavior and in my self-righteous indignation, I determined that I was the one who would do it. So, I walked into the locker room, opened his gym locker, and stole his baseball glove.

Yeah, I know. Stupid. But that was the best thing my angry fifteen-year-old mind could come up with at that moment as punishment for his bad behavior. I took a black permanent marker and blotted out his name where he had written it on the thumb of his baseball glove and simply wrote my name above it. Not a very clever attempt at concealing my act of thievery, but then again, I wasn't trying to conceal my actions at all. In fact, I *wanted* him to know that I had stolen his glove. I had never intentionally provoked a fight with anyone before, but I was willing to start one with Paul just to see how he would react and maybe finish the punishment process for his many perceived misdeeds.

I was patient. It was seven months later during the annual inter-class baseball tournament that the long-awaited opportunity presented itself. I used Paul's glove during our first game and left it lying on the bench where I thought he would see it. Sure enough, at one point during the game he walked over to the bench, picked up the glove, looked at the poor attempt to conceal the name of its true owner, saw the name of the thief clearly written above it, and then…he simply put it back on the bench and walked away. No reaction. No glaring, angry looks. Nothing was said. No acknowledgment of the fact that he knew it was his glove. My efforts at making his life uncomfortable for a few moments had apparently failed.

So…I kept the glove. During Christmas vacation of our junior year Paul decided to throw a party at his home in Sacramento for his classmates. About half of the thirty members of our class attended the party. It seemed that nothing had changed. Paul still needed to be the center of attention and was still trying to impress everyone. He had a copy of the newly-released Beatles album *Magical Mystery Tour* and proudly put it on the turntable for all to hear.

Afterwards, Paul pulled out his guitar and started playing the Arlo Guthrie song "Alice's Restaurant." I'm thinking, "Oh Paul, you are such a putz!" Since I was the only high school student invited to play in the combo of the school's acclaimed polyphonic choir and my guitar-playing skills were much better than Paul's, I gloated over the knowledge that all he could manage was the simplified version of the more intricate finger-picking arrangement from the record that I had mastered months before. As I continued in my self-important reverie, something happened that suddenly altered everything. My whole opinion of Paul Bonhoeffer was about to change forever.

Paul's father came into the room. I knew that he and his dad were not on the best of terms, but I didn't know how bad the situation had become until his father began to speak. I don't remember what the reason might have been for what he did next, but rather than waiting to correct his son in private, he chose to do it when the humiliation factor would be greatest. In front of the whole group–the people Paul most wanted to impress; the people with whom he had lived for two-and-a-half years and probably gotten closer to than any previous friends; the people whose opinions he seemed to truly care about–in front of us all, Paul's father *dissected* his son.

He was a psychologist who specialized in improving people's communication skills. That means he knew what to say, when to say it, and how to say it to get the maximum effect. With surgical precision and an ample vocabulary of razor-sharp words, he sliced and diced his son with a barrage of insults and name-calling that shocked everyone in the room. My mind recoiled and my body winced with each stinging remark.

I've heard angry parents go off on their teenage children on several occasions in my work as a family therapist, but nothing that rivaled what I witnessed that day. The disdain, the scorn, the contempt in his voice was gut wrenching and I watched as Paul's head began to drop and slowly descend toward his knees, lower and lower with each successive insult. He finally curled up into a ball of raw, traumatized adolescence and began to cry. Then his father calmly sauntered out of the room as if nothing of significance had happened, leaving behind the emotionally-dismembered remains of his broken-hearted sixteen-year-old son.

We all sat there in shock; numb and motionless, not knowing what to do or say. Within a few seconds Paul managed to reassemble himself, put a smile on his face and endeavored to continue with the party. But something significant had changed inside me.

I could no longer see Paul Bonhoeffer as the arrogant, self-absorbed person I had presumed him to be just moments before. He was a human being who had just suffered in a way that I would never have wished on anyone; a way that any teenager who had ever experienced rejection and humiliation could relate to. I now realized why Paul Bonhoeffer was the way he was. I could see that for the two-and-a-half years I had known him and very likely throughout most of the sixteen years of his young life, he had been constantly trying to prove that he was talented enough, smart enough, athletic enough, and victorious enough to merit his father's approval. What Paul Bonhoeffer deserved now was compassion, understanding, forgiveness…and to have his baseball glove back. But my sixteen-year-old pride and the fear of embarrassing myself by admitting my own bad behavior, were sufficient to talk me out of returning it.

We both left the seminary after our junior year. Actually, we were both asked to leave…well, not exactly *asked*. (The dean, Father Bruce, told me he didn't think I was priesthood material. At sixteen, he was probably right). We each completed our senior years at high schools in our respective communities sixty-five miles apart, so I didn't see Paul again. However, about two years later an event occurred that profoundly impacted me and made me realize that there were several transgressions from my adolescent past that required correction. In short, I knew I needed to find Paul Bonhoeffer and give him back his baseball glove.

I looked up his phone number in an old student directory I still had and called the number, only to hear, "The number you have dialed is no longer in service." Paul Bonhoeffer had moved. I called some of my former classmates, but no one knew where he might have moved to, nor had anyone made any effort to stay in touch with him.

I seemed to remember him saying something once about having family in Boston, Massachusetts. So, I went to the county library in my tiny hometown of Gridley, California hoping to find a Boston phone book. To my surprise there was a Boston directory in the library, and I found one listing for a Bonhoeffer, but it wasn't Paul's father. I wrote the number down and that evening I called, hoping that it would be a close relative of Paul's. But when I spoke to the man in Boston, I learned that he was neither acquainted with nor closely related to Paul and couldn't help me with my search. Discouraged, I became resigned to the fact that I might not be able to find him and return his baseball glove.

Four more years went by. I graduated from California State University, Chico with a major in psychology and a minor in music. I was married with two children and suddenly found myself on a career path that had never seriously crossed my mind before. I had planned to apply for graduate school in a counseling field. Instead, I found myself playing bass guitar and doing comedy and vocal impersonations of rock stars from the 1950s and '60s in an oldies rock 'n' roll show band called The Bop-a-Dips that I had joined six months prior to graduation.

While touring through the Pacific Northwest and performing in the Seattle area about a year later, I telephoned the hotel where my family and I were staying from a payphone in downtown Seattle. After finishing the phone call and looking down at the Seattle directory dangling from a wire in the phone booth, a thought suddenly struck me: "Maybe Paul Bonhoeffer moved to Seattle!" I looked up his name in the directory but there were no Bonhoeffers listed. From that point on I made it a habit to check the phone books in many of the cities where we performed, hoping that I might find Paul along the way. San Francisco, Los Angeles, Denver, Boise, Reno, Sacramento…a long list of towns large and small, but no Paul Bonhoeffer in any of them. Two years later I joined a larger '50s showband based in Orlando, Florida called Spun Gold and broadened my search to include many more states and cities all over the country. Still no luck.

More time went by. I finally left the music business after eight years of touring and resumed my original plans for graduate school. I still had the baseball glove and had used it occasionally for church softball games. My oldest son used it for Little League at one time, and it was beginning to show the signs of years of wear and neglect. The glove was consigned to the top shelf in my bedroom closet and each time we moved–a total of ten times over a twenty-five-year period–the glove also made the trip. Each time we packed up our belongings, my wife and I would come across it and she would say, "You need to get rid of that thing! It's worn-out and you never use it!" But I would always reply–probably with some guilt in my voice– "No, I need to find Paul Bonhoeffer and give him back his baseball glove."

Over thirty-two years had gone by from that autumn day in 1966 when I had taken Paul's glove until the spring of 1999. I was sitting at my desk in Provo, Utah where I was working as a social worker for the State of Utah and doing paperwork on the computer when a thought suddenly and inexplicably charged its way into my mind–a thought that I had not considered for many years. "There's a new way to find people," my conscience shouted, "and you are looking right at it! Maybe you can find Paul Bonhoeffer on the Internet!"

It was about 4:30 PM on a Thursday afternoon in mid-May. I went to a web site called Switchboard.com, not knowing how I would conduct the search because the web site asked for a name and a city or state of residence. Since I had no idea which city or state to put in, I just left that section blank. I typed "Paul Bonhoeffer" into the name section and nervously clicked "Search."

Suddenly, what I had attempted to do for years and had given up hope of ever accomplishing; what looking through scores of phone books had never produced; and what seemed to be a nearly impossible task to complete, was now accomplished in the blink of an eye with less than a minute's effort. There I sat, staring at his name, address, and phone number.

As incredible as it seemed, I suddenly realized that Paul Bonhoeffer was not living in some distant place at all, but was, in fact, living less than thirty-five miles away, in Sandy, Utah! I was dumbfounded. I kept staring at the monitor screen in disbelief. How could this be real? And why Sandy, Utah of all places? After a minute or two of mental stupor I realized that I actually had to call him if I was ever going to complete this thirty-two-year mission. I sheepishly dialed the number and anxiously waited for someone to answer. After four gut-wrenching rings, a male voice answered the phone–a voice that was vaguely familiar. I was speaking, to Paul Bonhoeffer.

"Hi Paul! It's Fred Dodini…from St. Pius?" His response was a chilly, "Oh yeah…what do *you* want?" I stammered and stumbled, trying to think of what to say next. I remembered that every five years since graduating, the class of 1969 from St. Pius X Seminary and Prep School held a weekend reunion, and this year–1999–would be the thirty-year class reunion. Paul had never attended any of them because no one knew how to contact him. I blurted out, "Well Paul, there's a class reunion planned for this summer and I'm sure everyone would love to see you again. Is it OK if I give the other guys your phone number and email address so they can let you know the details?" "Yeah, I guess so," he said, somewhat reluctantly. "That's great," I said. "And Paul, there's something else I wanted to discuss with you. Would you be available on Saturday evening if I come by your place?" "Yeah" he said, "I'll be here." We decided on a time and I told him I would see him then.

I drove home that night and went straight to my bedroom closet. There was the glove, still collecting dust in its usual resting place. When Saturday night finally arrived, I pulled the glove from the shelf, put it into a paper grocery sack, tossed a $20 bill inside to assuage some of my guilt, and headed off to his address in Sandy. When I arrived and rang the doorbell, Paul answered the door. I sensed that he was not in the best of moods and it soon became obvious that it had nothing to do with me. He invited me in and began introducing me to his children. His face lit up as he talked about his kids.

The atmosphere suddenly chilled when his wife entered the room and Paul introduced her. Their facial expressions were clear indicators that there were problems in their marriage. Then Paul and I walked out to the back yard and sat beneath a patio umbrella that shaded us from the slowly setting sun. We talked briefly about what he had been doing since high school. He had gone to college and was now an elementary school teacher. It turned out that the school where he taught the fifth grade was only yards away from a middle school I had visited only months before to deliver a motivational presentation to the students.

He hadn't been in contact with his father for many years and his marriage was not going well. He and his wife had separated for several months and had only recently gotten back together. The tension between them was obvious, and Paul expressed his concern that a divorce might significantly reduce the amount of time he could spend with his children. Clearly, his kids meant everything to him.

I listened patiently and empathetically, feeling more and more that my petty problems didn't begin to compare with the challenges he was facing. But after a few more minutes of catching up and talking about our lives, I sensed that the moment was right and I reached under the table and pulled out the paper sack. I reminded Paul about his missing baseball glove sophomore year and confessed that I was the one who had taken it. I apologized. There was little response. I reminded him again about the upcoming reunion and how much I sincerely believed everyone would want to see him again. He showed little interest, still absorbed in the sad feelings about his marital situation that were triggered by our conversation.

He loved to play golf and I learned that he worked at a local golf course during the summer where he could play for free. I suggested we get together for a game sometime soon. He responded with the obligatory "Sure" that included a blank expression and no enthusiasm. I told him I would call him and set it up (which, unfortunately, never happened) and then I left and headed for home.

I wondered whether Paul still felt any connection to the people and the experiences we shared together at St. Pius during what many of us who attended that school still consider to be among the most influential years of our lives.

The class members in charge of the reunion sent Paul an email with all the information but received no response. The designated weekend quickly arrived and I caught a flight from Salt Lake City to Reno, Nevada where I was met by two other classmates. We drove to a house the group had rented for the weekend near Donner Lake, California anticipating a relaxing and entertaining weekend renewing old friendships and debating politics and religion.

The kitchen and great room were located upstairs so we could enjoy a better view of the lake and the surrounding forest. We were all visiting and preparing dinner when someone looked out the upstairs window facing the street and noticed headlights approaching. We heard a car door shut and the classmate at the window said, "Hey guys, Paul Bonhoeffer just pulled up!"

The downstairs entrance door opened and closed, and footsteps were heard ascending the stairs. A group of us were standing in a circle at the top of the stairs involved in a conversation. My back was turned to the stairwell, so I wasn't aware when Paul reached the top of the stairs. A classmate standing opposite of me who was facing the stairs responded to Paul's arrival with a smile and a warm, "Hey Paul!" At that moment I turned around to greet Paul and was startled at first as I realized his face was only inches away from mine. He grabbed me in a bear-hug of an embrace and wouldn't let go. With heartfelt emotion he whispered into my ear, "Thank you for finding me! I needed to be here!" We both instantly burst into tears, and all the men in that room were suddenly and powerfully reminded of the unique brotherhood and bond we all shared as a result of the few short years we spent together at a small, obscure boarding school on Twin Cities Road in Galt, California.

"Thank you for finding me! I needed to be here!"-Paul B.

The weekend visit with my classmates was remarkable. Although our respective lives had gone in various directions that included a broad array of careers and experiences, we realized that we still had something significant in common with each another. There was no sense of competition or the need to impress. If anything, we felt greater connection and compassion for each other. When it came time to return home, Paul and I discovered we were both booked on the same flight back to Salt Lake City. We sat together and continued to talk all the way home. We walked down to baggage claim and continued our conversation for another twenty minutes until our wives began to complain about the delay. We didn't want to say goodbye. Even though we only lived a short distance apart, I was about to move to Indiana to start a PhD program at Purdue University and I think we both sensed we might not be seeing each other for a while.

Fast forward five years and it was time for the next reunion. Paul and I both made it to the get-together and picked up where we had left off just five minutes before (or so it seemed.) That was fifteen years ago, and our fifty-year class reunion occurred in June 2019. We have stayed in touch over the years and Paul has experienced some significant challenges in his life during that time. But he has also experienced some tremendous blessings as well. He seems genuinely happy about his life now, and I am happy, to see him happy.

"It ain't over till it's over"-Yogi Berra

If stealing Paul Bonhoeffer's baseball glove was the only thing I ever did wrong in my life, I would count myself very fortunate. But it's not, and I am still in need of improvement in many areas of my life. I look back over some of my impulsive and reckless decisions as a teenager and realize that a lot more could have gone wrong had I continued down that path. But I didn't. I chose another way. So can you.

Don't get too discouraged if you are disappointed with where you are on the continuum of good and evil right now. While the question of your location is important, it's the direction in which you are headed that ultimately matters most. Choose the right direction, and stick with it.

You can expect to face some significant challenges and opposition at various times in your life. Some of those challenges will occur because of your own choices, some as a result of the choices of others. Either way, don't give up hope. Do what is right and accept whatever consequences may follow. Hope for the best, knowing–as I have learned–that Providence will assist you with any sincere efforts to correct your mistakes.

God Doesn't Care Who You Were, Only Who You Are

I saw a movie several years ago entitled *Cowboys and Aliens* starring Daniel Craig and Harrison Ford that illustrated this point well. Craig played a former outlaw who, along with his girlfriend, were abducted by aliens from their home somewhere in the American Southwest around the 1880s. The extra-terrestrial beings examined the bodies of their human captives to identify their physical weaknesses so subsequent alien forces could follow this scouting vessel to Earth, conquer the planet, destroy its inhabitants, and plunder the planet of its gold.

Unlike his unfortunate companion who was incinerated by the aliens as a left-over lab experiment, Daniel Craig's character managed to escape his captors. But he was unable to recall any memories of the events other than an occasional flashback of images. He found his way to the desert town of Absolution trying to piece his life back together and to understand why he had some futuristic alien contraption strapped to his wrist.

With no memory of who he was or where he came from, he was befriended by a country preacher who stitched up his wounds and shared some homespun insight about the question of one's identity and destiny. He said, "I've seen good men do bad things and bad men do good things. Whether you're gonna end up in Heaven or Hell is not God's plan, it's your own. You just gotta remember what it was." Later, as he lay dying from an alien-inflicted wound, the preacher offered these final words of counsel to his amnesic friend: "God doesn't care who you *were*, only who you *are*." Sage insight. Likely gained through some life-changing experiences of his own.

Many of us will find ourselves in less desirable positions on the continuum of good and evil at various times in our lives. For some, the need for change becomes obvious after they look back over a long series of poor choices. For others, it comes as subtle insight gained through studious self-reflection or from a courageous and revealing conversation with a caring friend. This journey of personal progression and the need for continuous course corrections has been going on for a long time. It began long before we were born, and will continue long after we die. If we are paying attention, we will see reminders of this truth all around us.

Changing Course: The Allegory of the GPS

A few years ago, after completing a visit with one of our daughters and her family who live near Kansas City, Missouri, our daughter was driving my wife and me to the airport to fly home. Her GPS was programmed to give us directions to the airport. After driving about two miles from her home I suddenly realized I had left my cell phone charger on the table in her dining room. We stopped and turned around to go back to her home. However, the GPS continued to give us driving instructions to the airport. From high in the sky an all-seeing satellite would determine our present location and begin giving new directions to the desired destination.

"Recalculating," the pleasing voice of the young woman in the tiny box on the dashboard would say each time we ignored her instructions and failed to make the appropriate turn. "Drive point two miles and make a legal U-turn." Again, she was ignored. "Recalculating. Drive five hundred feet and turn right on Pleasant Valley Road." We turned left. "Recalculating." The instructions continued, but with no obedient responses from the driver. The GPS would say to go one way, and we always chose the opposite direction. The voice in the box never sounded impatient or frustrated with our lack of compliance. There was no hint of sarcasm. She just kept inviting us to choose a different path.

After a few moments, her instructions began to fall on deaf ears. No one was listening. We knew where we were going. Why listen to this know-it-all person who was obviously obsessed with wanting to make everyone go where *she* thought they should go!

About that time, I was jolted from my reverie when my wife commented, "It must be hard for the woman in the GPS to keep giving instructions and be repeatedly ignored."

It was a proverbial aha moment as my wife and I realized the parallel between our experiences with the GPS and our relationships with God.

The all-seeing, all-knowing Father of us all sees each one of us perfectly and understands the unique circumstances of our lives. His only concern is for our welfare. He understands exactly where we are on the path of life and offers the specific and individualized instruction we need at any given moment. "Take the closest exit off the Highway to Hell. Turn left onto The Road Less Traveled. Then turn right onto Paradise Drive." He knows every twist and turn in our lives and how to direct us toward our final destination— back into His loving presence.

Sun people understand the wisdom of listening carefully and following correct instructions. Moon people tend to get distracted by the scenery and begin to tune out the repetitive invitations to correct the course of their lives. They are enjoying the trip without much regard for where the path will ultimately lead them. Star people don't want to listen. They just unplug the GPS.

Life is a series of multiple course corrections and adjustments. Making mistakes is part of the process and so is correcting those mistakes. Like an airline pilot, reaching the correct destination involves repeatedly adjusting the path of flight by a few degrees here, a few degrees there, to follow the radio beacon that provides a straight line between the airplane and the chosen airport destination. If we have failed to pay attention to the warning signs that tell us we have traveled off course, the course corrections may involve dramatic changes. But by listening carefully and following instructions, sun people can avoid straying too far from the correct path.

Each of us has a built-in GPS-like mechanism that lets us know when we stray from the correct path. We call it the conscience. It is more than just an evolved biological function of the brain or a socially constructed set of rules. It is a spark of Providential light that connects each of us to divine wisdom and eternal law. A portion of this light is planted in every human heart and will brighten or dim depending upon the choices we make. The more we respond to it, the greater the amounts of light and truth we have access to and the more sensitive the conscience becomes. The more sensitive the conscience, the more easily we can distinguish between good and evil. The lesser the amounts of light and truth, the less we respond to those twinges of guilt that tell us we have done something wrong that needs to be corrected. That also means we will be less likely to recognize additional light and truth when we encounter it.

When we become aware of our options and where we are currently located on the path, it is our responsibility to adjust the course of our lives if we want to arrive at the solar destination. But for some, a lunar or stellar destination seems to be acceptable.

Crème Brûlée...or Jell-O?

One example of a change of direction occurred in the life of an acquaintance of mine who currently works as a life coach and motivational speaker. His star behaviors were not as obvious as some people's, so what he was doing on the outside, was not always a reflection of what was going on inside. For all intents and purposes, most who knew him considered his life to be one of happiness and success. He was a lawyer.

He went to an Ivy League law school and worked for one of the largest and most prestigious law firms in the country. He was well-paid, traveled internationally, was married to a beautiful and devoted wife and they had three beautiful and devoted children. He was well-trained in the art of litigation and used those skills proficiently–some would say, ruthlessly.

His law firm represented a large company that was involved in a series of lawsuits arising from a class-action suit. One particular trial involved a woman who appeared to have a legitimate claim. But trial lawyers are not hired to negotiate a win-win solution to a problem and he knew that if he couldn't successfully challenge the legitimacy of the complaint, he *could* attack the credibility of the person who filed it.

Artfully employing his cross-examination skills, he poked, prodded, and provoked the woman until he got what he wanted–an impulsive and emotional statement that cast doubt on the validity her testimony. That was all he needed.

After successfully winning the case for his corporate client, he gathered his things and prepared to leave the courtroom. The woman who had filed the lawsuit approached him and asked, "How did it make you feel to humiliate someone who you knew was telling the truth?" He offered no reply, and she walked away.

But those words wouldn't leave his mind. The sound of her voice and the self-incrimination it engendered in his conscience could not be erased. Something had changed and it could not be unchanged. He either had to go deeper into the darkness to find justification for his behavior, or he had to admit his mistake and correct it. As it turned out, twisting the truth and manipulating others in the courtroom were not the only things in his life that he had found ways to justify. He was also cheating on his wife.

While he later gave up the practice of law and confessed his infidelities to his wife (just before he moved out and divorced her), I was left with the feeling as he shared his story that there was little sense of sincere remorse on his part and that the changes he made were primarily self-focused. He seemed to show little regard for the impact his decisions had on his family and he described no effort at restitution or reconciliation. He appeared to be lightening the load of guilt his choices had created by transferring those burdens to the innocent victims of his choices. It felt like he may have moved from a star to a moon level, but there was still a higher level of light and truth that he had not yet accepted in his life. He could have had Crème Brûlée, but instead, he settled for Jell-O.

A Modern-Day *Les Misérables*

I witnessed a more sincere desire for a change of direction in someone's life in the fall of 1977 when I was nearing the end of my sojourn as a member of The Bop-a-Dips. We were performing at a club called The Candlerock Lounge in Sacramento, California. The bouncer at the club was a big, bear-of-a-guy named Butch who reminded me of Jerry Garcia of the Grateful Dead.

I struck up a conversation one day with Butch while the band was rehearsing. We each shared a little background about ourselves, but Butch's story was much more compelling than mine. He had been a member of the Hell's Angels for several years and as we spoke I could tell that those years were a source of a lot of painful memories for him. There was no sense of pride or bravado in his voice as he spoke about some of the bad things he had done during that time in his life. His head hung low as he began to share the deep feelings of regret that he constantly carried with him. Over the next two weeks we spoke more often and the conversations continued to go to a more personal and vulnerable level.

We spoke about our families. I was married with three children at that time, as was he. I was a naïve twenty-six-year-old boy and he was a world-wise and weary man, probably eight to ten years older. From our conversations it was evident that his biker years were well behind him and now his focus in life was his family. His huge body trembled as he expressed deep fears that he might be failing as a husband and a father, wondering how he could possibly support his family with little education and no marketable skills. After all, who wants to hire someone whose resumé reads like a character in the Marlon Brando movie, *The Wild One*. "Skills: drinking copious amounts of alcohol; defacing public property; snarling at, intimidating, and otherwise harassing innocent residents of small rural communities; selling drugs; beating people senseless (or worse); and driving off triumphantly into the sunset on a Harley." But that was not the man sitting next to me on a bar stool with tears welling up in his eyes.

He had realized that his life up to that point was a series of bad choices that now left him feeling trapped. He was a wannabe sun person trying to navigate out of a star environment. Tears continued to run down his beard-covered cheeks as he shared his concerns that with no other alternatives to make a decent living, he might do something that would put him back into Folsom Prison where he had previously spent time.

In his book *The Different Drum: Community Making and Peace*, psychiatrist and author M. Scott Peck wrote:

> *How strange that we should ordinarily feel compelled to hide our wounds when we are all wounded! Community requires the ability to expose our wounds and weaknesses to our fellow*

creatures. It also requires the ability to be affected by the wounds of others...But even more important is the love that arises among us when we share, both ways, our woundedness.

I don't know why Butch chose me as the person he could confide in about these things, but I felt privileged by his trust and humbled in his presence. Here was a penitent man who truly desired greater light and goodness in his life but who was struggling to know where to find it and how to hold onto it once he did. We bonded as friends and continued to correspond for many months after parting company. But like most long-distance friendships, we eventually lost touch with each other.

I have often thought about him and wondered how his life turned out. My imagination has come up with several possibilities. I prefer to think of him as a contemporary version of Jean Valjean from Victor Hugo's *Les Misérables*: a man who loved his family and may have felt that circumstances required him to do something wrong in order to provide for them. After leaving prison, Jean Valjean met Bishop Myriel who provided the former convict with temporary food and shelter and chose to see the goodness within him rather than to view him as just another unrepentant thief. The priest believed in Jean Valjean's potential, despite his past. That brief experience changed Jean Valjean's life forever. For Butch and me, someday our lives will intersect again and I will find out if our chance meeting affected his life as powerfully as it has affected mine.

How Is It Done?

As a therapist and life coach I have given a lot of thought to what motivates us to become sun people and how we can best encourage and support others who have chosen that same path. Around 350 B.C. the Greek philosophers Plato and Aristotle were equally concerned with this process. They pondered which methods they could use that would best help their fellow human beings achieve the pinnacle of human development: that is, to reach their full potential and become perfect human beings. They both responded to that question with somewhat different answers.

Plato determined that the best way to help people reach their full potential would be to describe all the characteristics of the perfect person. Those admirable qualities that would be expected to bring the individual the greatest levels of happiness and productivity. Others, seeing the advantages of becoming that kind of person, would naturally want to achieve the same for themselves and would mimic the life of the perfect person.

Aristotle saw it somewhat differently. He acknowledged that the path to perfection is a difficult one that will involve disappointment and failure at times. He sensed that imperfect people might become discouraged in their pursuit of perfection when they realized they didn't measure up to the example of the perfect person. They might mistakenly believe that an occasional failure would be proof that none of us are capable of perfection.

Aristotle suggested that the example that most of us would relate to and that should be held up for all to follow should be a person who may have struggled at times in his or her life and made some poor choices along the way. Maybe they even experienced willful disobedience and resistance to doing what was right from time to time, but never fully succumbed to darkness, never gave up, never stopped believing in their ability to correct their mistakes, and continued to make progress until the goal of perfection was eventually reached.

In fact, both philosophers were right. Both examples are necessary. We all need to have an image of what perfection looks like and the hope that even flawed human beings can achieve it. It was also Aristotle who wisely recognized that true happiness is not a destination, but is a by-product of our daily striving to reach our full potential.

The Law That Never Changes

Nearly three hundred years later, it was the Roman lawyer, political leader, and philosopher Cicero who offered what many consider to be the greatest insight of his day into the question of how each human being can maximize his or her potential.

Cicero believed that real happiness, growth, prosperity, and justice for us and our posterity, are to be achieved through living in harmony with what we refer to today as Natural Law. He defined Natural Law as "true law" when he stated:

> *True law is right reason in agreement with nature; it is of universal application, unchanging and everlasting. It summons to duty by its commands and averts from wrongdoing by its prohibitions...It is a sin to try and alter this law, nor is it allowable to repeal any part of it, and it is impossible to abolish it entirely. We cannot be freed from its obligations by senate or people and we need not look outside ourselves for an expounder or interpreter of it. There will not be different laws at Rome and Athens, or different laws now and in the future, but one eternal and unchangeable law will be valid in all nations and at all times. There will be one master and ruler, that is God, over us all, for He is the author of this law, its promulgator and its enforcing judge.*

At the beginning of the Nuremburg trials of Nazi war criminals after World War II, the defendants asked a legitimate and very important question of their judges. They asked, "Under which set of laws are we being judged?" Their position was, that although the things they were being accused of were heinous acts to some people, by German law they were still legal, and the German people were not accountable to the laws of any other nation or group of nations. After much discussion, the only suitable answer the tribunal could offer was that the defendants were being held accountable to an unwritten law that sounded very much like what Cicero described above.

As the great philosopher explained, the principles of Natural Law are not relative. They are not determined by subjective opinion or by a consensus vote among mortals. They are not even written down in a collection of dusty law books or on stone tablets. As American statesman Alexander Hamilton once expressed it, "They are written as with a sunbeam in the whole volume of human nature by the hand of the Divinity itself, and can never be erased or obscured by mortal power."

Natural Law is divine law. It is moral law. It is eternal and irrevocable. C.S. Lewis referred to this law as The Law of Human Nature or the Law of Right and Wrong. He wrote that this law is "a law we did not make but that presses down on all of us…something above and beyond the actual facts of human behavior…a real law which we did not invent and which we know we ought to obey."

Compliance with Natural Law protects individuals and societies from the negative consequences of wrongdoing. Individuals and societies who live in harmony with Natural Law will "prosper in the land" as the children of Israel were constantly reminded by their prophet-leaders. Not just prosper economically, but politically, emotionally, spiritually, socially, and in their physical health as well. Those who oppose Natural Law will experience the opposite; the loss of freedom, peace, health, wealth, and harmony in their homes and communities.

As constitutional law professor Dr. W. Cleon Skousen wrote, "Even in those nations sometimes described as pagan, there were sharp, penetrating minds like Cicero's who reasoned their way through the labyrinths of natural phenomena to see behind the cosmic universe, as well as in the unfolding of their own lives, the brilliant intelligence of a supreme designer with an ongoing interest in both human and cosmic affairs."

Thomas Jefferson referred to Cicero's concept of Natural Law in the Declaration of Independence when he wrote about self-evident truths and that all human beings are entitled to the freedom and equality granted to us by "the laws of nature and of nature's God."

Cicero believed that all human beings are endowed with some measure of this light; this Providential gift of right reasoning. Jefferson also wrote that all of humanity are endowed by their Creator with the ability to recognize the difference between right and wrong.

Cicero wrote that mankind also possesses the supernal gift of the ability to love. We can choose to add upon these gifts through sun choices, or we can choose star options and squander away whatever light we have accumulated. The more light and truth that we accumulate in life, the greater the ability to reason and love, until we reach our full potential. The perfected ability to rightly reason is called wisdom. The perfected ability to love is called charity.

As Plato and Aristotle indicated, for this perfecting process to occur there must be a standard; an example to follow. As Cicero stated, God is the standard. He is the example of someone who has perfected all the good traits and qualities that we as His offspring also possess. He has disciplined out of His life all the darkness and negative human traits that block progression. In addition to this perfect example, we are also surrounded in the world by examples of those who have made mistakes, even serious ones, but who have also corrected them and have advanced along the path toward greater light and truth.

From Rough Stone to Finished Work of Art

Perfecting our lives is like creating a great sculpture. The Roman poet Ovid wrote about a mythical sculptor named Pygmalion who could look at a piece of marble and see the finished sculpture trapped inside it. Similarly, when Michelangelo was once asked how he created such magnificent sculptures he responded that he would search until he found the right piece of marble, the one which he could look at and see the finished statue inside it. "Then," he said, "I simply remove everything that isn't part of that image."

To become a sun person we must understand what sun qualities and characteristics look like. We must keep our minds focused on the image of the perfected person that it is within our power to create. When we do, we will become acutely aware of what qualities, behaviors, appetites, inclinations, and ideologies don't fit with that image of the sun person we know we have the potential to become.

For example, I once heard an account of a married couple who attended a royal dinner of some sort in England attended by many dignitaries and government officials. The couple was reportedly seated next to a man from Scotland Yard who oversaw the department that investigated cases of the counterfeiting of British currency. In conversation, the wife said to the Scotland Yard official, "You must get the chance to study a lot of counterfeit money in your job," to which the man replied, "Oh no, I only study the real thing. I am so familiar with every detail of the real currency that I can spot a counterfeit quite easily."

Life provides us with a myriad of opportunities to choose among competing ideas and behaviors. For every correct principle that God has revealed, the Adversary has also created a counterfeit version. Sun people have enough light to recognize darkness, even when it is cleverly concealed in a counterfeit form.

When Cicero said of Natural Law, "we need not look outside ourselves for an expounder or interpreter of it," he did not mean that we do not need others to assist us in the search for truth, for he was one of the greatest teachers of his era. He recognized that good teachers can significantly help their students with the process of recognizing and understanding the statutes of Natural Law that are imprinted on every human heart.

As he also explained, Natural Law "averts from wrongdoing by its prohibitions." That means that complying with this law will reduce the number of negative consequences we experience because of poor choices. It will also decrease the amount of time we spend attending the school of hard knocks, where the accumulated residue of years of "stinking thinking" and bad behaviors are often chiseled away by adversity and misfortune.

There is a Greek word that Plato and Aristotle may have used to describe this process of correction and improvement. The word is *metanoeo*. It denotes a change of mind and a change of heart. The English translation of that Greek word is "repentance" and it is an indispensable part of the process of becoming a sun person. In addition to changing our minds and developing a fresh view about oneself, God, and the world, it also involves acknowledging our errors, making restitution to correct whatever we have done wrong, and making a concerted effort to not dwell on the errant thoughts nor repeat the destructive behaviors.

For some, this process of change may happen quickly and dramatically as the result of some life-altering experience. For others it is a gradual and continuous process of course correction and advancement that continues over a lifetime.

The First Step: Acknowledging the Need to Change

My wife Pat once taught a lesson to a group of women from our church about the importance of honesty in acknowledging our weaknesses and faults and about our dependence on the grace of God in overcoming them. As often happens, when we have heard the same principle taught repeatedly over the years we tend to pay less attention to the instruction. Pat was looking for a novel approach that would capture the women's interest and provoke more participation in the class discussion. She decided to use a treatment manual that I have used with some of my therapy clients that focuses on a particular behavioral problem. She stuck closely to the manual presentation, except that she replaced one word used throughout the manual with a different word. At the end of the class, several of the women commented about how much they gained from the lesson and how the group discussion was very helpful. Pat then informed the group that they had just completed Step 1 of the 12 Steps of Alcoholics Anonymous. She had merely replaced the word *addiction*, with the word *weaknesses*.

By acknowledging to ourselves that we are all vulnerable to various temptations in life and that each of us possesses certain weaknesses that lead to poor choices, we begin to recognize that we've all yielded to those weaknesses at various times in our lives and could be viewed as "addicts" in one way or another. The father of all addictions, the one that fosters and fuels all the others, is the addiction George Harrison described in the Beatles song "I, Me, Mine"–the addiction to self.

Since there are three kinds of people in the world, there are three kinds of addicts as well. Star addicts are unrepentant about their choices and seek to draw others down into the darkness with them. Moon addicts often have the desire to change, but they may lack the intention and discipline to maintain it. "The spirit is willing but the flesh is weak" and they find it difficult to say "no" to the marshmallow. Sun addicts are willing to patiently endure the discomfort of recovery and are committed to sobriety in its various forms by not indulging their weaknesses anymore. And once they have overcome their addictions, they look forward to helping others overcome theirs.

Step 4 of the 12 Steps asks participants to make a searching and fearless moral inventory of themselves. Several people have told me that they feel this to be the hardest of the 12 Steps and takes the most time to accomplish. In many ways it is a step that none of us will fully complete in this life. Making a moral inventory is something we need to be doing regularly throughout our lives as we strive to keep our lives in harmony with divine law through *metanoeo* and continued searching for greater light and truth.

This moral inventory is not a casual self-examination. Often it requires a very deep and sometimes painful exploration of our lives, our motives, our thoughts, and our behaviors.

The Body Is the Book of Life

I had an experience in January of 1976 that resulted in a scar on my right thumb that serves as a constant reminder of the need for self-evaluation.

I had graduated from college the month before and The Bop-a-Dips were only two weeks into our first extended tour and were performing in a club in Eugene, Oregon. The band house where we were staying was filthy and the beds were infested with fleas. Three or four days into our two-week engagement I noticed my right thumb was beginning to swell. What at first appeared to be a bug bite was now a painful infection and my thumb had swollen to nearly twice its normal size. Every time I bumped my thumb against my bass guitar while performing, a lightning bolt of pain would shoot up my arm and explode in my head.

After two nights without sleep and no reduction in the pain, I went to the hospital emergency room at 3:00 AM to get treatment. An older ER doctor who was probably in his mid-sixties was there with a young intern and it was decided that the senior doctor would need to lance my swollen thumb and clean out whatever infection he found inside. The numbing Novocain brought welcomed relief from the intense pain as the experienced doctor began to slice open my thumb. Finding a pocket of staph infection, he cleaned out the area, installed a drain, and prepared to bandage up my thumb. For some unknown reason, he paused and then said to the young intern, "I think I'll go a little deeper." That didn't sound good. As a musician I had good reason to be concerned about my fingers. I felt the pressure as he pushed the scalpel deeper into the left side of my thumb, deep under the nailbed and close to the bone. I can still hear in my mind the surprise in the young intern's voice as he said to his older and more experienced colleague, "Whoa! How did you know?" "I didn't," his colleague replied, "I just had a hunch." He'd found another pocket of staph infection deep inside my thumb, which had he not cleaned out, would have resulted in the infection continuing to spread with potentially more serious consequences for my thumb and my health.

Finding and removing darkness from our lives is not a painless experience, but don't let fear of the process cause you to postpone it. The pain associated with this kind of psychic surgery is short-lived in comparison to the pain that can occur in the future from neglecting to dig deeper and remove the foreign thoughts and behaviors that threaten our well-being.

Expect Opposition from Within and Without

As I mentioned, the greatest struggles in life take place within the confines of our own hearts. Louisa May Alcott wrote, "I ask not for any crown but that which all may win, nor try to conquer any world except the one within."

We have been told that the decisions made by our first parents in the Garden of Eden brought evil into the world and with it, tendencies toward selfishness, greed, immorality, and a host of other "fallen man" proclivities. However, that does not mean that having the propensity toward those negative traits means that we are slaves to them. Refining the human soul and eliminating those star qualities must be accomplished if we are to reach our solar potential.

There is an old Cherokee legend that tells of a conversation between a young boy and his grandfather who is trying to teach him this important principle:

> *"A fight is going on inside me," the grandfather said to the boy. "It is a terrible fight and it is between two wolves. One is evil; he is anger, envy, sorrow, regret, greed, arrogance, self-pity, resentment, inferiority, lies, false pride, and superiority." He continued, "The other is good; he is joy, peace, love, hope, serenity, humility, kindness, benevolence, empathy, generosity, truth, compassion, and faith. The same fight is going on inside of you, and inside every other person, too." The grandson thought about it for a few moments and then asked his grandfather,*

"Which wolf will win?" The old Cherokee smiled knowingly and replied, "The one you feed."

Graphic metaphors from the words of Jesus Christ such as "If thy right eye offend thee, pluck it out," remind us of how difficult this process of cleaning up our own lives can be at times and how seriously we should take it. Sometimes it feels like we must deny our humanity and that we are not allowed to make a mistake or have any fun in life. Not so. But the process of progression will always involve some measure of self-denial, delaying of gratification, and choosing which internal wolf to feed.

Opposition from without comes as a result of our associations with moon and star people. Moon people may have good intentions, but they lack dedication to the pursuit of greater light and truth. They may criticize your efforts or just appear apathetic to them. At times, they may even be among those closest to you.

Star people are not interested in advancing the cause of light and truth. They are all about promoting darkness. They are the people who look down from the lofty heights where vanity, conceit, greed, immorality, and superiority have lifted them. They use deception, criticism, doubt, fear, ridicule, shame, patronization, flattery, and other devices to discourage and mislead those who are making the courageous effort to incorporate principles of light and truth into their lives.

They may resort to malicious acts to try and destroy your reputation, your career, your relationships, or even your life. Their goal is to drag others into the same pit of darkness into which they have fallen, so they often conceal their ignoble purposes by cloaking them in noble language. Not recognizing this fact may place you as "sheep among wolves" at times, and can result in some very painful experiences. Nevertheless, sun people must continually strive to be "wise as serpents and harmless as doves" in those situations. Patience in the face of opposition is necessary to the refining process and you can expect to experience plenty of opposition on the path toward the sun. But keep in mind that these painful experiences and the suffering they bring can also be among the most powerful growth experiences in life.

Keep Looking Up. There Is Light at the End of the Funnel

I remember reading a lecture that was given by a university professor who described this refining process using an hour-glass-like figure resembling two funnels connected together.

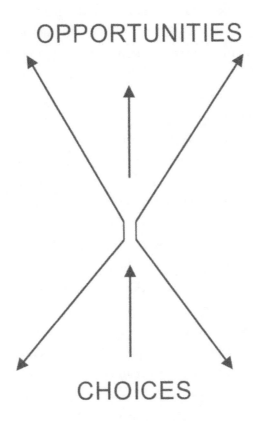

OPPORTUNITIES

CHOICES

Figure 2.1 The refining funnel

He explained that we all begin at the bottom of the hourglass, endeavoring to climb upward in our pursuit of self-improvement and spiritual advancement. As the sides of the lower funnel narrow, this represents the need to voluntarily reduce the number of choices in life that involve darkness and replace them with choices that invite greater light. Like a sculptor, we start chipping away at bad habits, recognizing erroneous thinking patterns, and disciplining our desires and appetites.

It may begin to feel like we are being required to sacrifice a lot, especially the self-indulgent behaviors that much of the star world describes as "having fun." Like the four-year-olds in the marshmallow study, we will have to decide whether we can trust those who have promised us that the rewards will be worth the effort and will be provided once the trial of our faith is over. We will have to distract ourselves from the temptation of immediate gratification and remind ourselves that not eating the marshmallow now, will result in a better outcome later. But as we do this, it may feel like we are limiting ourselves unnecessarily.

Others among the opposing forces from without will tell us we are being misguided, foolish, fear-driven, or prudish by limiting our choices and denying ourselves the gratification of some of our baser desires.

The process will eventually reach the point in the middle where the two funnels connect. We may feel we are being squeezed so tightly in this "strait gate" and "narrow way" that we feel constricted and uncertain whether the effort and sacrifice are worth it. We may ask ourselves, "Do I really want to put aside personal wants to focus on the needs of others? Do I really believe that sun people are happier than those with less light in their lives? Are the promised rewards worth the patience required to earn them?" So many questions with only faith and hope to guide our decisions.

Doubts creep in and resentment or embarrassment may begin to build until we either: (1) abandon the effort and reverse the direction we are taking, or (2) push our way through the doubts, accept the limitations that the path to the sun requires, and maintain consistent obedience to sun principles.

For those who choose the first option of turning back, regret becomes their constant companion. For those who choose the latter option, something happens that only those who have experienced it can fully appreciate and which is impossible for them to adequately explain to those who haven't. They emerge on the other side of the narrow passageway to the realization that the pathway now widens and provides access to forever-expanding amounts of light, truth, knowledge, and joy. The potential rewards are beyond our limited abilities as human beings to comprehend or express.

But we don't have to wait until the end of life to experience the rewards of sun living. Every effort we make on the path is rewarded by an increased measure of joy, peace, and confidence. Scientific research indicates that the anticipation of a positive event creates almost the same feelings in the brain as experiencing the actual event. Just imagining what the marshmallow will taste like when we get to eat it gives us much of the pleasure without the calories or tooth decay.

If you find yourself in a position where you desire to correct the course of your life and pursue something better, remember the words of Ernest Hemingway who wrote, "There is nothing noble in being superior to your fellow man; true nobility is being superior to your former self."

This process is not an easy one. Repentance is a solo activity that can be a difficult and lonely undertaking. In the James Taylor song "That Lonesome Road" he sings about the regrets that result when we fail to listen to others with greater patience and compassion. The singer laments some of the what-ifs of life and how things might have been different in his relationships with others if he had chosen to close his mouth and open his eyes more frequently, or to cool his head while warming his heart. Self-recrimination will not help nor will feeling sorry for yourself. The only way to free your troubled mind of regret is to walk down that lonesome road, without looking back, until the goal of sun living is achieved. (You can listen to the song on YouTube at https://www.youtube.com/watch?v=Gxg2NXzPSiw).

I know the feeling of having to walk down that lonesome road. There are defining moments throughout our lives when we each must make the choice between who we seem to be at the moment, and the person we ultimately want to become. Each of us will be tested. Each will have to pass through the narrow passageway. Just remember, there is light at the end of the funnel.

The Lesson

I have only shared the Paul Bonhoeffer baseball glove story a few times with couples attending a relationship seminar I teach and occasionally I have been asked what I feel I have learned from the experience. The answer has always been the same. One of life's greatest lessons is this: when you make a bad decision and the light within tells you it is wrong, don't let pride or anger or fear of embarrassment prevent you from correcting the problem as soon as possible. DON'T WAIT!

Some well-meaning people have suggested, "But it all worked out in the end! You found Paul Bonhoeffer and returned his glove and he would never have come to the reunion when he did if you hadn't. Maybe it was *supposed* to happen that way!"

No.

Regardless of the positive outcome, life might have been much better for both of us had I responded to my conscience as a junior in high school and decided to see Paul as a person of equal value, regardless of his behaviors, rather than as an object and an obstacle to my happiness. If I had recognized my own flaws earlier, I might have felt less inclined to obsess about his. And I also wouldn't have had to deal with over thirty-two years' worth of guilt and feelings of disappointment in myself that I experienced every time I saw his tattered baseball glove resting on the top shelf of my bedroom closet.

If you make the mistake of waiting, the second part of the lesson is this: NEVER GIVE UP in your efforts to correct the problem. There is no statute of limitations on apologies. As I said previously, if you maintain the desire to make amends and the willingness to act when the opportunity arises, life tends to provide additional chances to correct many of our mistakes.

Procrastination only extends the duration of our suffering and reduces the likelihood of our correcting the problem. As Will Rogers once said, "Even if you are on the right track, you will get run over if you just sit there." Waiting to correct our mistakes can also create obstacles for others who want to correct theirs and move forward in life. (Truck drivers have a name for people who sit at intersections and don't move, even after the light turns green. They call them "steering wheel holders." The motor is running, the car is in gear, their hands are on the steering wheel, and the light is green, but their foot is on the brake and they're not going anywhere. Neither are those waiting patiently behind them.)

If you want to pursue the path to sun-hood, I recommend following the motto of football quarterback Philip Rivers. It is the Latin phrase *Nunc Coepi*, which means, "Now I begin." Regardless of what mistakes you have made in the past, now is the time to begin correcting them. That requires discipline; the ability to say yes to good and no to evil. As a good friend once counseled a group of teens, "Discipline is doing what you don't want to do when you don't want to do it, because you know that you should." Sound advice for us all.

Throughout this book I will be making some suggestions on specific ways you can implement sun principles into your life as an individual, a spouse, a parent, and a community member. This is the first. I invite you to think about the people you may have harmed in any way during your life. A name (or several) should come to mind immediately. Contact them if you can. If contacting them is not an option, then contact a close member of their family. Acknowledge your mistake, apologize, and make restitution if possible. Even if they don't respond in a positive way, that's OK. You've done the right thing. If you need motivation, try watching some episodes of the old television series *My Name Is Earl*. That should help.

"We've Only Just Begun"–The Carpenters

And be patient. Sun-hood is rarely achieved during the average lifespan. Victor Hugo understood this when he wrote:

> When I go down to the grave I can say like many others, "I have finished my day's work." But I cannot say, "I have finished my life's work." My day's work will begin again the next morning. The tomb is not a blind alley; it is an open thoroughfare. It closes on the twilight; it opens on the dawn. My work is only beginning; it is hardly above its foundation. I would gladly see it mounting forever.

Aspiring sun people know that there is never a time when they no longer need to practice sun principles, or when they can give up encouraging others to do the same.

In Russian author Fyodor Dostoyevsky's novel *The Brothers Karamazov*, he addresses some of life's most important questions using the characters in his story of the Karamazov family to provide some excellent examples of the three kinds of people in the world. Two such characters in the book stand out in my mind: the Russian monk Father Kossima and his brother Markel.

Father Kossima's older brother Markel was seventeen years old when he contracted a fatal case of tuberculosis. In previous months, Markel had spent a lot of time with a political dissident and intellectual freethinker who taught at the local university and who had persuaded Markel to reject religion and any belief in the existence of God. The brothers' pious mother was heart-broken over Markel's harsh, atheistic comments. But as he grew closer to death he began to look more deeply into himself and his beliefs.

As he approached the veil between life and death, Markel began to see his existence and the relationships among people from a more enlightened perspective. To his friends who came to visit him he would say, "My beloved, my dear ones, what have I done to deserve your love, why do you love such a one as me, and why did I not know it and value it earlier?" To the family servants whom he had previously seen as something less-than himself but who continued to faithfully serve his needs, he now said, "If God would have mercy on me and let me stay among the living, I would serve you, for all must serve one another." And to his kind and saintly mother he would share the deepest and most enlightened awakening of his life when he said, "Dear mother…of a truth, each of us is responsible to all men, for all men, and for everything." Markel continued to practice sun principles until his last, dying breath.

For Father Kossima, even as a nine-year-old boy, watching this transformation take place in his brother's life had a deep impact on his own. He later decided to leave behind a self-focused star existence and to enter the monastery and dedicate himself to the pursuit of light and truth and to assisting others on the same path. Later in his life, as he lay dying himself, he reached out to those around him to share the same message of faith and hope that he had heard from his dying brother. As long as we remain alive, and for a period of time between death and the resurrection, it is not too late to change course and remember that we are never so far from God and each other that we can't retrace our steps.

Like Markel, as circumstances in our lives change, many people come to the realization that a deeper personal change is needed. I had a counseling client once who joined the Marines because he knew it was the most demanding branch of the military. He served for four years in Iraq and prided himself on his ability to endure pain. He also began to take pleasure from inflicting pain on others. In fact, he had a Latin phrase tattooed on his right forearm. It was a variation of a lyric from a song by the band Godsmack that read, "Tui poena est mei incunpitas." The English translation is, "Your pain is my pleasure."

But after returning to the U.S. and marrying a wonderful young woman and having their first child, he came to the sudden realization that learning how to become a better husband and father was what he really wanted. He discovered that learning to love openly, vulnerably, and joyfully as his wife and child did, was really the only way to transcend the pain of his former life. It is often the case when people seem to be at their lowest point in life that they are ready to embrace higher principles of light and truth. There is hope, even for confirmed star people. And if you are a sun person, you may be able to help them. As a wise leader once instructed:

> *It is my hope and my belief that the Lord never permits the light of faith wholly to be extinguished in any human heart, however faint the light may glow. The Lord has provided that there shall still be there a spark, which with teaching, with the spirit of righteousness, with love, with tenderness, with example, with living the gospel, shall brighten and glow again however darkened the mind may have been. And if we shall fail so to reach those among us of our own whose faith has dwindled low, we shall fail in one of the main things which the Lord expects at our hands.*

The Theme Song of My Life

As a senior in high school, I was uncertain about the direction my life was taking. As I pondered this dilemma, I began thinking about others who had come to similar crossroads in their lives and I began writing a song. It wasn't about me or even someone that I knew personally. It was a story of someone who lived nearly two thousand years ago. There is no record of this person, though I am certain that he lived.

The Apostle John tells of a woman who was caught in the act of adultery and brought by the scribes and Pharisees to Jesus for judgment.

Since the time that one of Israel's ancient prophets revealed to the people that the mortal mother of the Messiah would be named Mary, that name became the most popular choice for baby girls in all of Israel and Judea. That is probably why so many Marys are mentioned in the New Testament. Although this woman was never named, I decided that the possibility existed that she might have been named Mary as well.

Maybe her parents were devout sun Jews who hoped their daughter might be the one divinely appointed to bring the Messiah into the world. Or maybe they were social-climbing moon parents who named their daughter Mary because that's what all their Rabbi friends were doing. And maybe she was a good girl growing up, but then got involved with the wrong crowd in high school. Or maybe she was like Wendy Darling from *Peter Pan* and fell in love with a Lost Boy who wasn't ready to grow up. Or maybe she was an orphan without any parents to provide her with guidance who had to do whatever she felt was necessary to survive. I pondered numerous possibilities of what might have preceded that monumental moment in her life.

But as I wrote the lyrics, my mind seemed to focus on another untold part of the story; the part that happened after her encounter with the Master. I began to visualize a painful moment when this woman realized that she could no longer live by the star values of her day but had to change the direction of her life and follow the one who brought this new light into her life. She had to say goodbye to her old life, her old relationships, and begin a new life focused on truth, and on the person who had revealed it to her. It wasn't so much her story that I seemed drawn to, but the story of the unnamed man in her life. The song was suddenly about him and how this transformation in her life, had invited a transformation in his. I entitled the song, "My Mary."

I remember well the night my Mary woke me from our bed,
The dawn was fast approaching when she turned to me and said,
"I must leave you for another, for another's touched my hand.
And he's gentle, he's forgiving, and his vision leaves a brand.

Yes, they say his name is Jesus and he walks across this land
Healing people, and he's called the Son of Man.

I'm not sure I know the reason, that I know the reason why
I must follow him, for the answer surely lies
In the words that he has spoken and the gleam within his eyes.
He releases me, sets me free of my past life,
And the love that I have saved for him, now begins to cry.

So, I'll take my things and leave you, yes I have to leave this land."
And I cried for her, because I couldn't understand,
Why she was leaving me, to join this other man.
So I cursed her and I struggled to forget my lover's face,
And I despised that man from Nazareth, who came and took my place,
Preaching "Love your enemies my brothers, treat them in your place."

But the years have taught me many things, among them most of all,
That I could share the love she felt, not knowing him at all.
Yes, the love I've kept for you alone, my Mary, now I know,
The man who took your love from me, is asking for my own.
To walk a path that few have chosen, his seeds of love to sow.
So, my Mary I will join you, when His love begins to grow.

As I said, pursuing the path to sun-hood is more than just a momentary change in behavior. It goes much deeper than that. It is a way of being. As the song indicates, doing the right thing, as hard as it may be at times, assures us of the eventual attainment of lasting happiness and eternal growth. But not only that, it provides something that many others in the world who desire the same things are desperately in need of–an example to follow. We are here to work out our own destinies, but also to assist others in working out theirs.

As the great Italian poet Dante once wrote of those who fearlessly challenge the perilous darkness and blaze a trail leading to eternal glory, "Thou didst as one who, passing through the night bears a light behind, that profits not himself, but makes those who follow, wise." An excellent description of sun people.

So, stay on the road less traveled, the path that few have chosen. There will always be others on that lonesome road who will need someone else to help light the way. Be that light.

CHAPTER 3 Preview

This chapter continues to describe the sculpting process of adopting sun principles and practices while removing moon and star attitudes and actions from our lives. It offers several tools, including a decision-making model that will allow you to evaluate the belief system that drives your decision-making and assess the results those choices will produce in your life and in the lives of others.

CHAPTER 3

3 BELIEF SYSTEMS

Back in the early 1990s I heard a motivational presentation given to some high school students by Hyrum W. Smith of the Franklin Quest Company on ethical decision-making. It included a model that he called The Reality Model that explains why we do what we do and how to make better choices in life.

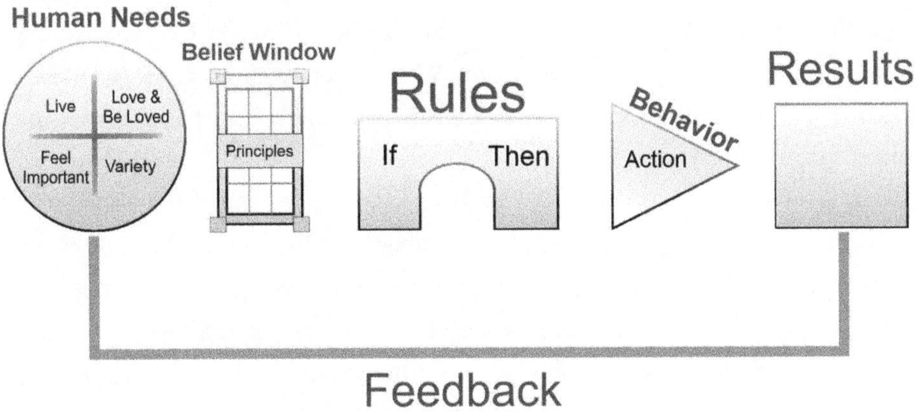

Figure 3.1 The Reality Model

As human beings, we have certain needs that we all share in common and that influence every decision we make in life:

1. The need to live.
2. The need to love and be loved.
3. The need to feel important.
4. The need for variety.

How this list of needs is prioritized and the intensity level of each need varies from person to person and can change at various times in our lives. How we choose to meet those needs determines whether we are living by sun, moon, or star principles.

To live we need food, clothing, shelter, and safety. As indicated in The Expanded Reality model in figure 3.2, some psychologists refer to this as the need for **certainty**–that we are confident about where our next meal is coming from and that we feel safe and secure in our surroundings and in our relationships.

The next need is the opposite of certainty–the need for **variety**. We need new experiences to challenge us and add adventure, growth, and emotional and spiritual depth to our lives. For some, variety is going from white sheets to a floral print or trying Thai food for the first time. For others, it may mean giving up your lucrative job on Wall Street to open an organic herb farm in Connecticut. Variety is the condiment, the spice of life–sometimes bitter, sometimes sweet.

The next need is **to love and be loved**. We have a need for connection with others. This is probably the most deeply rooted of all human needs. Some meet it through their relationships with other people while others may meet it through their relationships with their pets. Some may meet this need through their relationships with Deity. Either way, we all need to experience **love and connection** of some form. When this need is unmet it can be the source of the greatest loneliness and sorrow.

The next need is **to feel important**. We all need to feel wanted, needed, and to find a place where we fit-in in this big, wide, impersonal world.

Others have broken this down into more specific categories that include the needs for **growth, contribution,** and **significance**.

Life is pointless without growth. When a plant stops growing it begins to die. People are similar. We are here to progress and develop in body, mind, and spirit. This requires a variety of experiences that all contribute to our physical, emotional, intellectual, and spiritual learning and advancement.

There is a need for **contribution**–to give back in ways that benefit others. We want to be remembered and to leave a legacy, an imprint on the world of some kind, that is uniquely our own. As family therapist Cloé Madanes wrote, "Contribution is the human need that effectively regulates your other needs. If you are focused on contribution to others, you have the *certainty* of being able to contribute (there is always a way); you have *variety* (contribution is highly interactive); you have *significance* because you know you are helping others and improving their lives; the spiritual bond created when you help others gives you a deep sense of *connection*; and you *grow* by creatively helping others."

The first four needs of certainty, variety, love, and significance are essential for human survival. Madanes wrote, "They are the fundamental needs of the personality. Everyone must feel that they have met them on some level, even if they have to lie to themselves to do so." The last two needs of growth and contribution are the needs of the spirit and are necessary to achieve human fulfillment and what psychologist Abraham Maslow referred to as "self-actualization."

However, the remark by Cloé Madanes that the first four fundamental needs of the personality must be met by everyone "even if they have to lie to themselves to do it" seems to me to be a contradiction. I believe there is a seventh human need that has been overlooked by psychologists but readily recognized by philosophers and spiritual leaders for centuries–the need to know and embrace **truth.**

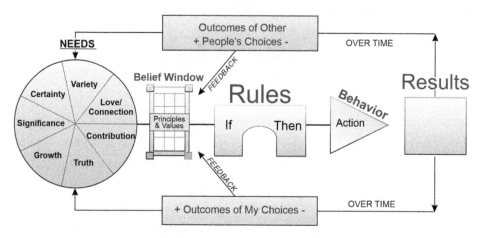

Figure 3.2 The Expanded Reality Model

We cannot expect to meet any of our human needs if we do not know truth and commit to living in harmony with it. It is only through living according to principles of truth in business, politics, finance, health, and a long list of other domains of life, that any measure of **certainty** can be realized. It is also how we learn to bridle our desires and appetites so we are able to choose a **variety** of activities that do not expose ourselves and others to unnecessary risks. It is only through compliance with true principles that we develop and maintain **loving relationships**, achieve lasting personal **growth,** and **contribute** to the betterment of others in meaningful ways.

> *We cannot expect to meet any of our other human needs if we do not know truth and commit to living in harmony with it.*

Significance that comes from being known for acts of generosity, bravery, and sacrifice produce lasting feelings of self-esteem and validation. Significance that results from deeds of darkness and evil is called infamy. In the end, it only produces feelings of worthlessness.

Truth is reality. We cannot make an informed and correct decision in life without knowing truth. But truth is more than just knowledge, it is a loving relationship. The great Russian philosopher and novelist Leo Tolstoy described it this way:

The hero of my tale, whom I love with all the power of my soul, whom I have tried to portray in all his beauty, who has been, is, and will be beautiful, is Truth.

Our relationship with truth requires commitment and fidelity. The amount of effort we make to ensure that the principles and values that constitute our belief system are true, will determine whether we are living by a sun, moon, or star belief system. It is the first step in making decisions that will meet our human needs and the needs of others in consistently positive ways.

Beliefs

Each of us comes into this world with the ability to distinguish between good and evil when we encounter them. But that ability is not fully developed at birth and takes years of growth and life experiences to mature. Over time, we each construct a belief system based on those interactions with parents, siblings, teachers, friends, religious leaders…the books we read, the Internet sites we visit, and the movies and TV shows we watch. Virtually everything we are taught and every experience we have in life has some principle or value associated with it. As we continue through childhood we begin to recognize the diversity of principles and values that are present in the world and we also begin to decide which ones resonate with us.

As we pass through our adolescent years, we begin to select the principles and values we will adopt and reject the ones we won't. We decide which ones we will place on our belief window and which ones we will jettison. By the time we complete those teenage years, our belief system is pretty well established. Those beliefs can change throughout life, but it usually takes a pretty significant experience to challenge our currently held beliefs, or many cumulative ones that gradually inform and reshape our belief system.

Some of those principles and values are placed on our belief windows consciously and intentionally, while others are there unconsciously as a result of some of our life experiences. For example, if a child grows up in an abusive home and is beaten, insulted, demeaned, or abandoned, that will have a negative influence on how he will see himself and others in the world–his internal working model of self and others. If she is indulged, spoiled, never taught compassion for others, and is never required to take responsibility for her mistakes and failures, that will also negatively influence how she sees herself and others. However, once we become aware of the unconscious ones and whether they are in harmony with the kind of person we have chosen to be, we are responsible to decide whether they remain on our belief window.

Rules, Behaviors, and Results

As the model indicates, once our belief system is in place, we next decide how those beliefs shape the **Rules** for our daily living. The rules are simple: *If…Then*.

It works like this. *If* I am in a situation and I need to make a choice, *then* I will do what my belief system tells me is most likely to meet one or more of my human needs.

What I do is called my **Behavior**, and those *Actions* will produce certain **Results**. As the arrow going from the **Results** box back to the **Needs** circle indicates, the results of my behavior are intended to meet my various human needs. As I continue to make daily decisions based on the principles and values that I carry with me on my belief window, over time, I will begin to see a pattern develop.

Either the **Outcomes of My Choices** are meeting my needs with consistently positive outcomes (+), or with negative outcomes (-). That provides feedback that either confirms the accuracy of the beliefs on my window and reinforces those beliefs and behaviors, or warns me of the inaccuracy of my beliefs and challenges the correctness of those behaviors. Sometimes the feedback is immediate–like when we race a yellow light in the belief that we will make it into the intersection before it turns red. *Crash*! (Or *flash* from a photo radar camera.) Sometimes the feedback comes days, weeks, or even years later–like when someone decides to drop out of high school in the 10th grade because he is 16 now, bought a *sweet* 2000 Mazda Protégé from the salvage auto auction, and has a *great* job at Blockbuster Video.

If I am wise and observant throughout my life, I will also pay attention to the **Outcomes of Other People's Choices** and whether their decisions have met their human needs with consistently positive or negative outcomes. That provides additional feedback as to the suitability of what's on my belief window.

(But we also need to be aware that psychosocial pressures exist that can cause people to ignore the evidence of obviously negative outcomes and continue engaging in self-defeating behaviors. For example, people who feel a strong need to please others or who want to gain acceptance into a particular social group may find it hard to reject obviously negative behaviors. They may be afraid of violating some dysfunctional family tradition–such as, children raised in families with multigenerational gang membership.)

Every day of our lives we will encounter situations that require a decision. Circumstances that produce stimuli which demand a response. Our beliefs determine our responses. Sometimes there are only milliseconds of time between a stimulus and our response, but that is when our decisions are made, and over time, how our destinies are shaped.

Since our human needs are universal and generally constant, they don't change significantly throughout our lives, though some may be more important at certain times in our lives than others. After we have made the choice to act in accordance with our beliefs and values, the resulting outcomes are outside of our control. The only components of the decision-making process that are truly under our control are:

1. Choosing the beliefs and values we place on our belief window.
2. How we apply those beliefs and values to our daily decision-making.

But there is another method for determining what should and shouldn't be on our belief windows other than just waiting to see the outcomes of our choices and the choices of others. Regardless of the source of a belief and how it got on our belief windows, beliefs that are not based on truth will never produce the outcomes we seek. They will never satisfy our deepest human needs.

Each person is responsible to examine the principles and values they encounter in life and to determine whether they are true or not. To do that they must understand that absolute and eternal truths *do* exist. They need to be aware that truth is not merely a social construction produced by the culture and the times in which we live, and that among all the existing beliefs in the world, there are many which are not true. As we increase our commitment to the discovery of truth, our sensitivity to recognizing it also increases.

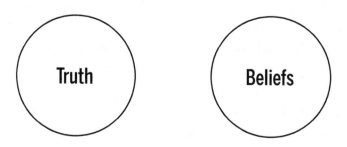

Your task is to examine the various beliefs that exist in the world and evaluate them against the standard of absolute truth before giving them any space in your life. Where beliefs and truth overlap you will find the principles and values that you want to install onto your belief window.

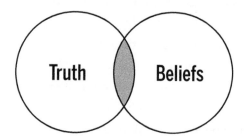

These are sun beliefs. Anything less than sun beliefs will produce results that will lead you further away from light and truth, and therefore, further away from happiness and fulfillment. (In chapter 8 we will consider how false beliefs in one area of our lives can infect other areas of our lives.)

One of the ways we can test the truthfulness of a belief is to apply the standard proposed by English philosopher G.K. Chesterton. He wrote that the test of the truthfulness of a belief is whether it produces behaviors that are *universal* and *reversible*. Universal means that a behavior would be appropriate and desirable for everyone to do. Reversible means that the behavior is one that we would not only apply in our interactions with others, but that we would also want them to apply in their interactions with us–The Golden Rule. Every major world religion includes some version of this concept among its doctrines.

When we choose to be a sun person, we are choosing to install sun beliefs on our belief windows and to behave accordingly. So, if there appears to be a conflict between their beliefs and their behaviors, sun people will change their *behaviors*, to be in harmony with their sun *beliefs*.

Moon people on the other hand, choose beliefs that are a conglomeration of truth and error. Their subsequent behaviors will produce results that may appear to meet some of their immediate needs, but in the long run fail to bring lasting happiness and growth. Rather than questioning the correctness of their actions, moon people will change their *beliefs* to accommodate their preferred moon *behaviors*.

Star people reject light and truth and carry a mixed bag of darkness-inspired beliefs that result in behaviors that produce consistently negative outcomes for themselves and others. But they will rarely admit it. While they are the first to accuse others of wrongdoing, they are the last to acknowledge their own.

> *Sun people will change their behaviors, to be in harmony with their sun beliefs.*

When a person senses what is right and wrong and chooses to do wrong, he looks for a way to justify his behavior–to make the wrong *seem* right. That's called "self-deception" and it is a common element of moon and star thinking.

Let's examine some common beliefs and which ones sun, moon, and star people choose to put on their belief windows. Then we'll examine the behaviors they promote and how the results impact us individually and as a society.

Competition vs. Cooperation

Among People

Charles Darwin published his book *On the Origin of Species by Means of Natural Selection* in 1859, explaining his theory of evolution based on the uniformitarian hypothesis: the theory that all forms of life have evolved gradually, over extended periods of time through the process of natural selection and survival of the fittest. In doing so, he unknowingly promoted a belief system about our nature as human beings that would impact society at several levels and in significant ways.

Darwin acknowledged that his conclusions were his best effort to explain the patterns he observed in nature and the perceived similarities and changes in the flora and fauna (plants and animals) that he had observed during his global travels. While using those conclusions to propose a theory that also explained the existence of humankind, he also acknowledged that there was the likelihood of some error on his part. (Since sun people are committed to the pursuit of light and truth, they also acknowledge that the best of us often make mistakes along the way.) It was a contemporary of his by the name of Thomas Huxley who held a more pessimistic opinion of human nature than Darwin. Huxley—referred to as "Darwin's Bulldog" by some—aggressively promoted the concept of a world driven by brutal, competitive self-interest for control of limited resources.

To many of the middle and upper classes of Victorian England and Europe, Darwin's book provided what one author referred to as a "consolation myth"—the myth that the upper classes did not need to feel guilty about their selfishness and lack of compassion for the poor underclasses of people because competition is built into human nature. They were just "doing what comes naturally" and shouldn't feel badly about it. A clear example of self-deception.

Huxley and others ignored much of what Darwin wrote about the more altruistic side of human and animal natures. Darwin acknowledged that, in many cases, it was cooperation among members of a clan, tribe, herd, pack, flock, etc. that produced consistently better outcomes for its members. While making his case for survival of the fittest through natural selection in his first book, in his next volume *The Descent of Man,* Darwin wrote extensively about the qualities of sympathy, cooperation, and altruism that exist in both the human and animal worlds.

Darwin hypothesized that altruistic organisms that are willing to make sacrifices for the welfare of others–a sun characteristic–tend to die earlier than selfish, competitive ones. He suggested that altruistic organisms would be less likely to pass their genetic endowment on to future generations as much as their more selfish competitors would. But this observation also threatened key aspects of his theory. What he may have failed to acknowledge is that there may be some things, other than genetic traits, that are passed on to future generations. These other things may contribute even more to their survival and advancement as a species. Maybe passing on sun values and character traits to future generations is more important to their thriving and surviving in a star-oriented world. Maybe doing so even changes their DNA for the better.

Darwin may have understood this. Prior to *On the Origin of Species,* he wrote that he considered sympathy, not competition, to be the strongest instinct in human nature, and the Golden Rule to be the cornerstone of morality among human beings. In *The Descent of Man* he used the term *love* ninety-five times when describing human relationships.

Love is not exactly a scientific term and despite years of research, no scientist has ever been able to determine what love is, what causes it to occur, and why it affects our moods and behaviors the way it does. But Darwin believed that love, in all its various forms–sympathy, conciliation, cooperation, sacrifice, altruism–are part of both animal and human natures in addition to competition. As author Thom Hartman stated in movie director Tom Shadyac's documentary film *I AM* (which I *highly* recommend for your viewing if you want to learn much more about this subject), "The basis in nature is cooperation and democracy. It's in our DNA!" Other scientists have reached similar conclusions. If cooperation is in our DNA, then competition and selfishness may be more of a conscious choice than a psychological imperative driven by a "selfish gene" as Huxley, Richard Dawkins, and some others have suggested.

While there does not appear to be any scientific evidence in support of the existence of such a gene in plant, animal, or human organisms, there are clear examples of competition at work in the natural world. However, the question that arises with the idea that natural selection and survival of the fittest has produced the best and brightest among the plant, animal, and human communities is this: *fit for what?*

If competition is supposed to produce the greatest leaders in the world, why have dictators produced some of the worst outcomes for themselves and their communities? Those who live by the sword eventually die by the sword, as do their civilizations. We have seen that drama played out repeatedly throughout human history.

It is especially sad to see a civilization that has experienced many years of cooperation-based leadership which has produced such great advancements for those civilizations, only to have one competition-based despot come along and destroy the whole thing. I know of no civilization that has prospered and progressed when its citizens spend most of their time and effort looking over their shoulders in anticipation of someone coming along to take away what they have worked so hard to produce.

Time after time we see that the greatest leaders were those who led with compassion and the conviction that sun principles produce the best outcomes for society. They taught their people sun principles, provided righteous examples by living them in their own lives, and left a legacy of sun values that formed the fabric of their societies. It is cooperation that has produced the greatest achievements in the arts, science, architecture, medicine, agriculture…in every area of human endeavor and has contributed most to the advancement of the human race. The spirit of competition and survival of the fittest promotes greed, selfishness, violence, the stifling of creativity and innovation, the theft of others' achievements, and the desire for power and control over others.

Adolf Hitler was a huge fan of Huxley's version of Darwin's theory and promoted it zealously in his infamous 1924 autobiography *Mein Kampf* where he outlined his philosophy and dreams for the future of Germany. He fostered ruthless competition among his highest-ranking and most loyal minions, often giving two people nearly identical responsibilities and then watching as they fought it out to see who would choose the most radical (and usually the most violent) methods and thereby curry favor with the Fuehrer. By maintaining enmity and competition among his subordinates, Hitler greatly reduced the likelihood that enough of them would ban together to eliminate him.

He applied the survival of the fittest concept to human beings in ways that Darwin would never have envisioned. The result was Hitler's support of the eugenics movement and the determination to eliminate any "inferior" human beings from the human gene pool by whatever means he and his henchmen deemed necessary. The harm he and others like him have caused throughout human history is beyond our ability to calculate. Others have applied social Darwinism's competition mentality to other aspects of human relations including business, politics, and even religion. As you will recall, it was cooperation that built the World Trade Center towers. It was competition that brought them down.

> *It was cooperation that built the World Trade Center towers.*
> *It was competition that brought them down.*

Examples of cooperation in the business field include Benjamin Franklin who never filed a patent on any of his inventions, hoping that others would build upon his ideas and efforts. Similarly, Elon Musk of Tesla Motors gave away his patents on electric vehicle technology to other inventors in the hope of speeding up the development of electric cars and thereby helping improve the environment for everyone. It was also Franklin's remarks to the Constitutional Convention of 1787 that allowed the participants to set aside self-interest and petty bickering to cooperate in creating the greatest system of government in human history.

Among Animals

In the animal world it is cooperation that allows a herd of red deer to decide when and from which watering hole they should collectively drink if they are to maximize their potential for survival. It is cooperation that allows a flock of migrating geese to fly much further than any individual goose ever could. It is a willingness to sacrifice her own life to protect the lives of her offspring that causes a hen to gather her chicks under her wings when danger is present.

Many of us have seen examples of one species of animal befriending another. Dogs that formed protective bonds with deer and elephants or that have raised orphaned kittens as their own offspring. Hippos that rescued African deer from the jaws of crocodile. A goat that served as a guide and caretaker for a blind horse. And the list goes on.

Cooperation among animals in their relationships with each other as well as in their relationships with human beings may extend to a deeper level of altruism than we humans understand. Native American and other indigenous cultures around the world seem to appreciate and honor the role animals play in our lives much more than contemporary Western Civilization does. Here is an excerpt from an Anasazi legend that describes what I am referring to. The words are those of an ancient and wise Native American offering counsel to our present generation:

"Perhaps it surprises you to hear the word peace applied to animals, since so many of them kill to survive. But observe them and you will understand. There are two ways to walk, [cooperation or competition] even in hunting. Let me explain with another legend—a story known among my people as 'The Legend of the Lamb.' It is said that before the foundation of the earth was laid, the animals gathered in a grand council to decide the order of their existence. How could they survive and multiply they wondered? What would be their source of food? Would they all eat grass? Then what would be left to cover the earth in softness? And who would inhabit the highest climbs and lowest vales? The debate grew loud and heated. Amid the clamor, the grand council failed to notice one among them who had made his way slowly to the fore. He called to them, 'My brothers and sisters of the earth.' All who were talking fell silent. Before them stood one who ate grass—a lamb. Not just any lamb, but the greatest of them all. 'My dear friends,' he began. 'You

are dear to me, as you know. I have come to know your hearts, each and every one. They will lead you to multiply and replenish the earth–from its tip to its depth. For this is the desire that is in you–the desire to fill the measure of your creation. But you must be free to do so. The birds must fly, the lion must roam the land, the fish must explore all the waters. You must not be bound to the grass. I will provide you the freedom you need by providing you all with food.' The grand council looked around in wonder. 'What food?' they asked, almost in unison. 'I will offer myself as food,' he said. My flesh and blood will sustain you wherever you need to go.' 'But how can it?' asked one. 'You will see,' said he. The grand council fell silent. The silence continued for hours. It was not a time for words, only for feelings. All were pondering the sacrifice of the lamb. Finally, out of the reverent stillness a dove took flight and lifted a song on the wind. 'This act must not be forgotten,' it sang. 'This act must be remembered still. Our lives must join in the offering; our acts must testify of his.' The dove lighted on the shoulder of the lamb while the music grew on the wind. The grand council joined in one voice and song, adding their words to the breeze. 'We too must offer as he has done,' they sang. 'We too must give, for each act of offering points to the act whereby life was given.' My young friend, do you see why I used the word peace to describe animals? Their deaths are sacred offerings. They make the same gift to you and me as they do to their fellow creatures. In similitude of the lamb, they give of themselves that others might live."

An example of the opposite behavior would be the beeswax-eating Honeyguide bird. Honeyguide birds are referred to as brood parasites. They are one of very few varieties of birds that lay their eggs in the nests of other birds. They lay their eggs in the underground nests of other bee-eating birds so the Honeyguide parents do not have to perform any of the normal parenting duties–like feeding and protecting their offspring. The mother Honeyguide incubates her egg inside herself a day longer than the eggs in the nest she invades. She then deposits that one egg in the nest of the other bird variety and never returns. The Honeyguide egg hatches a day or so before the other eggs. When the other eggs hatch, the newly-hatched-and-still-blind Honeyguide hatchling proceeds to use its sharp-pointed beak to locate and kill all of the other hatchlings. Believing that the Honeyguide hatchling is their only surviving offspring, the parents of the legitimate nest-dwellers give all of the food that would otherwise have been shared with their true offspring, to the murderous Honeyguide hatchling. (How do these birds sleep at night?)

So, while there are examples of animals who are the embodiment of cooperation and compassion, there are also examples of willful exploitation and competition for survival in the animal world, even when survival is not an issue.

Among Plants

While plants are constantly in the same hunt for food as animals, there is also variation in the ways they do it. Some compete and prey on their neighbors for nutrition while others seem to model their behavior after the Good Samaritan.

The *Cuscuta pentagona* plant, commonly known as "strangleweed" or dodder, is an example of competitive behavior among plants. When the seed sprouts it has no roots and has seventy-two hours to find food or it will die. It seeks out a source of nutrition by rotating in circles until it locates another plant it can attach to. Then it wraps around the host plant, pierces its stem, and begins sucking out its life juices—like a vampire. It also exchanges genetic information with the victimized host plant, allowing the dodder vine to influence the host plant's behavior in ways that further benefits the dodder vine. Like many predatory animals, the dodder vine can also choose among the available food sources, preferring the more vulnerable plants that are easier targets.

Similarly, the Spotted Knapweed sends its roots into the soil to absorb nutrition but also sends out a chemical through its roots that kills surrounding plants. This ensures that the Knapweed will have solo access to the nutrition in the soil and exercise dominion over its expanding territory. However, the Wild Lupin plant comes to the rescue of those plants victimized by the Knapweed by emitting its own chemical agent that protects surrounding plants from the Knapweed's poison. It is one of a group of plants called "nursing plants" that provide nutrition and protection to other plants.

Some plants communicate, cooperate, and demonstrate altruistic behaviors toward their next-of-kin as they participate in food-gathering. One of these is a plant called Searocket. Newly sprouted Searocket seedlings adjust the depth of their roots when they detect the presence of another seedling from the same mother plant. They reduce the depth of their roots in an altruistic act to share the nutrients in the soil with their sibling plants. They don't do that with non-related plants.

Then we have one of the best examples of cooperation in the plant world; the majestic Douglas Fir tree.

If you have seen the movie *Avatar* you learned of a tree that was not only connected with the deity of the Na'vi people, but was also connected with, communicated with, and supported all life on the alien moon of Pandora. This is not just science fiction, but is actually based on science fact.

Research conducted by Dr. Suzanne Simard of the University of British Columbia discovered an elaborate underground network that connects the oldest and largest Douglas Fir trees to all the surrounding fir trees and to certain fungi that live in the soil. The mother Douglas Fir tree absorbs the carbon-based nutrition that it takes in from the air through its needles and shares it by means of this underground network with the surrounding fungi and seedling trees. They often give the greater portion of nutrients to the younger trees that have less access to light and which are still somewhat dependent on their mother tree for sustenance. A family relationship is occurring among these trees as it also occurs among Searocket plants.

Is it possible that all life falls into the same three categories of sun, moon, and star? That all forms of life demonstrate intelligence and therefore, exercise choice to some degree? It has been said that wherever there is matter, there is also spirit. Animism is the belief that all objects in nature, even the universe itself, possess a spirit or soul that exists separately and apart from their material bodies. Where there is matter and spirit, there is life. Where there is life, there is consciousness. Where there is consciousness, there is intelligence and self-awareness. Where there is self-awareness, there is choice. And where there is choice, there is accountability.

> *Where there is self-awareness, there is choice.*
> *Where there is choice, there is accountability.*

The three categories of sun, moon, and star are determined by the levels of light and truth that are present. That is determined by the way each plant, animal, or person chooses to relate to those around it. At the sun level these relationships involve love, compassion, equality, and altruism. At the moon level self-interest often prevails over the mutual benefit of all. At the star level, self-interest is the only interest. At that level, conflict and death are the inevitable outcomes.

The prophet Isaiah once wrote of a time when "the wolf shall dwell with the lamb and the leopard shall lie down with the kid; the calf and the young lion and the fatling together; and a little child shall lead them." Isaiah foresaw a time when there would be a voluntary removal of all competition and a total commitment to cooperation among all forms of life. Survival of the fittest would be non-existent in such a world, as all would be "fit" for their role in that sun version of the world. And it won't take millions of years to accomplish either. It just requires the right choices.

A World in Competition with Itself

An example from recent history serves to describe what happens when the plant, animal, and human worlds do not cooperate with each other. In Communist China under the leadership of Chairman Mao Zedong there were periods of famine and starvation among the Chinese people. Millions were dying. At one point the chairman decided that sparrows were part of the problem. They were pilfering too much grain from the hard-working and undernourished Chinese people and he was going to put a stop to it. So, he ordered the extermination of the sparrows. Millions were killed, and the theft of grain ceased.

However, without the sparrows to eat the bugs, the crop-damaging insect population increased dramatically. So now the competition switched from man vs. sparrows to man vs. insects. So, Mao killed all the bugs–including all of the bees. Without the bees to pollinate the blossoms, the fruit and nut trees stopped producing fruits and nuts. For years there were areas of China with no bees left to pollinate the flowers, so each year an army of migrant farm-workers went into those areas armed with ladders and Q-tip-like applicators and pollinated all the fruit and nut tree blossoms by hand.

Rumor has it Albert Einstein once said that if the world's bee population were to die, the human race would follow in four years. Taken to this demonstrated extreme, a competitive, survival-of-the-fittest mentality between people and the rest of nature could one day lead to no survival at all.

Hold Theory Lightly. Grip Truth Firmly

Is evolutionary theory and its one-size-fits-all story of competition the ultimate truth about all life on this planet? As the scientific research indicates, the answer appears to be a resounding "No."

I believe that Darwin would join Dr. James Cahill of the University of Alberta who is spearheading much of this research on plants who said, "Killer competition is not the norm among plants. The idea that plants compete and that is all they do, is dead!"

Thomas Huxley once wrote, "A scientist has a bounden duty to hold his theory lightly and to part with it joyously when it conflicts with the facts." But with three kinds of people, there will be three kinds of scientists who define "facts" in differing ways.

Charles Darwin wrote in his summary of *The Descent of Man*, "False facts are highly injurious to the progress of science, for they often endure long; but false views, if supported by some evidence, do little harm, for everyone takes a salutary pleasure in proving their falseness. And when this is done, one path towards error is closed and the road to truth is often at the same time opened." I think if Darwin were alive today, he would be excited to join in the process of scientific inquiry and to see greater truth revealed and error exposed, even if some of those errors were his own.

Honesty vs. Dishonesty: "Keep Mine" or "Take It All"

A few years ago, I saw the worst thing I have ever seen on television. I know there are shows with lots of gratuitous violence and sex, and there are reality shows that promote competition, deception, manipulation, violence, and all the other kinds of star behaviors you can think of. But this…I was speechless. It was the game show from Hell.

It was called *Take It All* and I just happened to be channel surfing one evening in December 2012 when I came across the show. Howie Mandel was the host and the format of the show went like this:

The show starts out with five contestants who must estimate the retail value of certain high-value prizes. Like "white elephant" gift parties, there are opportunities to "steal" prizes that others have chosen. If you pick or get stuck with the lowest valued prize, you are eliminated. With each successive round, the prizes increase in value and one more contestant is eliminated, leaving behind any prizes they have previously accumulated. Initially it just feels like a high-priced office Christmas party game with the exception that the possibility exists that none of the white elephant gifts will be going home with any of the party-goers.

By the fourth round, the total value of the prizes and cash that the final two contestants have accrued can be as much as $300,000 or more, per contestant. They face off in a Final-Jeopardy-like showdown where they privately have to select one of two choices and put it on their video screens. They can either choose "Keep Mine" or "Take It All." Then they are each asked to reveal their choice. If they both choose "Keep Mine" they both go home with whatever prizes and cash each has accrued. Both are winners. If one chooses "Keep Mine" and the other chooses "Take It All," the one who chose "Take It All" wins and goes home with both sets of prizes and the other contestant leaves with nothing. If they both choose "Take It All" they both lose and both go home empty-handed.

Then something incredible happened. Howie reminded the contestants that this is a game and that lying is an acceptable strategy to win. I was shocked. I couldn't believe what I had just heard. While I was glad to see that Howie was somewhat uncomfortable giving that instruction, he still gave the contestants a minute to publicly talk to each other and employ the lying strategy if they chose to.

In the episode I watched, the two finalists were a young woman in her late twenties and an older woman, probably in her early sixties. Each tried to convince the other of her integrity and good intentions and sincere desire to see the other person benefit as well. As they spoke to each other there were compliments and teary-eyed expressions (mostly from the older woman) of how they felt there was a connection formed between them during the game and that each had looked out for the other during the earlier rounds of the game. You could tell that the younger woman was struggling to decide whether she could trust the older woman and she was open about her concerns. The older woman continually assured her fellow contestant that she had only the best of intentions, repeatedly saying that she felt a strong connection with the younger woman and was concerned for her welfare. Then they made their choices.

The young woman chose "Keep Mine" and the older woman chose "Take It All." The audience's reaction was a combination of shocked dismay and celebration. The family and friends of the older woman were ecstatic, while the family and friends of the young woman were stunned, disappointed, and angry. As the cameras panned the audience the people looked like they were applauding only because the applause sign was turned on. They all looked stunned by what they had just seen. How could any audience be expected to celebrate that kind of victory? The older woman won over $554,000 in cash and prizes because she lied to and deceived the more trusting younger contestant.

When interviewed after the show, the winner said that it was just a game and she did what she did to help her family. Really? So, it's socially acceptable now to lie and manipulate others if it helps *your* family? What about the *other* person's family? And what family members would be proud that their spouse or mother had just cheated another person out of her share of prizes that she had played fairly to win?

Is this where we are now as a society that we celebrate dishonesty and the exploitation of those who are naïve or trusting? Did the show's staff intentionally select people of modest means who might be more vulnerable to the allure of wealth and to the temptation to lie to get it? Is it considered entertainment now to watch the twenty-first century equivalent of a starving sin-eater as she compromises her soul to satisfy the society-induced hunger for game show stuff?

Howie and the show's producers were reported as saying that they see the show as merely a reflection of the greed that already exists in society and that they were not showcasing it. "These are two consenting adults who came in with nothing and are fully ready to play a game," he said. Seriously? Just a game? It's more than a game when people burst into tears or exchange angry looks when they lose on a game show because they have been betrayed by someone they trusted. The look of resolve on that young woman's face after she lost told the real story. Her integrity, her compassion, and her willingness to trust others had been used against her and she was not likely to trust another stranger again. And maybe not a friend, either.

When we introduce incentives into society that encourage dishonesty and the manipulation of others we are not merely reporting on their existence, we are encouraging their proliferation. Dishonesty and manipulation are becoming enthroned in the media as the strategies of choice to win in business, politics, relationships, and even game shows.

For sun people, maintaining their integrity and living with a clear conscience are greater incentives than a new Mercedes and a trip to Fiji. Well-intentioned moon people may fall victim to the siren song of the reality-show gigolo who promises happiness through victory while actually leading them down a path to moral degradation. Star people believe that it is acceptable to lie a little, to take advantage of someone's naivety, or to lay a snare to entrap a competitor.

Thankfully, *Take It All* received a substantial amount of criticism and was subsequently cancelled, but I still struggled with how anyone could defend this kind of behavior. Howie Mandel compared the game to the average person who plays poker on a Tuesday night with friends and relatives and bluffs to win and take their money. Sorry Howie, but you're wrong. Bluffing is an unemployed construction worker driving his parents' new BMW to his tenth high school class reunion. Bluffing is women who stuff their bras. This was out-and-out, premeditated lying.

When someone decides to write anywhere on their belief window that lying is a legitimate way to meet any of their human needs, that choice constitutes a clear effort at either trying to combine light and darkness–moon thinking–or a rejection of light and truth altogether–star thinking. That singular belief will influence many of the other beliefs on their belief window. And those beliefs will produce very predictable behaviors and negative results in the lives of the individuals and the societies that endorse them. In the end, everybody loses at the game of life when we play by these rules.

Changing the Rules

It is in facing these kinds of dilemmas in life that we learn what we are made of and what kind of person we are choosing to become. So, I began to ponder how I might respond to the "game show from Hell" situation. Was there really a way for someone to play this game without compromising their integrity and still produce a win-win outcome for both contestants? Is there really a way to protect ourselves from exploitation without exploiting others in return?

Some contestants might choose to disavow the whole premise of the show and storm off the stage in righteous indignation. Others might try to convince their opponent of their integrity and choose "Keep Mine," risking the likelihood of being taken advantage of and losing their share of the prizes. Still others might play the game to win, not trust their opponent, choose "Take It All" and then voluntarily split the winnings with their opponent if they won. I considered several possible options.

Four years later I happened to be listening to an episode of the PBS program *Radiolab* and learned how contestants Nick and Ibrahim navigated the same situation on a British TV show.

Take It All was not an original idea. There had been at least three versions of this game show produced previously for American and British television. Prior to *Take It All* the most recent version was a BBC game show called *Golden Balls* that aired between June 2007 and December 2009. At the end of each show, the final two contestants were given the same option–to choose a golden ball with the word "Split" inside in hopes of sharing the money, or to choose the ball with the word "Steal" inside in hopes of taking the entire pot.

As the pre-selection conversation between the two contestants began, contestant Nick shocked the audience and rival contestant Ibrahim by saying, "Ibrahim, I am an honest man and I am telling you now, 100%, that I'm going to choose 'Steal.' I'm asking you to trust me and pick 'Split' and I promise to split the money with you after the show. Or, you can choose 'Steal' and we both go home with nothing. Your choice."

Ibrahim suggested they both choose "Split" and share the money (though he later reported he was lying and had no intention of choosing "Split.") Nick listened and smiled and repeated his decision to choose "Steal." Each time Nick repeated his intentions, Ibrahim got more frustrated. He tried criticism and insults, thinking that would change Nick's mind. It didn't. This fruitless discussion went on for *forty-five minutes*. Even the audience began to get frustrated with Nick. But nothing swayed him. Nick was a rock. He never got upset; just continued smiling and confidently repeating his intention to choose "Steal." The show's host reminded Ibrahim that Nick had no legal obligation to keep his promise to share the money if Ibrahim picked "Split." Finally, he put an end to the pointless debate and demanded that the duo make their choices. Just as the two were reaching for their golden ball of choice, Ibrahim said with exasperation, "I tell you what…I'm gonna go with you!" He put down the first ball he had chosen and selected the other one. Nick had already chosen his ball. Then they each opened them, showing the word inside to each other and to the audience. Ibrahim chose "Split" and Nick chose…"Split"!

The audience was aghast and totally confused. What had just happened? Then it dawned on me. While Ibrahim assumed *he* was the one taking the risk, the truth was that he was *never* at risk of losing. He was either going to get half of the pot, or all of it. Regardless of his choice, he was guaranteed to win something. His opponent had already made that decision.

Suddenly, I understood something about sun people I had not fully appreciated before. Nick's behavior was not just a brilliant display of strategy, it was a display of character. Yes, his convincing rhetoric increased his odds of keeping half of the money, but it was *never* his intention to put Ibrahim's money at risk. It was *Nick* who took the risk by trusting *Ibrahim*, not the other way around. He had no more intention of causing harm to Ibrahim than King Solomon intended to cut a new-born baby in half to settle a dispute between two competing mothers. The mothers may not have known that, but the king certainly did. Was Solomon being dishonest by using that strategy? No, he was being "wise as a serpent, but harmless as a dove." In doing so he exposed star behavior and rewarded sun behavior.

I'll say more about the importance of vulnerability and trust in our relationships in future chapters, but the moral of this story is that sun people are willing to encourage others to be honest and trustworthy even when doing so may involve some personal risk. They will stand firm on correct principles and not waiver, regardless of the consequences. And they will create opportunities that invite others to do the same, just as Nick did for Ibrahim.

Howie Mandell concluded his interview about *Take It All* by saying, "I don't know if I'm teaching my kids right, but you have to go with your own instincts." Thomas Jefferson once wrote a letter to a friend by the name of Thomas Law saying, "I sincerely...believe...in the general existence of a moral instinct. I think it the brightest gem with which the human character is studded, and the want of it as more degrading than the most hideous of the bodily deformities." He also wrote to his friend Peter Carr saying:

> *This sense is as much a part of his nature as the sense of hearing, seeing, feeling; it is the true foundation of morality. The moral sense, or conscience, is as much a part of man as his leg or arm. It is given to all human beings in a stronger or weaker degree, as force of members is given them in a greater or less degree. It may be strengthened by exercise, as may any particular limb of the body.*

Some people appear to be going through life as vegetative couch potatoes wearing ear plugs, blindfolds, and oven mittens. Their moral sense is non-functioning and they fail to recognize the hideous spiritual deformities that result. The kinds of choices they make will reflect those moral handicaps.

But Nick seemed to be free of those moral disadvantages. In fact, as I listened to the remainder of the program, I was even more impressed with Nick when I learned that he was an experienced game show participant who regularly auditioned for these shows. He didn't play to win money and prizes for himself, but for the charitable organization he worked for and to which he donated all his winnings.

My mind scrolled back to the images of his demeanor and the look of serenity he maintained in the face of the criticism and mocking he received from his opponent, the host, and the audience. While they were all disturbed and distressed by the game, Nick appeared calm and confident. There was no hint of anger, fear, or smug self-righteousness. His example was a powerful reminder that those who have sun principles engraved on their belief windows can look forward to a heart at peace with the world, a conscience free of regrets, and the assurance that their choices will consistently produce positive outcomes for themselves and those around them.

Lie to Me...Please!

Sadly however, dishonesty is quickly becoming an acceptable, even desirable, component of our culture. Take vanity sizing for example.

When I was a child there was uniformity in sizing clothes for obvious reasons. If you know you wear a size 10, you want to be able to buy a size 10 item from any store or order it from a catalog with the confidence that it will fit. I learned recently about a large corporation that owns three different clothing store franchises. One caters to lower and middle-income customers, another caters to upper-middle-income customers, and a third caters to high-income customers. In the lower income stores a size 10 dress may still be a size 10. But in the middle income stores it is now a size 8. And in the high income stores it is a size 6. Same dress, same size, but with three different labels indicating three different sizes. Why?

Apparently, this corporation believes that people who are richer than most people are also vainer than most people and want to believe that they are thinner than they really are. "So, if the customer prefers to believe a lie, we will accommodate her. It's a win-win situation, right?" Just extend that reasoning to other areas of our lives and the answer becomes obvious.

Tech companies like Google and Facebook amass a huge amount of information about people based on their Internet activities and the company's computer algorithms create a profile for each of those people. Then they direct advertisements to those people about various products and services that they assume will appeal to them, based on their profiles. But it goes beyond just a marketing strategy. If two very different people with very different profiles do a Google search for the same topic or question, they will each receive different responses. Each person's response will be slanted to appeal to the perceived cultural or ideological biases of that person. These tech companies will tell their customers what they think they want to hear, even if it's not what they need to hear–i.e., the objective, unadulterated truth. Many are concerned that these companies control the dissemination of information in this way so they can influence our beliefs and decisions. Governments and political parties have caught onto this and are now using the same methods to influence elections.

We are creating a world where everything is Photoshopped, where fantasy and reality become so blended that people are no longer sure which is which, and where dishonesty is not only common, but expected. And as we know all too well, one lie leads to another and another and another. The eventual result is a world where no one believes anyone, about anything, anymore.

Dishonesty multiplies quickly within the society that tolerates it; from our personal and professional lives, to our civic lives. As nineteenth-century French economist Frederic Bastiat wrote, "When plunder becomes a way of life for a group of men, they create for themselves, in the course of time, a legal system that authorizes it and a moral code that glorifies it." And when one dishonest or manipulative law becomes a legal precedent, it often begets many others.

There are moon people who know that dishonesty is prevalent but they have either accommodated it or they have given up believing that it can be corrected and just don't care anymore. For star people, dishonesty is the easiest way to "take it all."

But for sun people, not achieving all of their economic dreams is not a curse, it is merely one of life's inconveniences. In fact, it is one of the great paradoxes that life often becomes less satisfying, less fulfilling, less secure, and less happy not just when things get significantly worse financially, but when they suddenly get substantially better. Just ask some lottery winners or entertainers who became overnight sensations.

A New Testament parable shared by Jesus addressed this issue masterfully when he told the story of a man who spent his life accumulating great wealth and worrying about not having a barn big enough to store all his goods and protect them from theft. He decided to tear down his small barn and build a much bigger and more secure one, only to die the next day. Heart attack I bet. Probably from stress. Too much worrying about his stuff.

Sun people understand what moon and star people fail to see and what I will address in greater detail in chapter 7; that having enough to satisfy our basic needs and being content with that will bring greater peace and happiness than taking it all.

Plainness vs. Complexity

It's the difference between a hand-shake agreement and a five-hundred-page contract written in legal-ese with a lot of fine print. It's the difference between The Constitution of the United States and the IRS Tax Code; between the Ten Commandments and the Halakhah.

Plainness means that things are explained using clear and simple language that the average person can understand. The terms and conditions of a sun agreement are clearly listed. What isn't spelled out is covered by a mutual commitment to the wonderfully simple and universally acknowledged sun contract: The Golden Rule.

Complexity often involves using terms that only a few people fully understand or that are used intentionally because they are difficult to clearly define. For example, moon and star governments have been known to write broad, vaguely-worded laws that can be used to target, intimidate, and control non-compliant citizens. For that reason, complexity is often the friend of star people who will use it to conceal, manipulate, or gain power over others.

Complexity often creates uncertainty, vulnerability, and confusion in our communications with others. (Think of the time you tried to read through all the closing documents for the purchase of your first home, or for a new app you wanted to download to your phone.) And the more complex things become, the greater the likelihood of conflict.

But one of the unique qualities possessed by many sun people is their ability to perceive simplicity and plainness in the midst of complexity; to condense a mountain of complex information into morsels that others can better digest and comprehend.

For example, my oldest daughter Matia is a math whiz. She majored in mathematics in college and became a high school math teacher. Like many of her math-teaching peers, she recognized that several of her students were flummoxed by the complex formulas and abstract concepts they encountered in high school algebra, geometry, trigonometry, and calculus. She realized that in order to help her students master those subjects, she would need to simplify the process for them. She could break down complex math problems into parts that were already familiar to her students and then show them how to use the formulas to connect the parts and find the answers–like Jesus would do if he were a high school math teacher. As history's greatest teachers have demonstrated, life's most profound truths can often be taught using the simplest of methods.

However, I'm also aware that several star individuals in history have spread some pernicious lies using simplistic expositions that many people failed to examine or challenge. Often, those were people who *wanted* to be lied to. But generally speaking, plainness and simplicity are the friends of sun people because they are committed to truth and transparency.

For many, reaching that simplicity and clarity of understanding comes only after wading through the complexity and chaos of the divergent philosophies of the world and distilling the precious sun truths that they discover along the way. Oliver Wendell Holmes Sr. summed it up this way: "For the simplicity on this side of complexity, I wouldn't give you a fig. But for the simplicity on the other side of complexity, for that I would give you anything I have."

My wading experiences have brought me to this conclusion: **as the problems of the world become more complex, the solution becomes plainer and simpler–a return to sun values.** When people are living by sun principles and values, they are better able to recognize solutions to their problems. When that happens, there is a sense of familiarity; of "duh! of course! how obvious! how simple!" Those who value honesty also value plainness and simplicity. No secrets. Nothing to hide. What you see is what you get.

Forgiveness vs. Revenge: The Story of the Three-Legged Cat

A three-legged cat once taught me a great lesson about forgiveness, resiliency, and love. It all began on a summer afternoon when I was sixteen years old.

I happened to walk into the garage of our family home that afternoon. Both of my parents' cars were gone as they were working at my father's pharmacy. Otherwise, I might not have noticed the cat.

Our home was built of cinderblock. In the garage, there were two places near the bottom of one wall where a block had been turned sideways to allow air to vent into the crawl space underneath the house. Wire mesh was attached to the block on the inside to keep various critters from getting under the house.

Figure 3.3 The garage wall

As I was about to walk back into the house, I noticed something moving inside one of the sideways cinderblocks. As I looked closer, I could see a medium-sized grey cat that was in terrible condition. It looked half-starved, its fur was all matted, and one of its back legs was totally severed just above the ankle and was hanging by a piece of skin. As I approached the opening and started to reach in to retrieve the cat, it began hissing at me and retreated as far back into the opening as it could. I decided to back off and not try to force the issue. I walked a few feet away to the middle of the garage floor and sat down. I stared at the cat and he stared back–like a game of chicken with each waiting for the other to make the first move.

After about fifteen minutes of this with no movement by the cat, I decided to go into the house and give the cat a chance to leave its hiding place. About thirty minutes later I came back out into the garage, only to discover that the cat was still inside the cinderblock. I went into the house and brought out a bowl of milk and placed it about two feet from the opening and sat down in the middle of the garage floor again to see if the milk would draw the cat from its refuge. The cat looked at me, then at the milk, and then back at me. Nothing. This went on for about another ten minutes with no response, so I returned to the house.

An hour or so later I returned to the garage to discover that the milk was gone and the cat was back inside the cinderblock. This went on for three days–me leaving bowls of milk and some cat food just outside the opening and then sitting in the middle of the garage floor waiting for about ten minutes to see if the cat would come out while I was there. By the third day he would leave the safety of the cinderblock and drink the milk while I sat there and watched, always with a close eye on me. With each day I would move a little closer to the food while the cat would eat. On the fourth day I was able to set the bowl down and sit only about one foot away. The cat came out of the opening and began to drink the milk. Slowly, I reached out my hand and stroked the cat's back. At that moment, everything changed. The cat trusted me. No fear, no hissing, no anger. After he finished the milk, I picked up the cat and took it into the house. My little sister had been following the events of the previous three days and we decided to cut the piece of skin holding the severed leg while she tried making an artificial leg for the crippled feline out of Popsicle sticks. After several failed attempts to attach it, we gave up and decided that the cat would just have to go through the rest of its life on three legs.

Now, my family owned several cats while I was growing up, but I have never heard a cat purr as loud as this one. When I would enter the family room and sit down on the couch, that cat would run across the room, leap into my lap, curl up, and start purring. His whole body would vibrate.

Animals can smile you know, and this cat had the biggest smile I have ever seen on any cat before or since. It managed to run and jump nearly as well as the other four-legged cats at our house and seemed to have no problems adjusting to its new surroundings.

How did he do it? How did he accept the loss of a leg and put behind him the painful memories of whatever had happened to him before I came along and coaxed him out of his hiding place in the cinderblock wall? How had he avoided the feline flash-backs, the kitty-catatonia, and the other psychological problems that are often present in the lives of people, and some animals, who have experienced severe trauma? He appeared to be genuinely happy. Even happier than our other cats which had never experienced hunger or abuse.

For years I have pondered that experience and what made that cat so emotionally resilient and able to experience real joy in the wake of such misery. I realized that no matter how much pain someone has endured in life, each person will decide whether he carries anger, fear, revenge, and hopelessness on his belief window or compassion, love, and forgiveness.

As difficult as life may be at times, how we respond to the circumstances we face is still a choice. If we allow what Caroline Myss calls our "woundology" to define our identities and direct the course of our lives we will never heal physically, emotionally, or spiritually from the challenges and opposition that each of us will face in life.

I once shared this story with a counseling client who began to cry as he recognized the similarities between the traumatized cat and his emotionally troubled wife who had recently done something that threatened the survival of their marriage. He described her as a "wounded bird" who was sequestering herself within their home, overwhelmed by feelings of anger, fear, and remorse. When I asked why he was crying he said, "I was afraid that you were going to say that you had tried to force the cat to come out of the cinderblock before it was ready and that it had run away and never come back." He was afraid that I was going to suggest a similar intervention with his wife. As we spoke, I began to realize something I had not consciously recognized before–that *my* decision had a lot to do with the *cat's* decision. My willingness to give the cat his space, to gradually and incrementally reach out and invite a compassionate relationship but not coerce one, and to let the relationship develop slowly was key to the cat's decision to trust, and eventually, to heal. That was exactly what we decided was the right thing to do for his wife.

Sun people are more concerned with reconciliation than revenge. They possess the ability to forgive even heinous acts perpetrated against them because of the light and love within them. They hold no "eye for an eye" approach to justice because they realize that only forgiveness can really free them from the traumatic memories and emotional baggage of life. Unlike moon people who may struggle to forgive and forget, or star people who vent their rage and aggression and make innocent victims of all those around them, sun people actually learn to love and trust more deeply and have more compassion for others as a result of their suffering.

That cat reminded me of Jewish psychiatrist Viktor Frankl who spent most of World War II in Nazi concentration camps seeing unspeakable violence and cruelty and anticipating imminent death every day. In his book *Man's Search for Meaning*, Frankl concluded that the meaning of life is found in every moment of living. Even in suffering and death, life never ceases to have meaning. He came to the realization that we may not be able to choose all of the circumstances of our lives, but we will always be free to choose how we respond to them. Frankl wrote:

> *A thought transfixed me: for the first time in my life I saw the truth as it is set into song by so many poets, proclaimed as the final wisdom by so many thinkers. The truth—that love is the ultimate and the highest goal to which man can aspire. Then I grasped the meaning of the greatest secret that human poetry*

and human thought and belief have to impart: The salvation of man is through love and in love. I understood how a man who has nothing left in this world still may know bliss.

My three-legged cat had apparently reached the same conclusion. Oh, that more human beings would do the same.

Punitive Justice vs. Restorative Justice

With every choice in life there are consequences. Sun choices bring positive consequences and rewards for ourselves and others. Moon and star choices bring varying degrees of negative consequences. When our actions negatively impact others, justice demands that we be held accountable for them. In doing so, people must also choose which approach to justice they will put on their belief windows.

Throughout human history there have been two primary approaches to justice that human beings have used: punitive justice and restorative justice. Punitive justice involves punishment in the form of inflicting physical and emotional pain and/or taking away people's money, freedom, eyes, teeth, hands (or other bodily appendages), or their very lives as payment for their crimes. It is based on what author Walter Wink refers to as the "myth of redemptive violence"–that violence is a necessary and appropriate response to bad behavior and that seeing the perpetrator of a crime punished in this way can be healing to the victim.

But rather than resorting to methods that return injury for injury, abuse for abuse, or pain for pain, restorative justice tempers the pain by providing opportunities for a change of heart by the perpetrator and a healing of the heart for the victim.

For example, one of the first twentieth-century applications of restorative justice at an institutional level began in the early 1970s in Kitchener, Ontario, Canada. A juvenile probation officer and a juvenile court judge decided that the traditional punitive justice model was not working with the youth in their community and that a new approach was needed.

They decided that two youth convicted of vandalism should be offered the opportunity to meet with the victims of their crime and work out a way to make things right. This intervention was the beginning of the first victim-offender mediation program and proved to be very effective at improving restitution completion rates, reducing fear among victims, and reducing repeat crimes by offenders. It quickly grew in popularity and has since spread to many jurisdictions around the world.

A similar model has existed for many years among the Maori people of New Zealand that is referred to as Family Group Conferencing. This involves bringing the offender(s), the victim(s), the tribal leaders, and any concerned members of whatever families are involved, to work out an agreeable resolution to the problems. Accountability is emphasized, but so is encouragement.

Restorative approaches to justice have existed throughout human history in various cultures and among various religions including aboriginal spirituality, Chinese religions, Christianity, Sikhism, and many more. Not only has it impacted the relationships within tribes and families, it has influenced the outcomes of world events as well. Take South Africa for instance.

After the fall of the Apartheid government in 1994 where the white minority had ruled South Africa since 1948, there was the need to address the thousands of incidents of torture, murder, and denial of basic rights to the black and colored majority in South Africa that had occurred during the forty-six years of Apartheid rule. In 1994 The African National Congress party, led by newly elected president Nelson Mandela, faced the dilemma of how to address these many crimes against the majority black, colored, and Indian residents of South Africa without further adding to the anger and resentment toward the white minority who had perpetrated them.

Drawing heavily upon the Christian principles of repentance and forgiveness, Anglican Bishop Desmond Tutu was instrumental in promoting a restorative justice approach to the problem. What the African National Congress decided to do was to offer amnesty to all those who would come forward and confess to all of the crimes they had committed so that the victims could be identified and the injustices they had suffered, acknowledged. This invited a spirit of repentance on the part of offenders and forgiveness and healing on the part of the victims rather than turning the victims into victimizers. Societal division and a spirit of revenge could have been the result had they decided to track down the offenders and aggressively punish their criminal behaviors. Instead, the desire for reconciliation and national unity were promoted and additional bloodshed was avoided.

That was also Abraham Lincoln's hope near the end of the Civil War when he issued a full pardon to all rebel combatants, their military leaders, and even to the Southern politicians who caused the war in the first place. That included a restoration of all their property rights–except of course, to their former slaves. The only requirement was that they would have to swear an oath of loyalty to the Union and to the Constitution and that the politicians would do nothing to try and reverse the Emancipation Proclamation or repeal the Thirteenth Amendment abolishing slavery.

You Are Welcome in Our Village

I remember a PBS documentary several years ago about a family from Great Britain who were invited to live in a small village among an African tribe. The family included a mother, father, and their ten-year-old son. There was no source of clean drinking water near the village, so water was trucked into the area each week from many miles away and then carried by hand to the village by the women.

One day the young boy decided to fill a water dish for a dog that roamed the village. But instead of dipping water from the storage container that the women had filled and pouring it into the dish, he dipped the animal's dirty water dish directly into the container, contaminating the village's weekly supply of drinking water. The women of the village were very upset by his thoughtless behavior and let him know of their disapproval.

It was decided that the village chief would go to the family's hut that evening to discipline the boy. The parents feared the worst because they had not been in the village very long and they were not familiar with the customs of this seemingly primitive African tribe. They scolded their son severely for his behavior and waited anxiously for the chief's arrival and his decision about the family.

That evening the chief came to the family's hut and asked the boy to join him as he walked to the edge of the village. They sat together on the ground and the chief put his arm around the boy's shoulder and held him close.

As they sat together under the stars, the chief repeatedly told the boy how much he was loved by the villagers and how appreciative they were of him and his parents for coming to their village. He also explained that the boy's behavior had offended some of the women in the village and that the young man would need to make things right with those who had worked so hard to provide safe drinking water for all in the village. He praised the boy for his willingness to correct the mistake and reassured him of his confidence that the boy would never repeat the error.

Together they walked back to the family's hut where he was reunited with his anxious parents. The family agreed to pay to replace the contaminated water and the boy was required to clean and sanitize the storage container. Then he was invited to assist the women in carrying the water to the village each week for several months so he could understand and appreciate their efforts on behalf of the people of the village. By applying restorative justice, the chief provided that boy with a life lesson he would never forget. By accepting responsibility and acting with integrity, the family forged bonds of love and commitment between themselves and the people of that village that were unbreakable. That's how sun people approach justice.

Just imagine what kind of young men and women we would have in our cities and towns, attending our schools, playing on our athletic teams, and participating in leadership roles if we all applied these same restorative justice methods in our homes, schools, churches, and courtrooms. There might be many more Jean Valjeans in today's world if there were more Bishop Myriels sitting in the judgment seats. And similarly, there might be more Bishop Myriels sitting in the judgment seats if there were more Jean Valjeans appearing before them in their courtrooms.

Conflict would virtually disappear in societies where the people have a restorative approach to justice written on their belief windows and where everyone applies a simple principle that I will address in more depth in the next chapter: that *people* are more important than *problems*, and when love is the guiding principle in the way we hold each other accountable for our actions, peace abounds.

So, where did the idea of restorative justice come from? Albert Einstein wrote in 1950 that he held an agnostic view regarding the existence of God because he could not believe in a Supreme Being who would use the system of rewards and punishments that Einstein saw recorded in the Bible as a means of controlling His children's behavior.

If Einstein had looked more closely, he would have discovered that famines, pestilence, wars, and fire and brimstone falling from heaven were only used by Deity as a last resort after his rebellious children had rejected all the offers of restorative justice that God had made previously. The same is true today in the court systems that offer restorative justice alternatives. For those who reject the opportunity of a more lenient and merciful restorative justice solution to their criminal activities, they have, by default, chosen the more punitive alternative.

Restorative justice is divine justice. The opportunity to accept responsibility for our actions, make restitution to victims, and reconcile with those we have offended is always the first option God offers and the one he encourages us to choose. When it comes to divine justice, the option of more punitive consequences for one's behaviors is always determined by the *offender*, not by the perfectly righteous and merciful judge of the universe. When we choose the levels of light and truth we are willing to live by, we are also choosing the severity of the consequences we will face when we transgress true principles. The greater the darkness, the harsher the consequences.

Restorative justice uplifts the mind and spirit, offers a healing of the heart, and invites everyone involved to become better people. It holds a prominent place on the belief windows of sun people.

Beauty

When sun people encounter beauty their first desire is to protect it, preserve it, and to share it with others. Moon people want to possess it for themselves; partly because they appreciate it, and partly because of the prestige that owning it will bring them in the world. Star people will deny it, debase it, or try to destroy it. Whether beauty is found in music, art, theater, films, the fashion industry, or simply in the natural world we see around us, there will be three responses to it.

Take buffalo for example. The tradition among the Lakota Sioux Indians of the Great Plains is that buffalos were among those animals who volunteered to descend from the spirit world to serve as food for mankind. For centuries these majestic animals have done just that–providing food and warm clothing through the cold winter months to appreciative Native American tribes. These people lived in harmony with their animal neighbors and killed them only when necessary, sharing the meat and hide among the tribal members.

When white hunters from the east discovered the enormous herds of buffalo that blanketed the Great Plains, they began killing them by the thousands and selling the hides. It got to a point where passenger trains traveling through the plains would stop on their journeys west to allow "hunters" to use these unsuspecting animals for target practice, shooting them from the comfort of their railroad cars and leaving the dead carcasses behind to rot on the prairie. This kind of wanton destruction nearly caused the extinction of this great animal.

Another example can be seen in the forests of California. For centuries the Giant Sequoia redwood trees of central California were revered by the Yosemite Indian tribe and known by the name *Wawona* in honor of the Northern Spotted Owl that the tribe believed to be the guardians of the forest. The magnificent beauty of these trees was shared among all of the Indian tribes of the area and only the Great Spirit was recognized as their owner. Not until 1852 when a hunter named Augustus T. Dowd came across them, did the rest of the world learn of their existence.

The first ancient sequoia seen by Dowd was named "The Discovery Tree." After surviving thirteen hundred years of the worst that nature could throw at it, the tree finally succumbed to the loggers' saw and was cut down one year later. The massive tree stump was turned into a dance floor that could accommodate a cotillion party of thirty dancers at one time. Drawings of the spectacular scene were published in East Coast newspapers and magazines to the awe and amazement of readers. But the question that remained for the loggers was, "What do we do with this thing now that we own it?"

They discovered that the wood was too soft and brittle to be used in construction and the massive weight of the tree caused it to shatter into pieces when it hit the ground. The trees were too big to mill, so in some cases the loggers strapped dynamite to them and blew them up into more manageable chunks of wood.

Because the wood has a high tannin content which makes it resistant to wood rot, it was used primarily for fence posts and in vineyards to support grape vines. Even after discovering the limited usefulness of the wood and the marginal yields they got from the massive trees, loggers continued to cut them down for another seventy years until conservationists like John Muir and others began efforts to protect the ancient trees. Finally, logging of Sequoia redwood trees was prohibited by law in 1980.

I will let you decide who belongs in each of the three groups of sun, moon, and star people. Certainly, not all hunters and loggers are star people and not all Native Americans and conservationists are sun people, but we can reach certain conclusions about ourselves based on the ways we choose to see the world around us and how we choose to use the resources it contains. This includes how we choose to see our fellow human beings—as objects for our personal use or as beings of intrinsic beauty and value.

Charles Dickens provided some timeless examples of these perspectives in his novel *Great Expectations*. When the character Miss Havisham is driven insane by her rejection and abandonment by her con-artist fiancé on their wedding day, she becomes obsessed with punishing other men for the pain inflicted on her by her fiancé. In an effort to destroy the beauty of true love for others, she engineered a romantic relationship between her cold-hearted adopted daughter Estella and an orphaned boy named Pip, using Estella to break his heart. At one point during one of his visits to her house, Miss Havisham shows Pip her brother's extensive butterfly collection. She tells Pip:

> *"Look closer if you wish. My brother's collection. He went to the furthest reaches of the earth in his quest for the purest specimen of beauty. And when he found it, he stuck a pin through its heart. He's dead now. Cholera. In the tropics. Struck down in his relentless pursuit of beauty. Perhaps it was beauty's revenge to stop his heart when he had stopped so many others."*

In the end it is Pip who restores our belief that beauty can still be found and appreciated, even though there is a lot of ugliness in the world around us.

There are many more instances in history and literature of similar responses to beauty in the world. These just serve as a few examples. The question is, what response to beauty do you choose to inscribe on your belief windows?

Using the Inspired Mind

One night in 1967 a deeply troubled twenty-four-year-old woman knelt in a small Catholic chapel in Chicago and poured out her heart to God as she had many times before, pleading for relief from the mental illness that shrouded her life in darkness and suicidal depression. As a result of a transformative spiritual experience that night where she felt the love of her Heavenly Father in a deeply personal way, she suddenly saw herself from a much more enlightened perspective: as a cherished and beloved daughter, struggling with a great burden, but capable of progression and growth. That experience enabled psychologist Dr. Marsha Linehan to eventually succeed in her own battle with mental illness and to develop a model of psychotherapy that she felt would help others with similar difficulties. The model became known as Dialectical Behavioral Therapy (DBT) and has helped many people achieve greater self-acceptance while also recognizing the need to make better life choices. She included as part of treatment the use of mindfulness meditation. This comes from Zen Buddhism and was part of her technique for helping people learn how to regulate their emotions and make more productive decisions. One of her methods she refers to as the Wise Mind exercise.

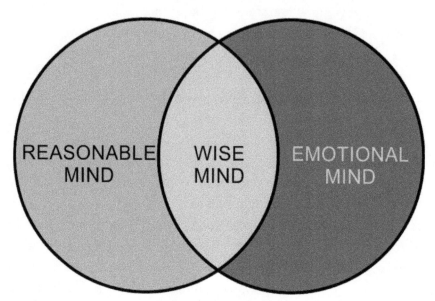

Figure 3.4 The Wise Mind

When the Emotional Mind dominates our lives and decision-making, we tend to make choices impulsively and without regard for how those decisions may impact ourselves and others. Incorporating the Reasonable Mind–the rational thinking process–into our lives means including logic and reason in our decision-making. Where the two overlap, Dr. Linehan refers to as the Wise Mind. It is in the Wise Mind that we find balance between emotion and reason and where we are able to make better informed decisions that are more likely to produce the positive results we seek.

For people who recognize they are engaged in problematic behaviors that are producing undesirable outcomes for themselves and others, the Wise Mind exercise is effective in helping them manage emotional impulsivity, employ critical thinking skills, and choose better behavioral options. But what about the people who aren't coming to therapy and who don't consider their choices to be problematic? Limiting the decision-making resources to the overlapping areas of the Emotional Mind and the Reasonable Mind alone, without incorporating morals and values, can produce some questionable outcomes at times. Let me share an example.

In order to protect his privacy, I will call him Seth. Seth was a seventeen-year-old boy from a middle-class neighborhood in a middle-class New Jersey community. He was of Jewish descent but was not a committed practitioner of his religion nor a firm believer in God. He was very intelligent and well-read about the religions of the world and loved to debate about religion and the existence of God, but it was purely an intellectual exercise. He considered himself to be a good person who was capable of empathy and who was not driven by anger, greed, or other negative human emotions. He was logical and reasonable in the way he conducted his business. In fact, he had a thriving business at the young age of seventeen that he anticipated would produce sufficient income to finance his college education and beyond. Seth sold cocaine.

But he considered himself to be an ethical cocaine dealer. In his logical mind, he was merely providing a product that many people desired and he was doing so in an ethical way. He did not sell to people who he knew were addicted or who had to pawn their parents' jewelry and stereo equipment to finance their drug habit. He charged a reasonable price and sold only good quality cocaine that was not excessively diluted or "cut" with other fillers to increase his profit margin. And his customers believed he could be trusted. His decisions were logical and not driven by emotional impulsivity. He was convinced that his emotional discipline, high IQ, and methodical thinking skills guaranteed his success and would allow him to beat the system. Oh…I nearly forgot to mention…his father was a cop.

One evening he was driving through a New Jersey neighborhood known for drug dealing activities when he was pulled over by a police officer because one of his taillights was burned out. The officer checked his license and registration and let him go. The next day he happened to mention to his father that he had been stopped the night before but that nothing had happened. Again, he thought he had beaten the system. His father knew better. With a knowing smile he explained to his son that he was "toast." "What are you talking about?" his son replied. "Nothing happened!" "Oh yes it did," his father retorted. "They know your name, where you live, the car you drive, and that you don't live in that neighborhood known for drug dealing. They know you are either a user or a dealer because, why else would you be there? It's only a matter of time now. Either quit the business or prepare to face the consequences."

He didn't, and he did…face the consequences, that is. That's when we met. He was arrested and his parents sent him to the wilderness therapy program where I was serving as the clinical director. I was assigned as his therapist and each week I would come out to the wilderness location where he and his band of fellow wilderness travelers were camping and spend the day talking about their lives, their choices, and their futures. We had some stimulating and intelligent conversations about his perspectives on life, but he seemed convinced that after doing his time "on the trail" he would go back to New Jersey and resume his life and his business where he had left off.

His parents were devout Jews, so we talked about his spiritual beliefs. As a logical thinker he said he could not believe in a Supreme Being whose existence could not be proven empirically. I remember one particular conversation about this issue that occurred on the third week of his six-week wilderness experience. Near the end of our conversation, I suggested that the only way I knew for people to find out for themselves whether such a being existed would be to seek a personal experience of some kind with him. We ended our conversation and I left him sitting by the mountain stream where we had been talking; the question of God's existence still unresolved.

The next week I encountered a very different young man. When I saw him, he seemed very excited to talk with me and we quickly walked along the stream to a private spot where he proceeded to climb onto a nearby boulder and proclaim like Moses of old might have done to the assembled tribes of Israel, that he KNEW that God existed! I asked him how he had reached that conclusion so quickly and with such certainty. He shared an experience that had occurred just a few days before.

While hiking with his group through a rugged mountainous area, he was climbing up a steep cliff face when the tiny ledge he was standing on began to crumble and give way. He felt himself beginning to fall and desperately tried to dig his hands and feet into the mountainside to stop himself from dropping the estimated thirty feet onto the rocks beneath him, but to no avail. He came to the sudden realization that falling off the mountainside and experiencing a serious or potentially fatal injury, was inevitable. At that very moment he said he felt "a force–like an unseen pair of hands," he said, that caught him in mid-air and lifted him back up onto a firm part of the ledge from which he had fallen.

He had experienced God in an unmistakable, undeniable, and deeply personal way. No more intellectual gymnastics about the irrationality of the existence of an unseen deity. Seth now knew first-hand. Like Marsha Linehan.

Given the spiritual nature of Dr. Linehan's own transformative experience, I was a little surprised that she did not include a third dimension in the Wise Mind decision-making process–the Spiritual Mind. So, I did.

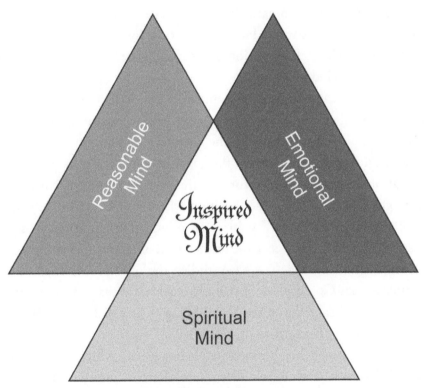

Figure 3.5 The Inspired Mind

From my perspective, if the Wise Mind is the result of the integration of the Emotional Mind and the Reasonable Mind, then where the Emotional Mind, Reasonable Mind, and Spiritual Mind overlap I will refer to as the

Inspired Mind. This involves allowing ourselves to experience the full spectrum of normal human emotions while tempering them with logic and reason and also honoring spiritual and moral values in every decision we make. All three components are necessary for the Inspired Mind to function correctly.

For those whose spiritual beliefs are the result of the overlapping of only the Reasonable Mind and Spiritual Mind, practicing a religion may be merely a logical choice that offers the most favorable odds for a desirable outcome. But the Reasonable Mind alone cannot fully comprehend the spiritual world.

For example, I met a man once who had researched Christianity and identified the two denominations that he believed had the best odds of being the Savior's true church. He began making donations to both of them, hoping to ensure himself a position in Heaven in the hereafter. Logical, but not exactly what God has in mind.

The opposite can also be a problem when one's religious feelings are the result of the overlapping of only the Emotional Mind and the Spiritual Mind. For those people religion may become a predominately emotionally-driven experience. It's about the rituals, the inspiring music, the pageantry, the grandeur of the church architecture, or the social interactions with others. That might also place them in a position where they could be more easily manipulated and exploited by hysteria-inducing, barnstorming pseudo-ministers. They may experience the exhilaration of believing they are "saved" or "chosen," but they may not have studied the scriptures enough to fully understand what God expects of them to qualify for that status. They may even become radicalized and feel that forcing their beliefs on others at the point of a gun is in harmony with God's will.

Did Seth's experience immediately change everything on his belief window? Would he forever make decisions from a sunnier vantage point— from the Inspired Mind? Not necessarily. Knowing God exists is not the same as knowing God. That process only begins when we are also committed to obeying God. While he was convinced now of the existence of a higher power in the universe and had added that reality to his belief window, Seth still had a lot more to learn about what that parent-child relationship really involves.

A spiritual awakening should do more than just change our thinking; it should change our feelings and behaviors as well. It doesn't just involve the mind. To an even greater degree, it involves the heart. It should invite a contrite attitude and produce feelings of gratitude, humility, and a desire to do good.

For Seth, he had yet to understand that other principles and values needed to be added to his belief window and how his old rules for daily living and decision-making would need to change to accommodate this sudden epiphany. So, two weeks later he went home…and six months later, he got arrested again.

As an eighteen-year-old adult with a second felony drug conviction, the consequences of his choices now became more dire and could potentially interfere with his education and career goals. Whether that was the reason for his change of heart or because he had finally done some serious thinking about the direction of his life after his experiences in the Arizona wilderness, I can't say with any certainty. But this time something significant had changed in him. He began to realize that a major course correction was necessary if he was to avoid more serious consequences in his future. And maybe he began to consider that the God who had introduced himself in such a poignant way was not interested in another lukewarm, moon level relationship with another one of his children–particularly this one. Lukewarm will not do. God will require us to be all-in at some point in our lives if we are to qualify to receive all he has to offer.

For everyone, life will inevitably provide a testing, refining, and defining experience. Several of them, most likely. And with those experiences, we will need to make an Inspired Mind decision, often when the only resource we have at our disposal will be the Spiritual Mind. The story of a man who lived over four thousand years ago illustrates this well.

I Will Trust. I Will Obey

His name was Abraham. He had lived an exemplary life of faith and obedience to the commandments God had given him. He had demonstrated that commitment on many occasions and his life had been miraculously spared several times because of it. He had received from God the promised

104 | SHINE Brighter

blessing of a son from the love of his life, his wife Sarah. Life was good and the integrity of his relationship with God seemed unassailable. Then he was commanded to do the unthinkable.

How could the perfectly loving, trustworthy, and all-knowing God of the universe ask this of him? Had Abraham not already sufficiently proven his humility, his obedience, and his loyalty to God? To be asked to offer his beloved son Isaac as a human sacrifice sent his Emotional Mind into a panic. He must have experienced a whirlwind of emotions, and at a level of intensity he had never previously known. Feelings of fear, abandonment, and revulsion swept over him. His body probably responded with nausea, trembling knees, and weakness in every joint and muscle. And although he was about one hundred and twenty years old at the time, at that moment he felt centuries older.

His Reasonable Mind was of no help. It was in chaos because there was nothing logical or reasonable about this divine demand. It was in direct opposition to everything he had ever known about the personality of God and the doctrines of eternity. There was nothing to hold onto; except the knowledge he carried with him in his Spiritual Mind.

Multiple memories of personal interactions with Jehovah and conversations with angels flooded his mind. Countless hours spent studying the writings of his ancestors Adam, Enoch, and Noah had brought him to a place of deeper understanding and filled his soul with light and truth. Even his name had been changed as a reminder of the sacred covenant he and Jehovah had entered into. Abraham fully intended to keep his promises to God, and he knew that God would keep his promises to Abraham.

Pondering the memories of these sacred experiences allowed him to transcend the turbulent Emotional and Reasonable Minds and allowed him to make the only decision that he knew was right. He would trust. He would obey.

Some have wondered why an omniscient God would put a righteous man like Abraham through such torture. With God, past, present, and future are one eternal "now," and Jehovah already knew what Abraham's decision would be. So why would God need to know how Abraham would respond? He didn't. Abraham did.

As we ascend the uphill path to the sun, we will inevitably reach a point where we "know as we are known"–where we will see ourselves with the same penetrating clarity with which our Heavenly Father sees us. It takes experiences like Abraham's to bring us to that point. All candidates for sun-hood will face something similar: an experience that tests the limits of their faith and spiritual endurance. These will be the defining and refining moments of our eternal lives. "The times that try men's souls," as Thomas Paine wrote. The best way to prepare for them will be to fill our Inspired Minds with truth, as Abraham did.

The path to the sun for most is typically a gradual one, though some may have a powerful change of heart because of a miraculous experience like Seth's. Either way, creating and maintaining lasting change in our lives requires a well-constructed foundation of light and truth that is continually being built upon. Additional light and truth are received incrementally–here a little, there a little–until full sun-hood is achieved. This process is aided when we carry Inspired Mind perspectives on our belief windows and apply them in our decision-making. **When we decide to allow ourselves to experience the array of human emotions, regulate them with reason and logic, and act in harmony with our deepest held spiritual values, our needs and those of the other people in our lives are much more likely to be met in consistently positive ways.**

As you read through this book you will see many more examples of sun, moon, and star principles that are present on people's belief windows and which are reflected in the choices they make. While we could continue to examine an endless list of the various options in this area, to further the learning process I suggest that an in-depth study of the lives and teachings of some of the prominent sun people of history would be worthwhile. People like Abraham, Moses, Cicero, Jesus Christ, Francis of Assisi, William Tyndale, Harriet Tubman, Elizabeth Jennings, Abraham Lincoln, Mother Teresa… there are many whose lives offer insight into sun living. The principles and values on their belief windows and the resulting choices they made during their lives provide some excellent examples for sun wannabes to follow and will help you with the next activity I am recommending. Please examine the beliefs on your belief window and consider these questions:

- Do they reflect Inspired Mind thinking?
- How have they influenced your behaviors?
- Are you satisfied with the results?
- Do they meet your most important needs in positive ways–positive for you and for the other people in your life?
- Are there some beliefs that you desire to replace now that you better understand the principles and values sun people carry on their belief windows?

Next, we will look at how our everyday choices impact the most important relationship in our lives.

CHAPTER 4 Preview

How do I love thee? Let me count the ways.
I love thee to the depth and breadth and height
My soul can reach, when feeling out of sight
For the ends of being and ideal grace.
I love thee to the level of every day's
Most quiet need, by sun and candlelight.
I love thee freely, as men strive for right;
I love thee purely, as they turn from praise.
I love with a passion put to use
In my old griefs, and with my childhood's faith.
I love thee with a love I seemed to lose
With my lost saints. I love thee with the breath,
Smiles, tears, of all my life! And, if God choose,
I shall but love thee better after death.

This classic poem by Elizabeth Barrett Browning describes a relationship between a man and a woman whose love and commitment transcends the conflict and chaos of the world as it has existed throughout human history. Done right, it can be a harbor from the storms of life and offers the greatest opportunities for happiness, fulfillment, and personal growth. Done wrong, it can feel like a dungeon filled with heartache, contention, and despair. It all depends on our choices. Sun, moon, or star.

3 KINDS OF SPOUSES

●●◀◀◀◀ ◀ ◀ ◀

Duri ng the five years I served as the clinical director for an outdoor behavioral healthcare program in Arizona I became acquainted with the unique culture and philosophy of experiential, outdoor-based treatment programs, usually referred to as wilderness programs.

Beginning in the late 1960s, Larry Dean Olson and his colleagues began taking teens and young adults into the Utah wilderness for thirty days and exposing them to the harsh realities of life in the wild while teaching them wilderness survival skills. Larry had gained this knowledge from his childhood fascination with Native American cultures and the years of study he put into mastering their primitive living skills. He let his youthful participants learn some of life's most important lessons from first-hand interactions with nature and from facing the natural consequences of their own choices.

Instead of the traditional counseling terminology, the staff made up a language of their own, using metaphors and imagery taken from nature and the Native American culture.

How's Your Walking?

In the Navajo culture, your life is referred to as your "walking" and as we move through life we are either "walking forward" and making good choices, or "walking backward" and making poor ones. If we discover that we have been walking backward in life, there are daily opportunities for a new beginning and a change in the direction of our lives. These treks into the wilderness provided real-life, uncontrived experiences that altered the way the teenage participants and their parents viewed themselves and others. They soon learned that life is more than walking the solo path of "me," but instead becomes a collaborative journey of "we." Keep this image in mind as we examine how relationships develop and progress, and what choices lead to becoming a sun, moon, or star spouse.

The HOUSE Model

Every person you will ever meet will fit into your life at one level of intimacy and trust or another. For any couple, the process of developing a trusting, intimate, and bonded relationship happens gradually, over time, progressing from lower levels of intimacy and trust (I/T) to progressively higher levels. Using the model of a house, let's look at how this process works.

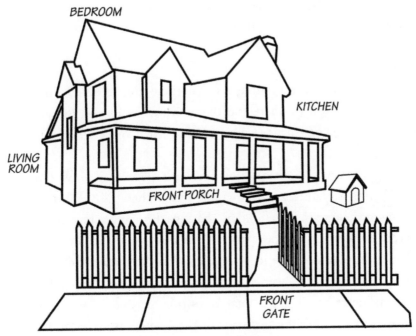

Figure 4.1 The HOUSE Model

The Front Gate

Relationships begin at the front gate. Front-gate-level relationships are with people who are just casual acquaintances. These people live on the "sidewalk" of your life, outside of the gate and outside of any meaningful involvement in your personal life. Typical examples of front-gate-level relationships are people like the teller at the bank you go to on a regular basis, the check-out person at the grocery store where you usually shop, the person who services your car occasionally, or who teaches in your child's school. You don't know much about them and they don't know much about you. For that reason, these relationships involve low levels of vulnerability and equally low levels of I/T.

But when we meet someone and realize that we are attracted to them for some reason, that we share something important in common, or that we just enjoy their company, we are inclined to want to get to know them better and to spend more time together. So, we open the front gate and invite that person onto our property. We take a risk by letting that person inside the protective fence around our home and our heart and onto the front porch. Not inside the house, just to the front porch.

The Front Porch

Each level in the house reminds us that there are necessary limits to the kinds of information we share and the activities we engage in with specific people, depending on their placement in our lives. We call those limitations, *boundaries*.

Front-porch-level relationships are with people with whom we are getting better acquainted. We increase our vulnerability a little more by spending more time together and by sharing a little more information about ourselves. In return, we expect the other person to do the same.

The front porch represents a zone between the public and the private; a shared area between the home and the community outside. Author Carson McCullers describes it as "a vital transition between the uncontrollable outdoors and the cherished interior of the home." It serves as a safe place where family members can interact with others in the community with limited risk, and where dating couples can get to know each other under the supervision of watchful parents.

This level also applies to workplace relationships. Most people would admit that workplace friendships are different from friendships with others outside of the workplace because of the competitive and hierarchical nature of the work environment, especially in the corporate world. If circumstances change at work and friends are vying for the same promotion or you are each in danger of losing your job due to staff reductions, you may sadly discover that your friend's career interests outweigh the importance of the friendship. I've had conversations with several people who reported losing their jobs because of personal information being used against them by competitive co-workers whom they considered to be close friends. Because of that risk, common sense would suggest that it is unwise to share a lot of sensitive, personal information with coworkers.

Front-porch-level conversations are limited to everyday activities. As Dr. John Van Epp explains in his book *How to Avoid Marrying a Jerk (or Jerkette)*, we begin the process of increasing openness by "sharing current events, established facts, and things we've seen and heard." In the past, people were much more cautious about sharing deep, personal, and vulnerable kinds of information or getting sexual on a first date. Society had clear boundaries to help protect young people as they learned how to gradually develop romantic relationships. But most of those traditional rituals and boundaries have been eliminated in contemporary societies and many young people are clueless as to how healthy relationships are developed. Instead, they are taking their cues from friends, TV shows, movies, magazines, and the Internet.

Healthy relationships develop gradually, over time, through a two-step process. First, we increase our vulnerability a little by spending more time with a person and sharing a little more information about ourselves. If the other person does the same and doesn't violate our trust, exploit our vulnerability, or misuse any of the information about us that we have shared, then intimacy and trust (I/T) go up a notch. We continue this two-step process of increasing vulnerability and building greater levels of I/T until something happens to tell us that the relationship has reached its appropriate level of I/T and is not likely to go any further. That becomes the boundary for that person.

For a dating couple, as they get to know each other better, they will determine whether they feel the relationship should move beyond casual dating to a slightly higher level of I/T. Either the relationship remains at the front porch and they simply remain acquaintances, or someone decides to open the front door and invite the other person into the house.

The Living Room

When someone invites another person into their home–literally and metaphorically–this significantly increases the level of vulnerability for the people who live there. Once your guest walks across that threshold they have immediate access to a lot more information about you. They see the way your home is decorated, the quality of the furnishings, the unique smells that each house has, the pictures on the walls, the books on the bookshelves, and so forth. This is all important information about the personalities of the people who live there.

Typically, the room we invite guests into the first time they come to our home is the living room. Living rooms are usually located just inside the front door. There is a reason for that. It's so you can control where that person goes in your home and how much information they have access to. While a modest increase in vulnerability is appropriate in a developing relationship, you still want to enforce clear boundaries to limit the amount of risk you expose yourself to until higher levels of I/T are established.

Living-room-level conversations involve a slightly higher level of openness and vulnerability. While we generally still focus on mundane, everyday kinds of stuff, our conversations involve a slightly increased level of personal disclosure. As Van Epp indicates, you begin to add more "personal perspectives, interpretations, and opinions to your facts." Living-room-level friends are closer than the front porch but are not yet considered to be life-long, bosom-buddies. They may also include some family members—those whom you have discovered through years of interaction cannot be fully trusted with your personal secrets or potentially embarrassing information.

As we spend a little more time together, we pick up more information about this person's personality, character, beliefs, and values through conversation and observation of their behaviors. We can then decide whether we feel comfortable sharing more of our own perspectives, beliefs, values, and experiences.

For example, let's say I was invited to an acquaintance's home for the first time and as I walked through the door I noticed that it was very clean and nicely decorated with furniture that was similar to my tastes. The walls were painted in a pleasing color that matched the carpet and the drapes, there was a bookshelf full of great literature that I have also read, and a print of a painting by an artist I particularly like, hanging on the living room wall. I would have gained a tremendous amount of information simply by walking through that front door. Finding out that I share so much in common with this person, I would probably want to invite them to my home as well. Their willingness to increase their vulnerability by sharing more about themselves will likely encourage me to do the same if I want the friendship to reach a higher level of I/T.

But what if I entered the home and it wasn't an environment that I am particularly comfortable with? The lime green 1960s shag carpet looked like it had not been cleaned since it was installed during the Nixon administration. The sofa had so many stains on it that it reminded me of a calico cat. There was no need for a book shelf because the only reading materials in the room were some copies of The National Enquirer laying on the coffee table. And prominently displayed on the wall in the living-room-place-of-honor was a life-size, Velvet Elvis painting surrounded by a halo of accent lights.

Does this mean that the person who lives there is a bad person? Not at all. But it does mean that we may not share enough in common for our relationship to move to a higher level of I/T.

Obviously, good relationships are built on much more than just common interests and similar tastes in home furnishings. The living room decor serves as a metaphor for the more important qualities I mentioned above of shared interests, shared values, personality traits that complement each other, or a strong commitment to a shared belief system. If those elements are missing, the relationship will likely not proceed beyond the living room level. If they are present, the next level in the house is the kitchen. If conversations at the living room level are considered mundane, that is not true of the kitchen.

The Kitchen

Kitchens are located at the center or rear of the home; deep within the home physically as well as emotionally. The kitchen is the place where family and close friends gather to share meals and celebrate holidays, birthdays, and other events. It is the hub of family life. Important conversations take place around the kitchen table and important decisions are made there. Parents teach their children important life lessons through the thousands of dinner-time conversations that occur there.

Kitchen-level relationships include our closest, *closest* friends and the few family members whom we know we can trust implicitly because they have proven their loyalty over time. These people would never get laughs at a social gathering at your expense by sharing potentially embarrassing information. These are truly the people who have your back and would probably "take a bullet" for you if necessary. They will hold you accountable for whatever poor choices you may make because they know that doing so is in your best interest. But they will also support you in the process of correcting them.

The distance between the living room and the kitchen is significant because it takes a lot of time and a lot of shared experiences to reach that level. Occasionally those experiences may involve conflicts or misunderstandings. A kitchen-level friend is someone who values the relationship enough to forgive minor transgressions by others and take full responsibility for their own errors. Few people that we meet will ever qualify as kitchen-level friends. In fact, most people tell me they can count on their fingers the number of kitchen-level friends that they have made in a lifetime.

These people know a *ton* about you and you know a *ton* about them. As Van Epp states, these conversations "convey more of the subjective, personal, and emotional content about your facts and opinions." Very high levels of vulnerability exist because of what these people know about you. But because they have proven their trustworthiness over time, there is an equally high level of I/T. **You cannot have one, without the other.** You cannot achieve the highest levels of intimacy and trust in a relationship without being willing and able to tolerate the equally high levels of vulnerability that it takes to get there.

It's an interesting paradox. The people with the ability to cause us the most harm and inflict the deepest wounds are actually the people we feel the safest with because they have proven their loyalty through years of experiences together. Even if there were problems along the way and conflicts occurred or hurtful things were said or done, because the parties apologized, took responsibility for their behaviors, and worked to reconcile as family members or friends, the relationship actually grew stronger as a result. With kitchen-level friends we don't have to worry about first impressions or whether we're having a bad day. They know us and love us despite our imperfections and weaknesses. And we love them equally, in return.

The Bedroom

The highest level of I/T, and therefore, the highest level of vulnerability, is represented by the bedroom. To better understand what I mean by vulnerability, I recommend a TED Talk. Go to https://www.youtube.com/watch?v=iCvmsMzlF7o. Social worker and author Dr. Brené Brown speaks about the power of vulnerability to create bonded, intimate, and trusting relationships. In her research she discovered a group of people she identified as having a deep sense of worthiness; of believing that they and others are worthy of love and belonging. She refers to them as "whole-hearted" people because they possess the courage to live their lives with openness and authenticity, the compassion to be kind to self and others, and the confidence to connect with others in deep and meaningful ways.

Vulnerability allows whole-hearted people to take the risk of saying "I love you," to be in a relationship without a guarantee that it will work, and to invest a huge part of themselves into the lives of others without the promise of reciprocity. Vulnerability is fundamental to connection, and as Brown explains, "What makes us vulnerable, also makes us beautiful." It is a quality that sun people possess in abundance and that is prominent in a bedroom-level relationship.

Partially because of the sexual connotation of the bedroom and partially because of the nature of the conversations that occur there, the bedroom level is reserved for husband and wife. This is where the most personal, private, and vulnerable conversations and experiences in life take place between spouses. It is at this level that we begin to peel away the layers of our lives like an onion, acknowledging our mistakes and trying to come to a deeper understanding of ourselves and the purpose of our lives. Our spouses should be our most trusted confidants and sounding boards in this process. Van Epp describes this level of communication as the place where you can "put your deepest feelings into words."

There is neither a need nor a desire for secrecy between partners at this level because secrecy of any kind (except, of course, for surprise events and gifts) interferes with the development of intimacy and trust. This does not mean that you have to share every idle or inappropriate thought that crosses your mind. There is no need to burden your spouse with the everyday temptations that we all face and that can be dismissed and forgotten. It is when those thoughts begin to dominate your thinking or influence your actions that you should feel obligated to seek out understanding and support from a caring spouse.

Sex

My mother was a nurse, so when it came time for the sex talk to be delivered to their two sons, I guess my parents decided she would do a better job with the topic. I was twelve and my brother was thirteen. I don't remember much about it (except for the graphic black-and-white pictures in her old nursing textbooks that she showed us of people dying from stage III syphilis.) But I do seem to remember what she said near the end of the lecture. It was something about sex being "a powerful physical, emotional, and spiritual experience. It is the bonding agent–the glue–that holds a marriage and a family together. Always treat it with respect."

Since sexuality plays such a significant role in our lives, I felt that this topic deserved a chapter of its own and began writing one. It was my intention to provide a comprehensive overview of the biopsychosocial aspects of sexuality including a summary of the current research on sexual orientations, gender identity, the consequences of the sexual revolution on society, and the personal implications of our sexual choices. Fifty pages and twenty-six thousand words later, I concluded that this subject deserves an entire book of its own to even *begin* to adequately address the topics of sun, moon, and star approaches to sexuality. Until then, let me just share a few thoughts on the role sex plays in our lives and relationships, and then I will discuss some specific areas of concern.

The Role

While the biological purpose of sex is reproduction, there is also a chemical component to the experience that contributes to the emotional bonding process. Sexual activity causes the pituitary glands in the brain to release a chemical called oxytocin that has been referred to as the "love hormone" or the "cuddle hormone" for its ability to create emotional bonding between people. Oxytocin helps establish the emotional bond between a mother and a newborn child. But it does much more than just facilitate the bonding process between people. It has also been determined to help speed up the healing process of wounds—both physical and emotional. It evokes feelings of contentment, reduces fear and anxiety while increasing feelings of trust and trustworthiness toward others, increases empathy and generosity, and reduces stress.

For women, their biggest doses of oxytocin are experienced when giving birth, breastfeeding a child, and through sexual activity. For men, we get much of our oxytocin through sexual activity as well as through many male-bonding types of activities like team sports. Given the powerful impact this hormone can have on people, one can understand why sex should be reserved for committed couples and why sexual infidelity is so harmful.

At the bedroom level of I/T, sex has the ability to strengthen the emotional bonds between couples and help them stick together through the many challenges that are a part of family life. At lower levels in the HOUSE, it can have the opposite effect.

Even with kitchen-level relationships, a "friends with benefits" approach to sex doesn't work. Oxytocin creates a bonding process with a person who, even at the kitchen level, does not share the same level of commitment and fidelity that a bedroom-level relationship demands. Instead of creating feelings of security and reduced anxiety, the results are often envy, insecurity, and hostility.

Having sex with a living-room-level or front-porch-level person means that one or both sexual partners will begin to form an emotional bond with someone they don't know very well. That creates a situation where the relationship is highly vulnerable, but woefully lacking in I/T.

For front-gate-level relationships, the partners will usually fight the normal emotional response that oxytocin creates by not allowing a bond to form. It's like the 1960s free love mentality...sex that is *free* of love, *free* of commitment, and *free* of responsibility. Reminds me of a lyric from a 1970 Stephen Stills song, "and if you can't be with the one you love, honey, love the one you're with." I can assure you, after eight years of touring as a rock and roll musician and seeing how many musicians live their lives, that love has nothing to do with what he is describing. Sex at the bedroom level of I/T can accurately be referred to as "making love" because of the emotional and spiritual bonds it helps create. But at the front gate level, having sex is more accurately described by one of several four-letter words, none of which is spelled l-o-v-e.

Moon and star people in society have progressively changed the role of sexuality from what it was intended to be. Instead of being an experience that elevates human beings emotionally and spiritually, for some it has become an experience that debases them. Sex was intended to be an experience that consummates the marital union and establishes and nurtures a covenant bond between the partners. But for many among the single-and-searching population, sex has become an introductory and perfunctory experience–like handing out business cards at a networking luncheon. And when it involves people who meet through the Ashley Madison Agency, it becomes something much more ominous.

Sexual desire can be stimulated by several things other than true love. And when love is not the primary motivating factor in a sexual relationship, don't expect the relationship to ever reach or maintain a bedroom level of intimacy and trust.

As Erich Fromm wrote in *The Art of Loving*:

> *Desire can be stimulated by the anxiety of aloneness, by the wish to conquer or be conquered, by vanity, by the wish to hurt and even destroy, as much as it can be stimulated by love...If this desire is not stimulated by love...it...leaves strangers as far apart as they were before–sometimes it makes them ashamed of each other, or even makes them hate each other, because when the illusion has gone, they feel their estrangement even more markedly than before.*

Neurons That Fire Together, Wire Together

Even in what some people may consider a committed relationship, when partners add physical pain, aggression, degradation, or fear to their sexual experiences, they are unknowingly changing their brains in ways that can turn sex into something sinister and destructive.

The brain has separate neural pathways for experiencing pleasure and pain as well as for emotional states like love, fear, aggression, shame, or embarrassment. When we combine sexual interest, arousal, and pleasure and their neural pathways with any of these negative emotional neural pathways, we create a situation described in Hebb's rule: "Neurons that fire together, wire together." This means that the brain begins to associate or fuse the two separate pathways together. Sexual interest and fear; sexual arousal and violence; or sexual pleasure and pain.

As this fusion of neural networks becomes more reinforced by repeated sexual experiences that incorporate fear, violence, or pain, some people may discover that they cannot experience sexual arousal without becoming aggressive or violent. Others may develop a tolerance for BDSM behaviors and be unable to experience sexual pleasure and orgasm without incorporating increasing levels of pain, aggression, or dominance into the experience. And still others may find themselves involuntarily aroused when they experience fear.

As psychiatrist Aaron Kheriaty warned:

> *Before making decisions about our sexual behaviors, we need to ask ourselves some questions about what we want to be doing to our brain and our body; what kind of neural tracks and networks do we want to be reinforcing through these behaviors? Do we want to be fusing sex and love? Sex and security? Sex and attachment? Sex and commitment? Sex and fidelity? Sex and trust? Sex and unselfishness? Or do we want to be fusing in our brain and in our experiences sex and violence? Sex and dominance? Sex and submission? Sex and control? We shape our brain by our choices. And we develop increasingly automatic and ingrained habits by our repeated choices. But the initial choice of which path we embark upon is up to us.*

Tragically, many sexual behaviors that for millennia have been considered dysfunctional or depraved, are now labeled as just part of the rainbow of sexual diversity.

Misuse It, You Lose It

There's another consequence for people who routinely choose to have sex outside the bonds of a bedroom-level, committed relationship with people with whom they have no desire to bond. They may eventually lose the ability to form a bedroom-level relationship all together. I saw this happen with some of the people I worked with during my years in the music business. One in particular stands out.

I'll call him Joe. He was a very talented singer who could sing anything by James Brown, Sam Cooke, Jackie Wilson, and just about any 1950s or '60s rhythm 'n' blues singer you can name. He had worked for years in Las Vegas and other show lounges around the country and traveled extensively. His was the stereotypical musician lifestyle that involved casual sex with women all over the country.

During the time we worked together he had a girlfriend he had been living with for several years, but he felt very little commitment to her and no obligation to be monogamous. They had an "understanding" he explained to me once. "When I'm in town, I'll be with you" he would say to her. But even that arrangement was routinely violated by him. She had stronger feelings for him, but had come to accept the fact that he was not willing to offer much in return.

My wife and Joe's girlfriend became friends and in the process of getting to know each other she would occasionally share some of the details of her relationship with Joe. There was sadness in her voice as she related that there was no holding hands or kissing or cuddling or any other commonplace expressions of affection and appreciation in their relationship. He didn't like that stuff. Sex was mechanical and a front-porch-level emotional experience at best. It added nothing to the levels of I/T in the relationship because it was all about his pleasure. Her body was merely a vehicle for his sexual satisfaction.

She had resigned herself to the likelihood that things were not going to get any better because he seemed incapable of real vulnerability and intimacy. His decades of promiscuous, free-range sex and regular viewing of pornography had extinguished his ability to form a bedroom-level relationship.

People can have sex with others at any level in the HOUSE model, but the results are never the same as a sexual relationship with someone with whom you share a bedroom level of intimacy and trust. That's because there is an inverse relationship (when one goes up, the other goes down) between the level of selfishness in someone's life, and the levels of I/T in their relationships. This is especially true when it comes to sex.

Sun people understand that the sexual drive is more than just a chemically-driven reproductive imperative. It is also the body's way of responding to the emotional and spiritual need for love and connection. At the bedroom level, spouses are willing to be patient with each other, to delay their desire for immediate gratification, and to respect the feelings and needs of their spouse. They can wait for the marshmallow. This exercise of self-restraint often increases the levels of passion and emotional bonding in the relationship when intimacy does occur.

Promises, Promises

Sun spouses bind themselves together by promises. Those promises are either outlined specifically in the marriage vows, or are considered implicit in the marriage ritual itself. Sexual exclusivity and fidelity, even on those days when couples may feel a lack of connection or commitment in the relationship, is an essential promise in a sun marriage. By keeping that promise, sun spouses are able to reach and maintain the highest levels of I/T. Without fidelity, bedroom levels of I/T cannot be achieved.

So, it is fair to say that sex can either contribute to a loving, bonded relationship when used correctly, or destroy intimacy and trust when used incorrectly. Even within the bounds of marriage we must be careful how we use it.

The Law

To summarize the sun perspective on sexuality, let me remind you of the sun law that governs its use. It is an element of Natural Law. As such, Cicero reminds us that it does not vary from city to city, continent to continent, century to century, or planet to planet. For those who are committed to sun principles and who seek a sun marriage relationship, adherence to this law is mandatory. For those who are comfortable with something less, they will likely question its relevance and trivialize its impact.

Individuals and societies who reject this law–even if done in ignorance–will lose the opportunity to receive the many benefits that come to those who observe it, and invite the many negative consequences that come to those who don't.

It's called the Law of Chastity. It is a clear, brightline rule governing sun sexual behavior. If you decide you want to consider it, a simple Internet search is all that is necessary. It's even on Wikipedia. But brace yourself. There is no wiggle room with this law. You either obey it as written, or you don't.

Bedroom Boundaries

A bedroom-level relationship requires strict boundaries around it to protect it. That is because spouses know things about each other that no one else knows; things others don't have a right to know. These boundaries keep the right two people inside the relationship, and all others outside.

To ensure that happens, sun spouses do not share bedroom-level information with lower-level relationships. That includes siblings, parents, children, best friends, co-workers, or anyone else with whom you have a lower-level relationship. Those people are not in a position to use that information in a constructive way and sharing it with them only invites them into a position in your life where they don't belong and can potentially cause harm.

That doesn't mean you can't seek advice from others on various relationship issues, but that doesn't require violating the trust and confidentiality of the bedroom. (An obvious exception to this rule would be when there are things going on in the relationship that could endanger the health or safety of a spouse or children, such as domestic violence, drug addiction, criminal activities, or other harmful activities.)

When Boundary Problems Occur

While everyone wants close, trusting relationships with family and friends (kitchen level) and one singular and most intimate relationship (bedroom level), not everyone knows how to create them. Some people have grown up in families where they didn't have close relationships with parents or siblings. They may have been bullied or ignored at school and had no close friends growing up. Their parents may have been distant from one another, fought, and experienced an ugly divorce. Those people have no examples of kitchen-level or bedroom-level relationships to draw from. They may have seen them in their friends' homes, but that may not be enough exposure to learn the attitudes and skills necessary to create those kinds of relationships in their own adult lives.

Those who have no examples of higher-level relationships and who fear that their emotional needs for love and connection are not likely to be met, often find themselves making one of two mistakes. First, they may decide to move into the living room full time, creating rigid boundaries and not letting anyone get close to them—ever. But why would an individual settle for that when something much better is available? Because it's safer there. The living room does not require the level of vulnerability that is necessary to achieve the higher levels of I/T. The conversations at that level typically do not go beyond the mundane and contain little, if any, vulnerable content.

I've known families who have lived their whole lives in the living room. It becomes a neglected and depressing place with grey wallpaper, worn-out furniture, and the musty smell of a rest home filled with lonely old people waiting to die.

The second mistake is to meet someone at the front gate and artificially take them immediately to the kitchen (or higher). Relationship-challenged people may be desperately hungry for a deeper connection with someone but they have not learned how to develop a healthy relationship; gradually, step-by-step, over time. They wind up driving potential friends away by having diffuse boundaries; that is, sharing too much vulnerable information or activities too soon, and expecting the other person to do the same.

You've probably met some of these people and felt like saying "Whoa! Too much information!" and looked for an escape from the conversation. The one place some people seem to be willing to take that kind of risk is on airplanes. You know the scenario…a captive audience, you'll never see that person again, and so on.

Diffuse-boundary people may find themselves in a relationship with a front-gate-level person whom they don't know, shouldn't be trusting, and who may be willing to exploit their naïveté and vulnerability for selfish purposes.

I had an experience along this line when my wife and I were first married and we had just moved into married student housing at the university I was attending. A young insurance salesman wanted to come by the apartment and talk to us about life and health insurance. He promised he would only take one hour of my busy Saturday afternoon, so we agreed. As you may already know, insurance salespeople are trained to ask potential clients to sit down together and talk at a specific location in the house–the kitchen table. Why? Because sitting at the kitchen table creates the illusion of friendship and a deeper personal connection. After all, we're talking about life and death, your health and welfare, and protecting your family.

For the first hour he pulled out a two-inch thick binder filled with pictures of his wife and kids. There were summer vacation pictures at the beach, Christmas mornings in front of the tree, birthday party photos, (at least there weren't any labor and delivery photos). I'm sitting there thinking, "I've never met your wife and kids! Those could be stock photos of some fictitious family that you bought somewhere for all I know! We're not friends! Why are you wasting my time!" One hour turned into two-and-a-half and I was getting frustrated. He finally promised to finish up and said he wanted to submit an application for me. "No obligation; just to see if you qualify," he said. "Yeah, right!" I thought. But I said "OK" just to get him out of the house and back to the front gate. Two weeks later he called to set up another appointment to discuss the insurance and when he arrived, he proudly presented me with my new insurance policy, all approved and filled out, adding, "Just sign here!" I said, "Wait a minute! I didn't approve this! You said you were just going to see if I even qualified with my meager, full-time student and part-time janitor income. I'm not signing anything!" He got angry and said that he had spent his own $20 to pay for the application process. When I said that was his decision and I knew nothing about any application fee, he got angrier and started making insulting comments about my parents (whom he'd obviously, never met.) I finally had to order him out of the apartment.

(Creating the impression of a kitchen-level relationship does not always have to be exploitative. For example, during the COVID-19 pandemic, celebrities often connected with their fans by hosting TV shows from their living rooms and kitchens. These often make-up-free celebrities demonstrated their willingness to be vulnerable and transparent with their audience. That helped create feelings of intimacy and connection for viewers feeling isolated and lonely while being sequestered in their homes.)

Boundaries are important for two reasons:

1. They help us establish a sense of our individual identity.
2. They protect us from violations and intrusions into our lives by others by letting them know where they fit into our lives.

Some people marry before they have adequately completed the step-by-step process and reached at least something close to the kitchen level before deciding to marry.

For example, occasionally I see spouses who have grown up with good examples of kitchen-level and bedroom-level relationships, who want the same for themselves, and who have learned what it takes to create one. But if they are not paying close enough attention during the courtship process, they may wind up marrying a living-room-level refugee from a troubled family who has very different expectations for marriage. What results is a tug-of-war between the two over who will control the relationship and whose needs come first.

The spouse who wants a bedroom-level relationship and can handle the level of vulnerability necessary to create one, will say to the living-room-level spouse, "Come up here! This is where real happiness is found!" The living-room-level spouse replies, "No way. Tried that. Got hurt. You come down here. It's all I have to offer."

The process of moving from the safety of the living room and jumping up to the bedroom level feels beyond that person's capacity for vulnerability. Because of this unwillingness to expose themselves to the higher levels of vulnerability necessary to advance to higher levels of I/T, the spouse who is camped out in the living room often reduces their expectations for love and connection in the relationship and denies them to their spouse as well. Because of this, they are also considered to have greater power in the relationship. Lesser need, equals greater power. But this is a self-focused, moon kind of power.

The bedroom-level person may feel forced to acquiesce and settle for an unfulfilling living-room-level relationship. That spouse is not going to have those important bedroom-level emotional needs met and will be vulnerable to trying to fill that empty space with lower-level relationships like children, siblings, friends, or co-workers. That person will also be more vulnerable to having an affair should they meet someone who seems to understand them and is better at meeting those deeper emotional needs.

However, the bedroom-level spouse has greater power at their disposal than they may realize–the sun power to help others heal.

The solution to this tug-of-war situation is for the bedroom-level spouse to use their influence to create a safe and nurturing environment for the living-room-level spouse. They invite the fearful spouse to begin sharing more personal thoughts and feelings and to begin increasing their vulnerability by addressing the unmet emotional needs that have caused them to hide out in the living room. It is the same gradual, step-by-step process that applies to building all bedroom-level relationships. Sun people are experts at creating them. In fact, they are often the only ones who can. Let me share an example.

Pillow Talk and a Troll Doll

I am friends with a couple I met many years ago who followed all the steps, dating each other and getting to know each other very well along the way until they were at a point where they were considering marriage. The woman felt that if her would-be fiancé was ready to discuss the possibility of marriage, he was entitled to know more about her–things that might affect his decision.

She shared the fact that her father had been an alcoholic throughout her childhood and her parents eventually divorced because of it. Because of the anxiety and rejection she had experienced growing up, she had difficulty discussing sensitive issues with other people and trusting them with personal and private information. She was also concerned that these trust issues might make sexual intimacy difficult for her.

They discussed these concerns and just before they got married, they decided on a strategy to address them…they went shopping.

But this was no ordinary shopping trip. They were looking for something special. Something that they could use to help them communicate about the intimate and vulnerable aspects of their relationship. She found an adorable Troll doll with spiked blue hair, big empathetic eyes, and a benevolent smile. It was about eight inches tall, dressed in an ancient Roman soldier's helmet and uniform of silvery fabric, and carried a sword. Forever afterward she affectionately referred to it as her "knight in shining armor."

They also found a heart-shaped pillow with the words "Pillow Talk" embroidered on it. They brought the two items home and placed them on a shelf in their bedroom.

From the beginning of their marriage, the couple used the doll and the pillow as tools to help communicate about sensitive issues. When the wife wanted to let her husband know she had a concern to discuss that required his full attention and understanding, or that she was comfortable and available for sexual intimacy, she could place one of the items on the bed or nightstand during the day to let him know in advance. His patience with her vulnerability and his sensitivity to her need for understanding and empathy when she shared her feelings with him, greatly increased the I/T in their relationship. After a few years, the doll and pillow had served their purposes and were no longer necessary to facilitate communication.

Today, after fifty-plus years of marriage, these objects stand as symbolic reminders of how two sun spouses can overcome whatever challenges may exist in a relationship and how sun levels of intimacy and trust can be achieved and maintained. That happens when sun partners are willing to place the needs of their spouse ahead of their own, knowing that the other spouse is willing to do the same in return.

For couples who are both stuck at a living room level of I/T in their relationship due to negative life experiences prior to marriage, they may have an especially difficult time navigating through the deep emotional waters that make up their lives. They will need help understanding how those early experiences have influenced their emotional development and to learn how to respond to each other in more compassionate ways. Until that happens, neither spouse will have the emotional reserves necessary to create a safe place in which the other can heal and grow. They may constantly find themselves in the tug-of-war scenario of trying to meet their personal needs in the relationship while also trying to protect themselves from the possibility of additional injury.

When Things Go Wrong: Healing a Damaged Relationship

Even sun relationships have their challenges. If there is an injury to a relationship and the levels of intimacy and trust drop, partners will also need to reduce their vulnerability. As I said before, you can't have a high level of one without an equally high level of the other. So when one drops, the other must drop too.

Suppose, for example, that my wife and I have a bedroom-level relationship and I do something really hurtful to her. Would she continue to trust me at the same bedroom level? Probably not. So, she reduces her vulnerability by sending me to that little alternative residence in the backyard known as *the doghouse*.

Who gets sent to the doghouse? Someone who has done something that offends another resident of the house. Being sent to the doghouse is a way of reducing our vulnerability by creating some emotional–and sometimes physical–distance in the relationship until the offended party can decide what should be the next course of action. If the violation is severe enough to destroy the bonds of I/T, my wife may decide to send me out the front gate and down the street. She's done. If not, she will have to decide where in the house our relationship is currently located–what the level of I/T is and what level of vulnerability she can tolerate. I have the same options. As the '70s British punk rock band The Clash sang, we each have to decide, "Should I stay, or should I go?"

If she tells me that she feels the I/T levels are at the front porch and that she feels she is living with a relative stranger whose behavior is foreign to the person she believed me to be, then we will have to begin rebuilding the relationship from that point. Rebuilding an injured relationship is done in the same way building the initial relationship was accomplished–gradually, step-by step, over time, through ongoing interactions that are appropriate to the corresponding level of I/T. The duration of the recovery period will be determined by the severity of the injury.

That isn't good news for me now, is it? That's because, with my demotion to a lower level in the house, I have also lost some of those bedroom-level privileges that come with the higher levels of I/T. That's part of the consequence we face when we violate our spouse's trust. We can't expect someone to be comfortable with sexual intimacy if the trust has been damaged. As much as we may all want to believe that a good dose of oxytocin will help the healing process and re-establish connection, remember that sex without trust does the opposite. So be careful about using make-up sex as an antidote.

If my wife decides to let me leap from the front porch back to the bedroom too soon, I will likely believe that the injury was not that serious and that my behavior was not that bad. If so, I will also be more likely to repeat it. I'll make the false assumption that our relationship is really back in the bedroom when truthfully, her trust level for me is still back at the front porch. She'll be faking it, and feeling worse about herself and more distant from me.

She may do the opposite. She may build a big brick wall in the living room and refuse to ever trust me enough to let me earn my way past it. If so, I will eventually give up trying to rebuild the relationship. To rebuild a troubled relationship, both parties must be willing to increase their vulnerability again, bit by bit, if they are to give each other the chance to restore the previous levels of I/T. If not, we'll either be stuck in a loveless, living-room-level relationship for the rest of our lives, or someone will reverse course and head out the front gate and down the street, looking for a new and more promising relationship.

The process of gradually increasing our vulnerability and restoring the previous levels of I/T can be much harder the second time around than it was the first, but it can still be done if both spouses are committed to the goal of rebuilding an intimate, trusting, bonded relationship. It can even become stronger than it was before the violation of trust occurred if both spouses accept responsibility for their poor choices, learn from their mistakes, and are willing to commit to living according to sun principles. It is always better to *mend* a relationship rather than *end* a relationship whenever possible, but that requires a commitment to sun principles on the part of both partners.

From Me to We. Finding Balance

As I explained in chapter three, we all have certain human needs that must be met to achieve happiness and personal fulfillment in life. Whether we choose to meet our need for love and connection in sun, moon, or star ways will determine the quality of our relationships.

Sun relationships achieve the highest levels of intimacy and trust because sun people consider the needs of others to be just as important as their own. They see life as a "walking of we." The greater the levels of light and truth in their lives, the stronger their connection will be.

As spouses ponder the human needs outlined previously—certainty, variety, love and connection, significance, growth, contribution, and truth— they may begin to recognize that each has some needs that are more heavily weighted than others and that may differ from their spouse's. For example, suppose a husband has a higher need for certainty and significance as he pursues his chosen profession and relies heavily on his income and status at work to meet those needs. That may result in conflict with his wife whose needs for variety and love/connection are more important at that time and who is relying on her husband to meet those needs. Once they understand their spouse's primary needs, both partners are in a position to do what they can to help meet them.

I have a set of scales from my father's pharmacy that is over one hundred years old. I remember seeing it every time I went into his store as I was growing up. He passed away in 2004 and those scales now sit on a shelf in my office as a reminder of the balance my parents demonstrated in their marriage. I regularly use them to teach couples that if they are equally committed to meeting the needs of their spouse, they will begin to adjust their own needs and establish a better balance in both of their lives. An experience shared with me by one of my sons-in-law offers a good example.

Wisdom in the E.R.

Jared is an emergency room doctor in the Chicago area. When he starts his late-night shift, he will often walk into the waiting room area and see a lot of sick, tired, scared, suffering, and frustrated patients and family members who have often been waiting for hours to receive treatment. The people would often look at him with angry expressions which would trigger a defensive attitude on his part. That is not the way most doctors want to start their shift trying to help sick and injured people in a stressful and emotionally-charged emergency room. So, he decided that the best thing to do for both the patients and himself would be to talk to them briefly before beginning his shift.

He would typically say something like, "I know you must be tired and frustrated having to wait here so long to get help. I am just starting my shift, but I will try and do whatever I can, as quickly as I can, to see that you get the help you need." That simple and sincere expression of compassion and concern is often all those people need to feel validated and to be willing to wait patiently until they can be seen. And it puts my son-in-law into a much better place emotionally to begin his shift.

Sometimes he has the time to chat a little longer with some of the patients and family members. With older couples, he often asks them the secret to a long and happy marriage. Sometimes the answers are funny, sometimes they are sarcastic, and sometimes they are profound. Recently he asked an older couple that question and the response was, "You know, most couples believe when they get married that they are 'equally yoked' and that they will grow and develop emotionally and spiritually at the same rate. Quite often, that is not the case. Each spouse will grow at different times and under different circumstances. There will be times when one person may be in a more emotionally and spiritually advanced place in his or her life than the other. You have to be patient and allow for that. The goal is to continue to grow…together." Profound.

Couples who understand this will experience a process that I refer to as cross-pollination, whereby each takes on some of the same qualities, perspectives, interests, and goals of the other. That is what unity and equality are all about—finding a way of turning two "mes" into one "we."

"Women Hold Up Half the Sky" –Mao Zedong

But there are others who struggle with this issue of unity and equality in their marriages. They may see their relationships as a competition for whose needs receive the highest priority, rather than as a cooperative effort that is more likely to meet both persons' needs equally—the win-win perspective that Stephen R. Covey wrote about in *The Seven Habits of Highly Effective People*. I have often wondered where this whole attitude of competition for control in male-female relationships began and what has fostered it. I think it started a long time ago.

Revisiting Eden

According to the Book of Genesis, when newlyweds Adam and Eve were placed in the Garden of Eden, the first commandment given to them was to "be fruitful and multiply and replenish the earth" with their offspring. But in their innocent and child-like state they lacked the knowledge necessary to accomplish that commandment. Then they were told about a particular tree that was planted in the midst of the garden whose fruit offered them the opportunity to increase their knowledge—exactly what they needed if they were to accomplish that pesky reproduction requirement that seemed so important to their Heavenly Father. But gaining the desired knowledge would come with a price. Along with learning about good, the knowledge of evil would also enter the world, and death along with it. For the rest of their mortal lives and throughout the lives of all of their descendants, Adam and Eve and their posterity would be faced with having to make choices between good and evil and accepting the possibility of failure. That was God's plan. It had always been the plan.

Like the HOUSE model, in order for relationships to grow and progress to deeper levels of intimacy and trust we must be willing to take risks, exercise faith, and face the challenges and opposition that are essential components of the mortal experience.

The desire to grow in knowledge, experience, understanding, and wisdom is an intrinsic part of every human being—male *and* female. How we choose to respond to that desire determines whether we become a sun, moon, or star person. Adam and Eve made a decision that gave them the opportunity for eternal growth and progression. The only concern may have been how they reached that decision.

What if Eve had responded to the Serpent's enticement to eat of the fruit of the tree of the knowledge of good and evil by saying something like, "You know, you make a pretty strong case for eating this fruit. Hang on a second while I run this idea by my husband." The conversation between Adam and Eve might have gone something like this:

Eve: *Adam, I just had a conversation with the serpent about the fruit of the tree of knowledge of good and evil, and...*

Adam: *Yeah, me too. He tried to talk me into eating it a little while ago. I totally shut him down.*

Eve: *Seriously!? Why didn't you talk to me about it?*

Adam: *I dunno. It didn't seem that important at the time.*

Eve: *Not Important!? Of course it is! And it would have helped me to know that you had already said 'no' because I was really tempted to say 'yes'!*

Adam: *YES!? Why would you even consider it? You know what Father said would happen if we did—death! What's there to talk about?*

Eve: *Then why did He put the tree here in the first place?*

Adam: *Hmmm...you know...that's a good question.*

Eve: *Father would never put us in a situation that could potentially destroy us unless there was a wiser purpose. I don't think He brought us here to just eat fruit and tend the garden forever. There's something more important that we're missing in all this; we're not seeing the bigger picture. Knowing about good and evil and experiencing them both must have something to do with it.*

Adam: *That's deep. You're right. There are two trees that are different from all the others with two special kinds of fruit. On the one hand, there is the fruit of the tree of knowledge of good and evil. With evil comes death and separation from God. On the other hand, there is the fruit of the tree of life that offers eternal life in the presence of God. Can we have one, without the other? Can eternal life even be achieved without knowledge? And it's not just about us. It's about the children we're supposed to have too.*

Eve: *Great point, Adam. I don't think eternal life can be achieved without knowledge. And like you, I've been thinking about the commandment to be fruitful and multiply too. That is a really important thing we're supposed to do, and in all honesty, I have no idea where babies come from.*

Adam: *Well, I've been giving that some thought, and...*

Eve: *And what?*

Adam: *...I have no idea either.*

Eve: *OK. So, we agree that we can't obey that commandment unless we have more information. And we both agree that gaining more knowledge is a good thing, even if it means experiencing some pain and sorrow in the process. In fact, maybe experiencing good and evil, joy and sorrow, health and sickness, pleasure and pain, life and death is the only way to gain the knowledge we need. This is a real dilemma. If we keep the commandment not to eat the fruit, then we can't keep the other commandment to be fruitful and multiply. What's the greater good here?*

Adam: *I think you're right, Eve. You know me, I tend to be more black-and-white in my thinking, but together we make a pretty wise team. We can wait until Father returns and discuss it with Him, but I kinda think He has already given us all of the information that he intends to. I think we're supposed to figure this out and decide for ourselves. To make the decision to put ourselves at risk to achieve a greater good is something only we can decide to do. When Father married us He never said anything about 'until death do you part,' so we have to have faith that He has a solution to this death problem. But remember, no matter what differences may exist between us, and no matter what evil the serpent and the world outside of Eden throws into our path to try and pull us apart, we stick together and hold onto each other. We never let go. No blaming each other afterwards. I promise to always be there for you, if you promise to always be there for me. It's the only way this whole plan is ever going to work. Promise?*

Eve: *Promise. OK. Here's yours; I've got mine. Ready?*

Adam and Eve together: *1…2…3…*

Unfortunately, it didn't happen quite that way. But I believe that if Adam and Eve had counseled together about this decision they would still have made the same choice. And we should be grateful that they did. Without it, none of us would have the opportunity to experience the challenges of mortality and someday qualify for immortality and eternal life.

The only error that I see on Eve's part was that she did not consult with Adam before making her decision. But she was a child; an innocent child without any experience or understanding of deception or evil. She likely didn't fully understand either–until after the deed was done–that when she made a choice that affected her life, she was also making a choice that affected Adam's.

The sequence of who decided what and when it was decided is irrelevant to some degree. What they understood was that starting this installment of the human family was a joint responsibility that would require a united effort on both of their parts to accomplish. I believe they both struggled over their choices and that tears were shed by both of them in the process of making this monumental decision. But I also believe that they left the garden hand in hand, united and prepared to meet the challenges of mortality in a new and very different world.

One of the hallmarks of sun spouses is their willingness to counsel together over any decision that will impact their lives and the lives of their children. They also share a commitment to carry the burdens and responsibilities of those decisions, together. This is not a power-based, hierarchical relationship, but a relationship of cooperative equals.

When I took engaged or married couples backpacking into the wilderness for the five-day retreats I used to conduct, one of the things I would tell them is that I wanted them to consider themselves as if they were Adam and Eve–alone in the world and totally dependent upon each other. You would be amazed how differently couples interact when they act as if their fiancé or spouse is the only other person on the planet and that cooperation is essential for their survival. You can't just ignore the other person when you are angry or upset with them and go hang out with friends or tell yourself that there are plenty of fish in the sea. You learn to appreciate each other's unique talents and to be grateful for their companionship. Pride is also less likely to disrupt the equality and unity in the relationship.

This sense of mutual interdependency is an integral part of a sun relationship. Novelist Louis de Bernières described this kind of interconnected love beautifully in his book *Corelli's Mandolin* when he wrote, "Your mother and I had it; we had roots that grew towards each other underground, and when all the pretty blossoms had fallen from our branches, we found that we were one tree and not two." (Think of the Douglas Fir tree.)

I had a conversation with my wife about this one day while we were weeding around some of the fruit trees in our yard. My wife was complaining about not being strong enough to push the shovel deep enough into the soil to loosen up the weeds so she could pull them out, so she had asked me to help. I asked her if she thought the world would be different if women were just as physically strong as men. She thought for a moment and said that if that was the case, women would probably be less inclined to rely on men and men would be less inclined to step up and take on the role of protector and provider for their families. As author and Director of the Institute for Marriage and Public Policy, Maggie Gallagher stated, "Most human societies, for most of human histories, devoted enormous energy to giving social meanings to gender, creating in each sex a profound need for the other. We are engaged in the reverse process of attempting to raise men and women who do not need one another, and I fear we are succeeding."

There are good reasons to be concerned about the direction in which the world is headed regarding marriage and family relationships. At the same time, I am confident that there will always be sun people around who understand that the marital relationship offers a level of connection and support between the sexes that transcends any other form of human interaction.

Equality

A hallmark of a sun marriage relationship is that both partners see and treat each other as equals. Our roles and responsibilities may vary, but it was not intended that marriage should involve the authoritarian hierarchy that has been common in the past.

For millennia, various cultures have placed men in positions of superiority over women. Maybe this was due to men's greater physical strength, men's desire to protect women, or some men's desire to control women. Or possibly, it may have something to do with God's edict recorded in Genesis 3:16 when He said to Eve, "thy desire shall be to thy husband and he shall rule over thee." I was intrigued recently to learn from a Hebrew scholar that the Hebrew letter *Bet* (ב) which is commonly translated as "over" in this verse, more accurately means "with," as in ruling as a family. To rule together–while allowing for variation in responsibilities and roles– seems to be in greater harmony with the spirit of the Biblical teachings about marital relationships. A unified and egalitarian couple who desire to see each other succeed in his and her roles is much more likely to achieve their goals and produce a bedroom level of intimacy and trust than a strictly hierarchical relationship. The misuse of power is much more likely to occur in hierarchical relationships and much less likely to occur when couples see each other as equal partners on a joint mission as husbands and wives.

In an effort to remind her husband John Adams of her concerns about the roles of women in American society, Abigail Adams wrote a letter to him in March of 1776 as he and a few other notable Founding Fathers were preparing the Declaration of Independence. She was fully aware of the significance that document would have on future American families as she wrote:

> *I long to hear that you have declared an independency. And, by the way, in the new code of laws which I suppose it will be necessary for you to make, I desire you would remember the ladies and be more generous and favorable to them than your ancestors. Do not put such unlimited power into the hands of the husbands. Remember, all men would be tyrants if they could. If particular care and attention is not paid to the ladies, we are determined to foment a rebellion, and will not hold ourselves bound by any laws in which we have no voice or representation.*

While I'm certain John Adams would disagree with the generalization that all men are capable of being tyrants since his and Abigail's relationship was described as one of mutual respect and deep affection, I can certainly see her point. The feminist movement of the last century might be seen as the rebellion Abigail referred to, but remember that there are three kinds of women as well as three kinds of men, so there are also three kinds of feminists.

Sun feminists–male or female–want equality of *personhood* for both genders. They honor and value the unique qualities each gender possesses and recognize the interdependency Maggie Gallagher described as something natural and good.

Moon feminists want equality of *power*, which translates into wanting men and women to be equally free to engage in their choice of behaviors, be they virtues, or vices. This perspective denies the obvious and intrinsic differences between men and women and can turn a cooperative relationship into a competitive one. Moon feminists mistakenly believe that equality between the sexes is best achieved by promoting some form of androgynous uniformity. In reality, it can only be accomplished by composing a harmonious blend of our unique male and female characteristics and roles.

Star feminists don't want equality. They want revenge.

Whether we elevate or demote a spouse, we create imbalance in the relationship. By seeing our spouse as inferior we are more likely to take over all of the decision-making responsibilities and fail to encourage initiative and accountability on the part of our spouse. By seeing them as superior we may be inclined to blindly follow and overlook bad behaviors.

Men and women are different, but equal. Different strengths, different vulnerabilities, different chemistry, different physiology, different temperaments...the list goes on, and there are volumes of scientific research that support these facts. Part of creating a bedroom-level relationship involves acknowledging and understanding those differences and working to support the growth and utilization of the strengths, while protecting the areas of vulnerability.

For example, men and women are wired differently when it comes to emotions and therefore, they do not deal with conflict the same way. Some psychologists have said that men's greatest emotional vulnerability is to feelings of shame and failure. So, when they experience conflict with their wives, they have a tendency to feel emotionally overwhelmed more easily. They may feel that they are failing, and retreat from the conflict.

For women, their greatest emotional vulnerability is said to be the fear of being abandoned, unsafe, and uncared for. (I am speaking generally and this may not be the case for every man or every woman, but it gives us a better understanding of how men and women differ in this important area.) Since women seem to tolerate the emotional soup of conflict more easily, they tend to want to stay in the conversation longer and hopefully, resolve the problem. But when a husband retreats, the wife feels abandoned, so she pursues him to try and reconcile and reconnect. When the wife shares her feelings of being abandoned, the husband feels more shame and failure so he retreats even more, making the wife feel *more* abandoned and increasing her pursuit even more, etc., etc., and the cycle continues. This cycle can be very harmful and could be easily avoided if men and women simply understood their differences in vulnerability and agreed to act toward each other in ways that do not trigger or exploit those vulnerabilities.

Meeting the Needs That Matter Most

Part of what defines sun people is the desire and commitment to nourish others and to be an influence for good in their lives. When two spouses take the time and make the effort to really get to know each other in a deep way–travel upward through the HOUSE model–they will become more aware of their spouse's strengths *and* weaknesses. A sun person would never exploit those weaknesses for personal advantage. A star person would do just that; look for the weaknesses in others and take advantage of them for personal gain. A moon person would probably be reluctant to invest the time and effort to learn about those things in the first place, or they might just be indifferent to them.

Knowing about your spouse's needs and weaknesses gives you tremendous power. As I said, increased I/T requires an equal increase in vulnerability. If a sun husband knows his wife is vulnerable to fears of being unloved and uncared for and that she has a high need for love and connection, he would make extra effort to do things that assure her of his love and appreciation for her. That would definitely increase the I/T in the marriage. A star husband might use that same information to punish her by withholding his love and affection when she does things he doesn't like.

As Dr. Gary Chapman indicates in his book *The 5 Love Languages*, understanding our spouse's deepest needs and the ways he or she most experiences love, increases one's vulnerability. But it also provides the best opportunities to increase I/T in the relationship. Sun spouses will use that information to serve and protect their partners. Star spouses will use that information to manipulate, coerce, or punish their partners. Moon spouses will usually act the way a friend did when I invited him and his wife to attend a marriage enrichment workshop I was teaching. He declined to attend the classes or to even read a book that I had recommended saying, "I don't want to learn anything more because then she will expect me to change. I'm OK with the way I am and she needs to be satisfied with that." His wife tried to hide her disappointment, but I could see it in her eyes.

Although my friend has since changed his negative attitude about self-improvement, at that time he was demonstrating a defining characteristic of some moon people: their lack of desire to learn more, to increase the levels of light and truth in their lives, and to adjust their behaviors accordingly. To reach a bedroom level of I/T in a marriage requires valiant efforts to improve both individually and as a couple. That's why moon marriages have a tendency to get stuck somewhere between the living room and the kitchen. They settle for something much less than they could have achieved had they been willing to make the effort.

Resolving Conflict

When conflicts develop in relationships they tend to follow a pretty predictable cycle. How we deal with conflict reflects which category we are in—sun, moon, or star—and determines the levels of intimacy and trust we will achieve.

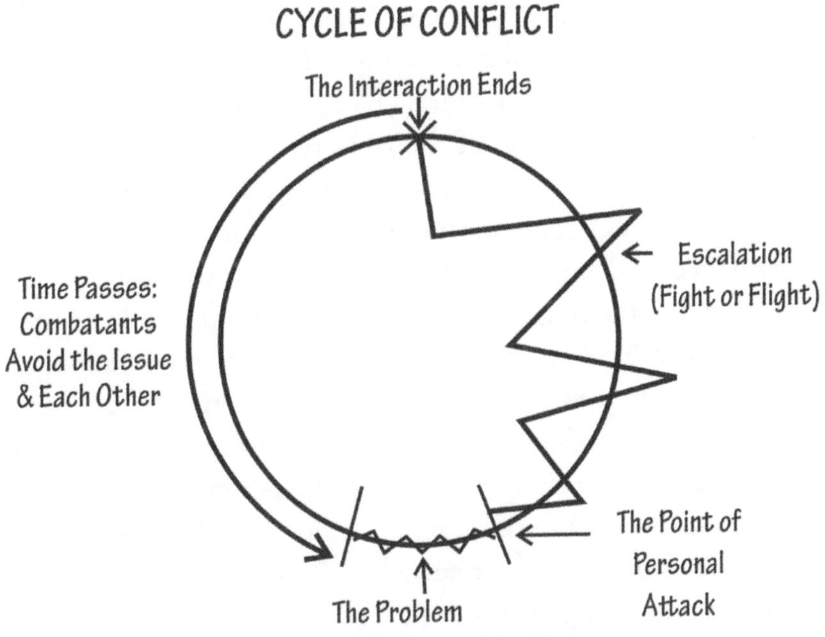

CYCLE OF CONFLICT

Figure 4.2 The Cycle of Conflict

As we go through the experiences of daily living there will inevitably be times when decisions must be made about issues that a couple may not completely agree on. Using figure 4.2, I will refer to those issues as *problems*. As indicated in the diagram, when a problem occurs it can create tension in the relationship as the couple discusses the problem and how to resolve it. However, if the couple are able to remain amicable and are willing to consider each other's opinions and needs, they can usually find a solution to the problem that they can mutually agree on and implement. The more problems they are able to solve, the easier the process becomes. The intensity of the tension gets less and less and the amount of time it takes to resolve the problem is also reduced, thereby shrinking the problem area on the cycle. So, even if a really serious problem occurs, the couple is able to tackle it successfully because they have been successful at solving so many lesser ones. Life is easier, the loyalty and confidence in the relationship gets stronger, the I/T increases, and the couple has now created a culture of success. A culture of peace. A culture of equality. A sun culture. But if that doesn't happen, something else does–something much less desirable.

A problem occurs and the couple begins to address it. The tension begins to increase and no solution seems to be in sight. Then something happens. One or both of the partners says or does something that changes the complexion and direction of the conversation. It shifts from a "we" perspective to a "me" perspective. This is referred to as **The Point of Personal Attack,** and it occurs when someone says or does anything that makes the other person feel criticized, blamed, ignored, minimized, or rejected in any way. At this point, the couple is no longer discussing the problem; they are now discussing each other. Whether the personal attack was intentional or not, when someone feels they are being attacked it triggers a response in the amygdala section of the brain known as the fight-or-flight response. When that area of the brain is turned on, the pre-frontal cortex area of the brain that controls our rational reasoning ability shuts down, so more of the brain's energy is transferred to the amygdala. We stop searching for solutions and instead, start looking for an escape from the perceived threat.

If the response is *flight*, the person will try to end the conflict by either physically escaping the situation, changing the subject, or caving in to their partner and agreeing to something they don't believe is right, just to avoid further conflict. That may end the conflict temporarily, but it will not usually resolve the problem. It may send the false message to the more assertive spouse that he or she is always right because the flight-oriented spouse keeps giving in. That invites lower levels of I/T and more passive-aggressive kinds of behaviors from the person giving in.

If the response is *fight*, the person feeling attacked will fight back. From that point on, the conflict escalates. That can involve more anger, insults, name-calling, and bringing up past failures and other unresolved issues. It can potentially get physical. In a violent relationship, at the high point in the escalation, someone gets hurt. If the relationship is not physically violent, it begins to feel emotionally violent and the conversation has to end. Now the spouses are feeling angry, scared, and wounded, and are unable to talk to each other or reach any resolution to the problem. So, they stay away from each other for a while, waiting for the emotions to calm down and hoping that the problem will disappear–which rarely happens. And because life is full of problems, eventually another problem arises, or the previous problem returns, and the cycle begins again.

> The relationship is ALWAYS more important than the problem.

But if they failed the last time, they are more likely to fail again. As they repeat the cycle over and over again, the tension between them as they discuss the next problem begins at a higher level of intensity and increases faster. As a result, the Point of Personal Attack comes sooner…and sooner… and sooner, until the relationship gets to a point where the couple has very little tolerance left for each other. They have created a culture of failure rather than one of success, and now virtually any comment is construed as "getting on my last nerve."

Compliments are viewed as sarcasm, and any effort at a positive interaction is viewed with suspicion and seen as an effort to camouflage some selfish, ulterior motive. If the conflict continues, it can result in what is called a "parallel relationship." That means two people who may be living in the same house, but who have no relationship. Their I/T levels have dropped to the front porch or lower, and they live in separate, parallel worlds where neither one is willing to interact with the other in any meaningful way nor communicate about anything but the most trivial of issues.

With a *fight* response the problems are obvious because all of those around the couple are witnesses to the escalating conflict. The harm to the relationship and to the individuals is visible on the outside because it is all expressed in their angry words and actions and their distancing themselves from each other.

But with a *flight* response the damage to the individuals and to the relationship is less visible. It takes place on the inside. The person who controls all the decision-making authority may begin to believe they are always right because the other spouse always seems to agree with them and there are no obvious objections. Life appears to be free of conflict and problems seem to be resolved quickly. But the truth is that the person in control begins to exclude their spouse from the decision-making process. The compliant spouse then begins to feel undervalued. The controlling spouse becomes more prideful, domineering, and self-focused. They gradually become less aware of the compliant spouse's needs and their responsibility to help meet them. The compliant spouse loses self-esteem; is less likely to stand up for their opinions as an equal partner in the marriage; and begins to feel unloved, uncared for, and unimportant.

The corrosion taking place inside each spouse may not be visible to those around them, but it is there and just as harmful as the other, more aggressive approach to conflict. So, whether the response to feelings of personal attack is *flight* or *fight,* either way produces harm to the individuals and to the relationship if the conflict is not resolved in a mutually respectful way.

The key to resolving conflict in positive ways and to reaching and maintaining the bedroom level of I/T is for both spouses to understand and be committed to one simple principle. That principle is this: **the relationship is ALWAYS more important than the problem.**

By the relationship, I do not mean merely staying married and avoiding divorce. I mean having a balanced, loving, intimate, soul-satisfying, sun relationship. For those who are willing to put the relationship first, they will discover that they have the ability to solve any problem life can throw at them. *Any* problem. But for those who mistakenly consider a problem to be more important than the relationship, they will never solve the problem, and the repeated conflict will eventually destroy the relationship.

Think back to conflicts you may have had with various people in your life. In cases involving a front-gate-level or front-porch-level relationship, you were probably more concerned about getting justice than about reconciling with that person. That is due in part to the lower levels of intimacy and trust involved at the lower levels in the HOUSE model. But if it involves a kitchen-level or bedroom-level relationship, you were probably more willing to extend mercy and to do all you can to preserve the relationship.

Since sun people are all about serving the needs and best interests of others, reconciliation is their goal whenever possible. But it takes two to reconcile. Two people who agree that the relationship is always more important than the problem. Two people who are willing to choose a sun way of being over the lesser alternatives and demonstrate that decision through their actions.

As family therapist Cloé Madanes asserted, "Choice is action. Compassion only exists in the compassionate deed; violence only exists in the violent act; love is only present in the loving gesture." It is in the everyday *actions* we choose in life that the kind of person we are becoming is revealed. Choosing the integrity of the relationship over prideful self-interest is central to becoming a sun spouse.

Five Steps to Resolving Conflict

Once the commitment to sun principles has been made and the belief that the relationship is always more important than the problem is etched on our belief windows, then some relatively simple actions should be all that is necessary to resolve problems—*any* problems, for *anyone*. Simple? Yes. Easy? That depends.

Step one is to stop the escalation of the conflict. As indicated in the diagram in figure 3.7, the point at which a problem becomes unmanageable is the Point of Personal Attack, when the fight-or-flight response kicks in. It is then that new and more immediate goals emerge:

1. To defend yourself and your position from attack.
2. To win the argument and avoid the embarrassment of admitting you may be wrong.
3. To get back at the other person for past offenses.

The more intense the response and the longer you delay in stopping the escalation, the harder it gets. As indicated, the emotions of fear and anger are powerful and are not easy to control once they take over your brain. But if both parties are equally committed to the relationship, then they are also equally responsible for the escalating conflict. Whichever party first recognizes the fight-or-flight response in themselves or in the other person, is obligated to stop the escalation. Their responsibility is to neutralize the new emergent goals, encourage a change of heart, and re-focus on the importance of the relationship.

Since I have a penchant for sports metaphors, allow me to offer one.

We have referees on the court in basketball games to keep the game from turning into a brawl. But on the playground when I was a kid there were no referees. So how did we manage to play the game and still keep it fair? **We called our own fouls.** The honor system.

If a player went up for a shot and felt that they were hacked in the process, they would call a foul on the opposing defensive player. The offensive team would keep possession of the ball and the game would continue. Even if the defensive player disagreed with the call, the benefit of the doubt went to the offensive player who called the foul. Why? Because keeping the game going and having fun was more important that arguing over who was most at fault. After all, what is more important, the game or the foul? The relationship, or the problem?

Now, if a player repeatedly called a foul every time he missed a shot or turned over the ball, the players on both sides would get tired of it and eventually invite that player to leave the game. The same thing applies to our relationships. If you want a sun relationship you have to honor sun principles. Anything less continues the conflict until the relationship weakens and becomes a parallel relationship, or no relationship at all.

Please remember that calling a foul is *not* an accusation. ("You fouled me you *jerk*!") It is more like an admission of discomfort. ("Ouch, that hurt!") Whether the person hurting is yourself or the other party, calling a foul is intended to diffuse a situation by inviting empathy into the conversation, not antagonism.

What happens after a foul is called by a referee? The game stops momentarily.

Step two is to take a timeout. A timeout gives both parties time to reflect on what just happened and prepare to reconnect in a more positive way. If the foul is called sooner, before the emotions get ramped up, the timeout may only need to last a few minutes or even seconds. If the parties wait until things have already escalated, more time will likely be necessary to calm everybody down again.

Decide on how much time is needed and use the time productively. If you use it to plot your revenge like petulant children often do when sent to their bedrooms for timeout, you will only add to the problem. Instead, start first by asking yourself how you were feeling when the personal attack occurred; whether you were in a bad mood because you had a tough day at work or because someone cut you off in traffic. After this self-assessment, then put yourself in the other person's shoes and consider some of the difficulties they may be dealing with, or some of the good things they have done for you recently. Experiencing empathy is the best way to diffuse negative emotions.

Step three is to talk about what happened. Not about the initial problem that started the whole conflict, but about what caused the personal attack. Before you can resolve the original issue, you have to resolve the more important issue–the relationship is under fire and trust needs to be restored. Share your perspectives and insights gained during the timeout about what contributed to the personal attack and reconcile the relationship. There is a simple communication tool that can help with that conversation. It is called the Speaker-Listener method (S-L).

The S-L is a structured way to have a conversation that reduces the likelihood of conflict. One person begins as the speaker and the other as the listener. Speakers speak, and listeners listen–*only* listen. They do not interrupt or allow their minds to wander. They do not begin thinking about their rebuttal to what the speaker is saying. The listener's job is to understand what the speaker is trying to communicate to him or her.

Speakers need to learn how to condense their thoughts into a brief, comprehensive, and coherent monologue that the listener can easily understand. By brief I mean in two minutes or less. Any longer than that and there will be too much information for the listener to process and remember, and the speaker is more likely to get off topic and bring up a bunch of unrelated and unnecessary information. Speakers address the issue from their own perspective using "I" statements rather than more accusatory "you" statements.

Once the speaker is done, the listener then reflects back to the speaker the information they received while also including what they have picked up from the speaker's non-verbal communication; like facial expressions, tone of voice, or body language. No critiques, no sarcasm, no rebuttal, no personal opinions thrown in. Just reflect accurately and objectively what the speaker has communicated. Then they reverse roles and repeat the process.

The reason for using such a structured approach is to ensure that the conversation stays focused, addresses the real purpose, and doesn't drag on until it invites another personal attack. If that happens, then another foul is called and you start the process all over again until successfully completing the conversation without triggering a negative response. Tedious? Sometimes, but remember that the goal is to create empathy and restore connection and trust in the relationship. The more you practice it, the easier and more natural it becomes.

Step four is to revisit the original problem. Now that a connection has been re-established, you should be able to return to a discussion of the original issue. I recommend that you also use the S-L for that conversation for the same reasons listed above. You do not have to agree with each other. This is the time to express your honest opinions about the issue so both parties know each other's perspective. Then the fun part begins.

Step five is to list options to solve the problem. Brain storm. Anything goes on the list; even silly, impossible options. Laugh as much as possible. Eventually you will begin to narrow the list down to a few reasonable options and pick the best one. Both parties commit a 100% effort to the solution. If after a while that option genuinely does not seem to be working, continue going down the short list until you find one that does. Problem solved. Then move on.

Occasionally there will be times when both parties feel very strongly about their choice of solutions. That's called a tie. Since ties often occur in many life situations, we all need a designated tie-breaker. Sometimes the best option may be to table the decision until more information is gathered. But eventually, ties must be broken and a decision has to be made.

There are nine members of the Supreme Court to avoid ties. Every football game begins with a ritual to decide who gets possession of the ball first. So, we flip a coin; play "rock, paper, scissors"; or use some other method of resolving the impasse. When the decision is made and the tie is broken, then we pull together as a team and focus on the game–that is, the relationship.

Few relationships are free of any problems and the likelihood is that even great relationships will experience the occasional unresolved conflict. That is not the problem. It's when a *pattern* of ongoing, unresolved, and escalating conflict develops that relationships are at risk. When you choose your way of being you also choose how you will deal with conflict. You can employ the star practices of criticism, contempt, defensiveness, stonewalling, and belligerence that psychologist Dr. John Gottman warned against, or you can employ compassion, patience, understanding, and humor.

Angel Face

There is a legend that tells of the fateful day when Adam and Eve were required to vacate the Garden of Eden. Just as they were about to step outside of its protected precincts and into the lone and dreary world, their Heavenly Father called them back and gave them a special gift that He knew would help them deal with the challenges that life in mortality would bring them. He gave them a sense of humor.

An abundance of laughter is an indication of a healthy, happy, committed relationship. The absence of laughter is a clear indication of a troubled one. As Russian comedian Yakov Smirnoff has said about marriage relationships, "When things are not working, laughter is the first thing to go. The second thing to go is intimacy. The third thing is your house."

The ability to laugh at yourself is an indication of a person who possesses good measures of humility and meekness and who has concern for the well-being of others. As Steven R. Covey quipped, "If you can laugh at yourself, you will make it easier on your companion and on your children, who have to live with what you do and don't do, and with what you are and are not."

My wife and I certainly try to apply humor generously and frequently. I remember one hot Arizona summer afternoon in 2012 when I had just come into the house after working in the yard for a couple of hours. My wife was seated at the desk in our kitchen doing something on the computer as I walked in and sat in a chair beside her. The pungent odor of male perspiration filled the air. My wife looked at me with that wrinkled facial expression we've all experienced when smelling something repugnant and blurted out, "You stink!" I responded with a look of suave sophistication and a Casanova-like cadence in my voice and said "Well, you know some women find that odor arousing!" She suddenly got an excited look on her face like a standup comedian who has just been fed the perfect setup line by someone in the audience as she shouted, "That's a LIE! A lie sweaty man tell women!"

We both burst into laughter. Laughter releases a dose of oxytocin into the brain, and we have already discussed what oxytocin does for our relationships. So, as I looked into her glistening eyes, I saw an oh-so familiar expression of joy on her face. When she smiles it isn't like what you might see on the face of a typical beauty pageant contestant, but one that engulfs her whole face and engages every muscle in it. Laugh lines appear at the sides of her eyes and her cheek muscles rise, pushing the skin beneath her eyes upward and reducing the openings for her eyes to less than half their normal size. Unlike the toothy smiles you see in cosmetic dentistry advertisements, hers is a smile that is about two thirds teeth and one third gums. Her smile is an image that is forever branded upon my mind, my heart, my soul. To me, it's the face of an angel. In fact, if you were to look up my wife's name in the contact list on my cell phone you will not see Patricia listed anywhere. Under speed dial number two is the listing "Angel Face." As I looked at her I felt a sudden emotional rush as my mind suddenly reached back in time and retrieved thousands of compressed memories of similar events throughout our many years of marriage.

I remembered the many experiences we shared as parents attending our kids' births, baptisms, sporting events, choir performances, Junior Miss pageants, graduations, weddings, and the births of our grandchildren. I remembered sitting next to her in the hospital as she faced the painful task of childbirth with faith, courage, and determination. I remembered the wise counsel she has given over the years, not just to our children, but also to their father. I remembered the painful looks of sorrow, frustration, and on a few occasions even anger, when I said or did things that offended her. I also remembered her words of encouragement as she supported me through the darkness and difficulties of the most painful experiences of my life.

I could never express my level of appreciation nor repay her for all that she has done for me. She is indeed a pearl of great price and there was no way I could even begin to place a value on the years of joy, laughter, hardship, and friendship we have shared together. Like the Grinch whose heart grew three sizes that fateful Christmas day, on that hot summer day a deep feeling of gratitude swelled within mine.

The Heart of The Matter

You could read every self-help book ever published about how to improve your marriage, but without a softening of the heart toward your spouse, you will never benefit from the principles and skills they teach. Over the years I have worked with nearly one thousand couples and, sadly, a minority of them have embraced the simple truth that the integrity of their relationship is *always* more important than the temporal concerns and problems we encounter in life

Sun relationships are only possible when each partner first decides to become a sun individual. That is a process that should begin long before you start looking for a potential spouse. I say that because it takes a sun person to recognize, attract, and appreciate another sun person. Similarly, moon people attract moon people, and star people attract star people. If we settle for becoming something less as individuals, we can expect to achieve something less in our marriages.

The questions you should ask yourself before making the decision of whom to marry should not just be "Is she the one for me? The one who will meet my deepest needs and bring blissful happiness into my life?" More importantly, it should be, "Am I the one for her? Am I the kind of person who will commit to loving and helping my spouse reach her full potential?"

It is within family relationships that we are best able to experience and fully understand what is meant by the saying, "It is better to give, than to receive." Far too many couples get the order reversed and miss out on the mind enlightening, heart expanding, and soul-exalting experience that marriage is intended to be. It is not easy; it was not intended to be. It will require the best you have to give, and then some.

It is in marriage that sexuality is sanctioned so that its procreative and bonding powers can be fully employed. It is there that we develop patience, humility, a willingness to sacrifice for the welfare of others, and all the other sun qualities. We are to be helpmeets, caregivers, and caretakers of each other. But unlike the children at Bing Nursery School, you don't have to wait to receive the rewards of a sun relationship. You just have to decide that you truly want one and act accordingly. The rewards begin immediately.

So, when you are tempted to take the easy way out, to let pride or selfishness reduce the levels of intimacy and trust in your relationship and send you or your spouse out the front gate and down the street, remember that life is a "walking of we."

Men and women were never meant to be alone. From the Book of Genesis account describing the relationship between our first parents, we come to understand that marriage was never intended to end at death and that the fundamental unit in eternity is not the individual, but the family.

Believing this should impact our choices regarding where we focus our time and energy in this life. For sun people, the focus will always be on their relationships. For moon people, worldly things can get in the way. For star people, people are just objects for their use and relationships don't matter.

I once saw an interview with twelve-time Emmy award winner and acclaimed actor, writer, director, producer, author, and TV pioneer Carl Reiner and his similarly acclaimed son Rob as they spoke about their family life in the midst of the glitz, glamour, pressures, and excesses of show business. The senior Reiner said that there was nothing more important to him and Estelle, his beloved wife of nearly sixty-five years, than producing good children who could contribute to making the world a better place. In speaking about their three children he said, "There is nothing more important than sending wonderful people out into the world. It's the best thing I have ever done."

Some religious scholars have suggested that the questions our Creator will ask each of us when we stand before Him for judgment will not be about any of the temporal things many people tend to believe are so important. He won't ask about our career successes, the honors we received, our prestigious college degrees, our financial achievements, or any other worldly accomplishments.

The first round of questions will involve a searching examination of our relationship with our spouse and whether we have contributed, to the best of our ability, to their happiness and growth. The second round of questions will be similar and will focus on our role as parents and whether we have done the same for each of the children entrusted to our care. Finally, there will be a round of questions about whether we have used our time and talents to contribute in positive ways to the lives of the people in our communities, states, countries, and the world.

The Highest Relationship

For people of faith, there is another relationship level in the HOUSE model than exceeds even the bedroom level of intimacy and trust. I'll call it Heaven.

Our relationships with God progress in much the same way as our relationships with other people. In this case, it is God who stands at the front gate, waiting for us to walk by on the sidewalk of life. He invites us into a relationship and asks us to exercise just a little vulnerability at first by entering the front gate, for which He generously rewards our fledgling faith. He asks us to spend more time with Him, to get better acquainted, to share experiences together, and to learn about His qualities and the tremendous spiritual benefits that this relationship offers to those who are willing to pursue it.

We determine the boundary. If all we are willing to accept is a front-porch-level relationship, then He will honor that decision. No coercion, no threats, just an invitation to move to something higher and better. He invites us to cross the threshold and enter His living room where we can learn much more about Him and how He lives. Our conversations and interactions become more personal, more frequent, and more vulnerable. He asks us to increase our trust, to sacrifice more of our temporal desires, and to develop a deeper relationship that offers much greater potential–that of discipleship.

Between the living room and the kitchen will be many years of experiences that will test our commitment to this singular and extraordinary relationship. Some will progress toward the kitchen, while others will stall and get stuck at a moon level somewhere in between. For those who persist in building this relationship, intimacy and trust will grow as we encounter the challenges of life together. Eventually the relationship will progress from that of master and servant, to one of deep friendship.

As we approach the bedroom level of intimacy and trust we will begin to experience a level of communication and connection that feels like a marriage relationship that has achieved the supernal sense of oneness that the scriptures describe. The still, small voice of the Holy Spirit will become as familiar and uplifting as the whispered expressions of love and gratitude we share with our spouse at the most intimate and vulnerable moments of our lives.

And as I mentioned, at some point in time, what happened to Abraham will likely happen to each of us. We will be asked to endure something that will require greater faith than we think we are capable of. We will come to that moment of understanding—as did Abraham—that our relationship with God must transcend everything else.

To become sun people we must fully accept the responsibility of freedom of choice, with its possibility of failure, and place our eternal destinies in the hands of just one person. Everything we seek as sun people depends on His success. Without it, there would be no possibility of a resurrection, no forgiveness of sin, and no hope for eternal life. Talk about vulnerability.

So, we either push on, accepting these terms, trusting in His promises, and enduring to the end so we can reach the summit of intimacy and trust that extends high above the bedroom, or we lose our confidence, weaken our commitment, and settle for something less.

The choice is yours. But contemplate again what C.S. Lewis wrote: "Aim at heaven and you will get earth thrown in." In this case, if we aim at Heaven by applying sun principles in our relationships with God, we will likely do the same in our relationships with family and friends. The result will be getting bedroom-level marriages with our spouses and kitchen-level friendships with our family and friends, thrown in.

Your next activity is to determine where in the HOUSE model your relationship with your spouse is located and what levels of vulnerability, intimacy, and trust you have generated. If you are not happy with the results, follow the steps I have outlined and make it better.

CHAPTER 5 Preview

Parenting was the first and foremost responsibility given to the world's first couple. All other responsibilities in life are appendages to it. It also provides the most challenging and transformative experiences in life. Transformative for parents, as well as for their children.

This chapter will examine what sun, moon, and star parenting looks like and how our parental choices will impact the lives of every generation that follows us.

CHAPTER 5

3 KINDS OF PARENTS

A Star Trek Approach to Successful Parenting

Captain's log: Star date 2021.9.

Star vessel Z-10n has come upon an emerging civilization that is struggling to maintain the stability and functioning of its basic societal unit referred to in their indigenous planetary language as the "family." We have observed increasing fluctuations in cultural norms and that many within this society are challenging the traditional values and practices honored by their ancestors. As a result, the structural and moral integrity of this essential organization is in danger and that of the entire civilization along with it. While we have successfully navigated through our own times of upheaval and social uncertainty centuries ago, the Prime Directive prevents us from intervening directly in the affairs of this civilization to correct the problems they are creating for themselves. Instead, we have determined that it would be appropriate to work behind the scenes by quietly introducing our galactically time-tested approach known as the Prime Directive of Parenting to select members of this society

*in strategic nations throughout this world in the hope that the
information will eventually be embraced by the citizenry on a
global basis.*
End of Captain's log entry.

For those of you who are old enough to remember the old Star Trek
television series you will understand the dilemma the crew of the starship
Enterprise faced. As they traveled around the galaxy discovering new
civilizations, they often came across worlds on the verge of self-destruction
because of their bad societal decisions. To "beam down" and take over
leadership of these developing societies would be to deny them the freedom
and responsibility of determining their own destinies. To fly away and ignore
them would be to disengage and fail in their responsibility as a member of
the Galactic Federation of Planets to adequately protect new civilizations
from their own immaturity and vulnerability. They had a responsibility to
help other civilizations learn how to achieve a peaceful, cohesive society of
their own without force or coercion.

Wouldn't it be great if an advanced race of beings from another world
were to distill their accumulated wisdom in family living into a simple format
that was understandable and applicable to everyone? If they arrived in a huge
starship, interrupted all audio and video transmissions on the planet to share
their message, and looked like Yoda or Gandalf we would probably respond
immediately to their counsel and instructions. But if it happened the way I
described above…well then, maybe not so much. Nevertheless, here it is for
your consideration and perusal… *The Prime Directive of Parenting.*

There are two parts to the Prime Directive of Parenting:

1. Parents are to *keep their children safe* physically, emotionally, and
   spiritually.
2. Parents are to *prepare their children for adulthood.*

That's it. Simple. The greatest concepts can usually be expressed in
simple terms. The question is, how do we apply these simple instructions?

Keeping Them Safe

The Prime Directive of Parenting recognizes that our first responsibility as parents is to protect our children from the physical, emotional, and spiritual threats to their safety that are common to this world. We are also to do this in ways that respect their free will, honor their personhood, and prepare them for an autonomous life as an adult.

The two elements of the Prime Directive of Parenting are interconnected, which means you cannot separate them. The strategies you use to accomplish the first part must also be appropriate for accomplishing the second part.

To begin with, let's identify the four basic styles of parenting. They are (1) Authoritarian, (2) Authoritative, (3) Permissive, and (4) Disengaged.

Authoritarian

Authoritarian parents rule with an iron fist. "My way or the highway" is a phrase made popular by authoritarian people in general, but particularly by authoritarian parents. At the star level they use their superior physical power as well as their control over everything their children need or want in life to dominate and control their children's behavior. They use abusive levels of corporal punishment, threats of violence, and excessive removal of privileges to coerce compliance.

Rather than teaching their children sun beliefs and values and encouraging critical thinking skills and self-reliance, they indoctrinate them in their authoritarian ways of thinking. One of the most shocking examples of this kind of indoctrination that I have personally encountered was reported to me by an adult client who described an incident that was repeated several times throughout her childhood. When her father was upset with her mother for some perceived violation of his Draconian rules, he would force the children to sit and watch as he administered "discipline" to their mother. He would beat her bloody and then send her out of the room to clean up, leaving the red evidence of his seemingly justified disapproval on the living room carpet for the children to see. Then he would repeatedly say to his traumatized children, "Love is pain; pain is love," and require them to parrot the same phrase back to him.

Authoritarian star parents put excessive expectations on their children, demanding total compliance to their rules and superior performance in athletics, academics, or other pursuits. They bask in the glow of their children's accomplishments and take it very personally when their children do not live up to their expectations.

Whether their children are viewed as obstacles that interfere with the parents' efforts to meet their self-centered needs, or as tools they use to meet those needs, authoritarian star parents never see their children as equal human beings, entitled to equal human rights, regardless of their age. Rather than becoming autonomous, confident, and caring adults, the children of authoritarian parents are likely to be rebellious and resistant to authority, lack compassion for others, be prone to anger and depression, and treat others the way they were treated growing up—as objects to be controlled and manipulated.

The key word here is *excessive*. Authoritarian parents are excessive in their discipline and the demands they put on their children. There is no balance between high expectations and unconditional love. Everything is conditioned upon compliance.

At the moon level, authoritarian parents can be controlling in a different way. They tend to be over-involved in their children's lives, sometimes to the point of handicapping them. While their intentions may be good, over-protective "helicopter" or "snow-plow" parents often deprive their children of the character-building challenges that children must face if they are to develop self-confidence and emotional resilience.

Authoritarian moon parents often confuse keeping children safe with controlling them. They implement policies intending to protect them that, in reality, may be preventing them from developing the emotional and spiritual muscles necessary to face the temptations and challenges they will encounter in the adult world.

Another way moon parents let the world get in the way is a common phenomenon we see in many homes today. David Brooks describes it well in his book *The Road to Character* when he writes of the current trends in childrearing of over-praising and over-incentivizing children.

Children are bathed in love, but it is often directional love. Parents shower their kids with affection, but it is not simple affection, it is meritocratic affection—it is intermingled with the desire to help their children achieve worldly success.... It is not simply 'I love you.' It is 'I love you when you stay on my balance beam.' ...Lurking in the shadows of merit-based love is the possibility that it may be withdrawn if the child disappoints.

Some authoritarian moon parents can become so emotionally enmeshed in their children's lives that the children begin to feel more like the parents at times. I remember a classmate in my home town who was a talented athlete and was especially good at basketball. He was probably the highest scoring guard to ever play for my small-town high school basketball team. His father sent him to all the basketball camps, made him practice for endless hours, and—according to some of his close friends—required him to score a certain number of points per game or face punishment.

Each year our rural community organized an invitational basketball tournament that included some of the best high school teams in Northern California. During one game this classmate got into a minor scuffle with a player on an opposing team. His father came charging out of the bleachers, ran up to the opposing player, grabbed him by the throat with one hand, and prepared to punch him in the face with the other. The classmate had to pull his father away from the opposing player and his father was then unceremoniously removed from the court by the coaches and the security staff.

The last time I saw this father was at his son's bedside in the hospital where the son was being treated for injuries from a solo drunk driving accident. Dad continued to lecture and berate his son, who laid there expressionless. Although it was evident that this father was concerned about his son, by this point in his life, this discouraged son had effectively tuned-out the sound of his father's voice.

Authoritative

There is no sun version of authoritarian parenthood. Sun parents are *authoritative*. They teach their children the importance of sun principles and values; model those beliefs in their own lives; establish rules clearly founded on those beliefs; and enforce those rules with consistency, patience, and love. They do more than just teach sun principles. Instead, they instill in their children an appetite for sun principles. A hunger for light. A thirst for truth. As a result, when the children of sun parents reach adulthood they will continue to feast on sun principles throughout their lives.

Authoritative parents understand what investment advisor R.C. Peck described as two of the most important needs that children of all ages have, and that their parents must meet if their children are to thrive:

1) **They need to know the rules** and why those rules are important.
2) **They need to feel they belong**; specifically, that they belong to their parents and family.

Sun parents do not always provide their children with the answers to all of life's questions. Rather, they assist their children in finding the answers for themselves. The answers we obtain through our own efforts are usually the answers that maintain lasting value. Sun parents allow their children to progressively make more of their own choices while making sure they experience the natural consequences of those choices.

Sun parents neither under-praise nor over-praise their children. They provide recognition and encouragement for their children's efforts and successes, while providing accountability and correction in restorative ways when their children break the rules. They are the parenting equivalents of the tightrope-walking circus family The Flying Wallendas. They are masters at balanced parenting.

The healing balm of forgiveness is applied generously in authoritative households by all their members. Children raised by authoritative parents set high, yet achievable standards for themselves and others. They are disciplined, motivated, honest, hard-working, and they provide inspired leadership when placed in positions of responsibility. They truly live by the Golden Rule in their relationships with others and they fully understand and apply the relationship principle that I mentioned previously—that the relationship is always more important than the problem.

Authoritative parents understand the responsibility of protecting their children while also preparing their children for adulthood. They apply what I refer to as the Inoculation Paradigm. Using a medical metaphor, this means that if they are to develop sufficient physical, emotional, and spiritual immunity to the increasingly toxic ills of the world, our children must be exposed to a dose of those "diseases." Like getting a small-pox vaccination to prevent your child from getting a full-blown case of the disease, children need to be exposed to enough information about the evils and ills of the world–in addition to a much larger dosage of what is good and true–if they are to develop some measure of immunity to them.

To do this, authoritative parents must be fearless communicators who regularly invite conversations with their children about virtually any topic of concern in today's world. Sex, drugs, rock 'n' roll, politics, religion, tattooing…there are no taboo subjects in authoritative homes. Dinnertime in authoritative households is a protected and sacred time for having these kinds of discussions in a relaxed environment, and authoritative parents take full advantage of those opportunities.

Authoritative parenting is the best way to honor and implement the Prime Directive of Parenting and sun parents will be the most successful at keeping their children physically, emotionally, and spiritually safe.

Permissive

Permissive parenting is like being stuck in San Francisco in the late 1960s. (Since I attended college in the San Francisco Bay Area in 1969, I know whereof I speak.) Along with the infamous Timothy Leary invitation to "Turn on, tune in, and drop out," other key themes of the 1960s included "Do your own thing," and "If it feels good, do it!" This was often interpreted to mean do whatever you want to, without regard for laws, morals, common sense, and the welfare of self or others. The permissive approach produced a lot of hedonistic, self-absorbed, and unmotivated individuals, some of whom fried their brains on drugs. At the same time they were messing up their own lives, they were also passing around STDs to their friends and acquaintances like movie popcorn.

Permissive parents have never read the book by Dr. David Walsh entitled *NO. How Kids–of All Ages–Need to Hear It and Ways Parents Can Say It.* They seem to want to believe that children think and act like adults, or that their childhood ignorance and impulsivity will only produce harmless experiences that add to their growth and pose no serious threats to their physical, emotional, or spiritual safety. Saying "It's all good!" regarding our children's misadventures and mistakes in the form of shoplifting, drinking, drugging, premarital sex, daredevil activities, and academic failure invites some painful learning experiences with some negative consequences that often cannot be reversed.

Permissive parents make the mistake of believing that loving their children unconditionally somehow requires tolerating bad behavior. That is definitely *not* the case. In fact, authoritative parents know that part of loving their children means wanting the best outcomes for them by correcting their errant behavior. It is only when people are consistently obeying sun principles that lasting happiness and fulfillment can be achieved.

Children need to be taught a clear set of principles and values by which they can judge between right and wrong. They need to be recognized for their successes in honoring those principles and held accountable when they don't. Parents need to establish appropriate limits on their children's behavior so that their children will learn self-control and be able to voluntarily maintain those limits when they reach adulthood.

It is in adolescence and young adulthood that our children will be exposed to more emboldened star people preaching an ever-expanding and more deceptive array of star beliefs. Our children will need to be strong enough to "take a punch" when star people start swinging at their sun belief systems. They will need sun GRIT–what Angela Duckworth defines as "the passionate commitment to, and perseverant application of" sun principles. Permissiveness and self-indulgence are moon parenting perspectives that will not prepare children for the adult world and the challenges they will inevitably face.

I could compose a long list of examples of how moon parents tend to let the world get in the way during the process of parenting their children, but many of them fall into the same category: too much concern about how they are perceived by others, and too little concern about what's best for their kids. They fail to understand that if they do not establish and reinforce principles of light and truth in their lives and the lives of their children, each successive generation has the tendency to lose more of that light and truth and have less to pass on to their posterity. This gradual, downhill decline is how moon people become star people over time.

Disengaged

Disengaged parents are usually star parents. (Except, of course, those who act that way because of mental illness, traumatic stress, or similar problems.) Their focus in life is on themselves and they show little regard for the safety and happiness of others, even their own children. There is a song recorded by Johnny Cash that reminds me of this style of parenting. It was based on a poem by Shel Silverstein about "A Boy Named Sue."

It tells the story of an absentee father who runs from the responsibilities of parenthood. Abandoning his three-year-old son and the boy's mother, he leaves his child with a painful reminder of his inept parenting by saddling his son with a name that is certain to cause him to experience rejection, harassment, and ridicule. He names him Sue. The result for the boy was a life of embarrassment, anger, conflict, violence, and a vow that he would hunt down and kill the man "who gave me that awful name."

"Well, I grew up quick and I grew up mean," was the boy's description of his life. He developed street smarts, but no compassion, no connection with others, and no purpose in his life. Life was about survival and revenge.

Eventually, the long-anticipated day arrives and he comes across his father in a bar in Tennessee. A fight to the death en*sues*. (Sorry, I couldn't resist.) Just as the son is on the verge of fulfilling his murderous vow, Dad tells Sue that he did his son a huge favor by giving him a girl's name. He credits that decision with producing a tough and strong man who should be *grateful* to dear old dad for the name! This father apparently had no confidence that his son stood any chance of surviving in the cold, cruel world without learning to be tough and mean. So, he did what disengaged parents and star people in general do—he looked for some way to justify his star behavior. As I mentioned, star people must find some way to make the wrong, seem right.

(For the complete poem go to http://famouspoetsandpoems.com/poets/shel_silverstein/poems/14827).

The children of disengaged parents can grow up angry, rebellious, aggressive, lonely, aimless, purposeless, hopeless, and disengaged from others—very similar to the children of authoritarian parents. Sue was a "chip off the old block" and had become just like his father.

As the old saying goes, "You can pretend to care, but you can't pretend to show up." Sue's father didn't care, so he ran from his responsibilities as a father. Teaching his son to be tough is not preparing him for the most important roles men have in life—of becoming loving husbands and fathers.

But I have also learned that we have to be careful about how we judge others in this area. I had a conversation in the early 1970s with a young man who had just returned from a stint in the Peace Corp. He had been serving in India among families who were members of the lowest caste in Indian society, the Untouchables. While visiting the home of a desperately poor family who had a couple of older children and who had recently had a third, he was shocked by what he considered to be a blatant case of child abuse. Instead of seeing brightly colored mobile-like objects hanging above the infant's bed as he was accustomed to seeing with the children of many American parents, these parents had hung a piece of barbed wire that would surely cause pain when the child reached up to grab it. When the Peace Corp volunteer asked the parents why they would do such a hurtful thing, he was not prepared for their answer. They calmly explained to him that as a member of the lowest caste in India, their child would experience nothing but pain and heartbreak throughout his life. By introducing him to pain from the very beginning of his life, they felt they were doing him a favor and preparing him for the greater pain that would inevitably follow.

Maybe that was the "different point of view" the boy named Sue was referring to that suddenly turned a violent exchange with his father into a mutual appreciation hug-fest, but the two circumstances seem very different to me. One involved a star parent who shirked his responsibilities as a father and who was willing to cause serious harm to his son to save himself from pain. The other involved well-intentioned sun parents who probably would have sacrificed their own lives if it meant better lives for their children. Regardless of the specific behaviors involved, you will have to decide whose intentions were compassionate and whose were not; who is the sun parent and who is something less.

Parenting and the Family Ship

I have discovered recently that there are a lot of similarities between parenting and shipbuilding. The challenge for shipbuilders throughout history has been to find the balance between building a ship where the joints that hold it together are strong enough to provide strength and safety, but flexible enough to allow the ship to adjust to rough waters. As author J.E. Gordon pointed out in his book *Structures: Or Why Things Don't Fall Down*, if the joints are too rigid the ship may not be able to withstand the pressures from turbulent seas and may break apart—like several poorly-designed welded steel ships did during World War II. If they are too flexible, the ship will leak excessively and may sink.

Authoritarian parents are too rigid, and their families will break apart when confronted by the many challenges that life will throw at them. Permissive parents are too flexible, and their families will discover that the errant philosophies and destructive behaviors common in the outside world are seeping through the cracks between the timbers that make up their family ship.

Disengaged parents don't bother to build a ship.

Authoritative parents have figured out the balance between strength and flexibility. Their family ships may appear to leak a little from time to time when under pressure, but they hold up during the storms of life.

Please understand that being an authoritative sun parent is not a guarantee that all your children will become sun people, nor is being an authoritarian, permissive, or disengaged parent a curse that will guarantee that your children will all turn out to be moon or star people. I have known many sun people who have survived an ugly upbringing, and I have met star people who came from the best of families. We all have moral agency. We all get to choose the kind of person we want to be. But being an authoritative

sun parent gives children the best opportunities to make the wisest choices–
the choices that will bring them the most happiness. As a society, we owe
them that opportunity.

The Changing Roles of Sun Parents

Loving a child invites a degree of pain and sorrow into our lives, particularly
when our children's own misguided choices invite pain and sorrow into theirs.
There is a long list of things children and teens can do to put themselves at
physical, emotional, or spiritual risk and parents have to be prepared to deal
with them. And while doing all we can to keep them safe, parents should
also realize that their role as protector must change as their children grow.
If our children are to be prepared for the adjustments of transitioning from
childhood into adulthood, we as parents must also adjust along with them.

From Quarterback to Spectator

Dr. Kevin Theriot once described the changing roles of parenthood using
a football metaphor that many of the parents I have coached have found
helpful in understanding their changing roles as parents.

When children are first born they are entirely dependent on their
parents or caregivers and remain that way for several years. So, between
birth and about eight years of age, kids are the players and parents are the
quarterbacks. Like Peyton Manning (or your quarterback of choice), parents
are choosing the plays, throwing the passes, handing off the ball, reading
the defenses, calling audibles…they are in charge and are running the show.
Children's future success depends on how parents use this time to establish
a foundation of principles and practices that install desirable attitudes and
beliefs onto their children's belief windows.

But when children reach about eight years of age, something changes.
Their brains and their moral reasoning ability have developed to a point
where they are better able to distinguish between right and wrong. As a
result, they are now more accountable for their choices. From age eight
to about fourteen or fifteen they continue developing an increased sense
of individuality and separateness from their parents. And because of that
change, parents are pulled off the field and their uniforms are taken away.

Instead, they are given a cap, a clipboard, and a whistle. They are no longer quarterbacks; they are now coaches.

Not that they weren't also coaches when their children were young, but now that is all that they get to do. They don't run out onto the field and take over when their children mess up a play. The coach's job is to teach, train, drill, motivate, discipline, and prepare their players. But once they take the field, the players are responsible for the outcome. Their heads are either in the game, or they're distracted and uncertain. They either know how to play their positions with confidence, or they don't. If the players have been properly coached, they will have a sense of purpose in life and will take responsibility for the choices they make. If not, they will struggle to figure out who they are, and why they are.

When children reach the age of fourteen or fifteen they enter what psychologist Erik Erickson calls the Identity Formation Stage of development and they get serious about breaking the apron strings and establishing themselves as individuals. That includes selecting a value system that they consider to be their own—a system that may or may not be in harmony with what they have been taught by their parents. While the teaching process continues, at that age, parents give up their clipboards and whistles and are given a set of pom-poms instead. They are now cheerleaders.

Cheerleaders may be on the sidelines like the coaches and players, but they have minimal impact on the outcome of the game. Their job is to smile and cheer with never-diminishing enthusiasm, regardless of the outcome of the game. They celebrate their team's victories and share in the sorrow of their defeats. Though they may shed tears of compassion for the struggling and sometimes disheartened players, they never leave the sidelines or turn a blind eye to what is taking place on the gridiron or say insulting things about the players behind their backs. They stay. They cheer. They try to reinforce what the coaches have taught and motivate the team members. They love their players despite their sometimes-lackluster performances. And between games, they are confidence-builders and empathetic listeners.

This goes on until children reach the age of eighteen or nineteen and (hopefully) complete high school. Then parents give up their pom-poms and are escorted from the sidelines to a seat in the bleachers. They are now only spectators and the players on the field will only be aware of their presence if they look for them in the crowd or strain their ears to hear the familiar voices of Mom and Dad amongst the many others in the boisterous world around them. If parents are to continue to participate in their children's game of life, it will only be because their children invite them to. It won't be as quarterbacks or even coaches; it will be as consultants.

But remember, there are three kinds of spectators just as there are three kinds of quarterbacks, coaches, and cheerleaders.

Sun spectators cheer loudly and passionately. They sit in the bleachers with other loyal fans and would never mock or harass the opposing team's players or fans. They are there to support their players and to remind them that, win or lose, it's how they play the game that matters most.

Moon spectators would rarely risk embarrassing themselves by painting their faces and being loud and ostentatious. They might also get discouraged if their child's team wasn't playing well and would probably go home at half-time if defeat seemed likely.

If star spectators show up at all, they are usually so obnoxious that no one wants to be around them.

My wife and I have discovered that this transition can be a very positive one for both parents and children if we have successfully completed our jobs of keeping them safe and preparing them for adulthood. We can watch as they take on the challenges and responsibilities of adulthood. We can celebrate their successes and mourn their failures from the slightly less vulnerable position of the bleachers. And we can become assistant coaches for our grandchildren without the responsibilities and pressure that the head coaches endure. If parenting is a game, then these are the roles we play; and the Prime Directive of Parenting provides the rules.

No Apology Necessary

It is important for parents to remember that you never need to apologize for applying the Prime Directive of Parenting. When you need to intervene in your child's life and provide guidance, correction, or discipline, you should speak authoritatively, with confidence, and with compassion when you tell your child:

As your parent, I am bound by the Prime Directive of Parenting to keep you safe and to prepare you for adulthood. I will not hesitate to act decisively whenever I see that you are at risk physically, emotionally, or spiritually, or when I believe you need to understand something that is essential to your happiness and success in the adult world.

I call this the Parental Oath of Office. I encourage all parents to put that statement on a plaque or parchment with all the family signatures at the bottom and hang it on your living room or kitchen wall where it will serve as a daily reminder to both you and your children of what you are committing to do for them. Repeating that statement to them whenever you feel it is appropriate will radically reduce the amount of resistance you get from your children. How can they argue with that statement? If they try to, just point out that everyone signed it and it can't be rescinded. After all, it's the *Prime Directive of Parenting*! It's galactically tested and approved!

But also remember, to apply it appropriately you must be in a sun state of mind. Your intentions and your way of being must be responsive, not resistant; restorative, not punitive; compassionate, not selfish. If you are angry when you apply the Prime Directive of Parenting it sends the message that you are more concerned about control and compliance than you are about loving, nurturing, educating, and preparing your children for independence and self-reliance as adults.

Preparing Them for Adulthood: Enter to Learn, Go Forth to Serve

There are several schools, colleges, and universities in the United States that have chosen as their school motto, "Enter to Learn, Go Forth to Serve." If life is the great school, then the home is the most important classroom. It is here that the most significant teaching and learning takes place.

While protecting our children may be a vitally important service we provide to them, teaching them how to live prudently, productively, and piously is the way we most successfully satisfy the two interwoven requirements of the Prime Directive of Parenting. And as every teacher knows, you cannot adequately teach what you haven't first learned yourself, nor model a "yearning for learning" if that same desire is not also burning within you. The greatest teachers in my life have been those who taught sun principles and values along with the imparting of academic information.

With that thought in mind, I began to scan my memory banks for examples of the best teachers in history whose lives most reflected the criteria of having been passionate students as well as dedicated teachers who taught moral principles while also imparting knowledge. They are the instructors who epitomize the motto, "Enter to Learn, Go Forth to Serve." Such a person would be a great example for sun parents everywhere to emulate. I believe I found him.

The Pride of Hampton

He was born a slave on a plantation in Franklin County, Virginia, though he was never certain of the exact year, month, or day. He never knew his father. Opportunities for education in the South were not only non-existent for African slaves prior to their emancipation at the end of the Civil War, but illegal as well. But with freedom came an unquenchable thirst to learn to read and to gain an education, regardless of the sacrifice. He remembered as a child carrying the school books for one of the young mistresses from the plantation and watching longingly as she joined her classmates in the schoolhouse, thinking that "to get into a schoolhouse and study in this way would be about the same as getting into Paradise."

"Booker" was the only name he had ever known growing up, but on his first day in a real school classroom he suddenly realized that not having a second name was not going to satisfy his teacher when the roll was taken. Thinking quickly, he confidently responded to the teacher's request for his full name with "Booker Washington." When he discovered some years later that his mother had given him the second name of Taliaferro at birth, he incorporated it, making his full name Booker Taliaferro Washington or Booker T. Washington as the world would soon come to know him.

Booker T. Washington knew as a young man that education was the key to raising himself and his people out of the hopelessness of slavery and elevating them to a position of equality with others. When he learned about the Hampton Normal and Agricultural Institute in Hampton, Virginia in

1872 and its program to provide moral training and a practical, industrial education to southern blacks, he made up his mind that he would endure whatever sacrifice was necessary to get to Hampton and to get admitted into the school. He would later become its most celebrated graduate.

In 1881 he was asked to begin the Tuskegee Institute in Tuskegee, Alabama in the hope of replicating what had been accomplished at the Hampton Institute. What he had learned from his saintly mother growing up and while a student at the Hampton Institute provided the foundation for everything he did and everything he taught at Tuskegee. He was a sun person if ever there was one.

There is an old saying that reminds parents that "more is *caught*, than *taught*" when it comes to teaching our children. This means that they will learn much more from watching how we live *our* lives, than they will from our lectures telling them how to live *theirs*. Or as legendary UCLA basketball coach John Wooden was fond of saying:

No written word or spoken plea
Can teach our youth what they should be.
Nor all the books on all the shelves.
It's what the teachers are themselves.

I will offer a brief description of some of the beliefs and values that were important elements of Booker T. Washington's way of being, how they were reflected in his life, and why they are so important for parents to teach and emulate today

The dignity of hard work and the importance of self-reliance.

At Tuskegee, the students and faculty were expected to perform manual labor. From foundation to chimney, they built all but a few of the more than twenty buildings that existed on the campus at the time Booker wrote his autobiography in 1901. They built a brick kiln and persevered through several failures until they learned how to produce good quality bricks for their own use and to sell to others in the community. Then they learned the art of brick masonry so they could lay them properly. They provided most of their own food by raising livestock and growing grains, fruits, and vegetables. They even designed and assembled their own mattresses and most of their own furniture. When some parents complained that they only wanted their children to learn from books and shouldn't be required to perform such hard, manual labor, Booker respectfully set them straight on the matter. No student escaped that responsibility, even the ones from more privileged families. And they were all better for it.

Maintaining honesty and integrity, even in the face of great difficulties.

After his first year at the Hampton Institute and with a debt of $16 that he still owed the school, he had no money to return home to West Virginia where he hoped to find higher-paying work during the summer vacation so he could pay off the debt. All he could find in the Hampton area was a job as a waiter at a restaurant that paid little more than the cost of his room and board and didn't allow him to save any money. One day during his last week of working at the restaurant he found a $10 bill under one of the tables. As he later recalled in his autobiography *Up From Slavery*, "I felt it to be the proper thing to show the money to the proprietor. This I did. He coolly explained to me that, as it was his place of business, he had a right to keep the money, and he proceeded to do so." In spite of the many times Booker Washington felt anxiety over the financial challenges he faced during his life and especially during the early years at Tuskegee, he never allowed fear or discouragement to cause him to compromise his principles. As a result, there were miraculous events on multiple occasions that allowed the school to always meet its financial obligations.

Standing up for what is right, even when facing opposition for doing so.

After becoming the nation's most prominent spokesman for the black community, Booker was asked to write an opinion piece for the Christian Union Magazine about the intellectual and moral qualifications of black ministers in the South. It was not very complimentary and provoked a lot of condemnation from black ministers and black newspapers around the country. In time, the various church leaders discovered he was right and subsequently raised their training standards for the ministry. Reflecting on this encounter with criticism from members of his own race, he wrote, "My experience with them, as well as other events in my life, convince me that the thing to do when one feels sure that he has done the right thing and is condemned, is to stand still and keep quiet. If he is right, time will show it."

With freedom comes great responsibility.

Booker wrote about the memorable day soon after the Civil War had ended when all the slaves on the plantation were called together to the "big house" and the Emancipation Proclamation was read to them by a stranger from the North. They were told that they were now free and could go when and where they pleased. Booker then described the scene:

> For some minutes, there was great rejoicing and thanksgiving and wild scenes of ecstasy… The wild rejoicing on the part of the emancipated colored people lasted but for a brief period, for I noticed that by the time they returned to their cabins there was a great change in their feelings. The great responsibility of being free, of having charge of themselves, of having to think and plan for themselves and their children, seemed to take possession of them.

The care and appropriate use of our bodies.

As a slave, a bath consisted of an occasional swim in the nearby river. While a student at the Hampton Institute Booker learned of the value of regular bathing with soap and water. "I learned there for the first time some of its value," he wrote, "not only in keeping the body healthy, but in inspiring self-respect and promoting virtue." Booker had never even seen a toothbrush let alone owned one prior to going to Hampton. But "the gospel of the toothbrush" as General Samuel C. Armstrong at Hampton had called it, was considered by Booker to be "a part of our creed at Tuskegee" and an essential tool all students at Tuskegee were required to own and use as part of their daily healthcare routine.

He took offense at the suggestion made by some Southern whites that black women had a reputation for being promiscuous. (Given that black female slaves were often not allowed to decide if, when, and with whom they had sex, I am not surprised that it took a while for them to feel they had regained control over that aspect of their lives.) And although he never mentioned anything in his autobiography about any problematic sexual behaviors among the students at Tuskegee, I am certain that the Bible study classes at Tuskegee addressed the proper use of their bodies' procreative powers.

While the people in Booker's day struggled primarily with the abuse of alcohol, today's families are facing an ever-increasing list of legal and illegal mind-altering alternatives. Not only do we have numerous pharmaceutical options to choose from, but our society has begun removing the prohibitions on the recreational use of marijuana and potentially, may someday do the same for other street drugs. Booker had no use for any substance that clouded his thinking or separated him from the real world, as difficult and demanding as it can be at times.

It was Aldous Huxley in his 1932 novel *Brave New World* who warned all future generations of the dangers of dependence on drugs to solve our problems. While Karl Marx considered religion to be the opiate of the masses, in Huxley's futuristic world, the universal happiness drug *soma* had become the religion of the people. Similarly, in today's world there are many who seek for courage from a bottle of alcohol, consolation from a syringe of heroin, insight and expansion of understanding from a tab of LSD, and relief from anxiety and stress from a bowl of marijuana. Instead, Booker made it a daily practice to avail himself of spiritual resources. This helped him to find greater purpose in his life and courageously face the many challenges that confronted him throughout his life. He never felt the need to escape them.

Another current trend in society is the popularity of tattoos and body piercings. Some see their use as decorating the body while others see their use as defacing it. Booker considered the human body to be a sacred gift that should be respected and cared for. He understood the importance of teaching his students about the need for self-discipline in the use and care of their bodies as well as in all other areas of their lives. In this age of "body hacking" I can't think of a time in human history when it has been more important for parents to teach their children the same values.

Being true to oneself and resisting the temptation of trying to impress others by appearing to be something we are not.

When Booker was a young student at his first real school, he was confronted with two difficulties. One was the problem of his name, as I mentioned earlier. Being a slave also meant having no real family history; no lauded name that would be a herald of his future success; no heritage that would provide him with advantages that others might not receive. He would have no unearned status that he could depend on "to do for me what I should do for myself." Instead, Booker resolved, "because I had no ancestry myself, I would leave a record of which my children would be proud, and which might encourage them in still higher effort."

The second difficulty was poverty. With poverty often comes the moon desire to impress others, which can cause worldly things to get in the way of more important things. As a child, it was the desire for a store-bought cap like the ones worn by the other boys at his first school that presented a problem for him and his mother. She explained to him that she didn't have the money for a "store hat" and instead, made him one out of two pieces of "homespun" (denim) fabric. Booker later wrote:

> *The lesson that my mother taught me in this has always remained with me, and I have tried as best I could to teach it to others. I have always felt proud, whenever I think of the incident, that my mother had strength of character enough not to be led into the temptation of seeming to be that which she was not—of trying to impress my schoolmates and others with the fact that she was able to buy me a 'store hat' when she was not.*

As author Malcolm Gladwell explains in his book *David and Goliath*, it is easier for poor parents to say "no, I can't" when denying a request from a child for something that is a want rather than a need in life. It is much harder for middle and upper-income parents to do what is best for their children by saying "no, I won't" when confronted with the same request. Teaching children the value of money, the wisdom of thrift, and the importance of delaying gratification is missing in many homes these days and children are struggling because of it. Sun parents are willing to say "no" when appropriate because they understand it will help their children in the development of sun qualities.

David Brooks wrote about the qualities of character that make people like Booker Washington and his mother unique. Citing the philosophy of Rabbi Joseph Soloveitchik and the rabbi's book *Lonely Man of Faith*, Brooks wrote that to achieve success you build on your strengths, but to build character, you must transcend your weaknesses.

The lives of Booker and his mother reflect that deep desire to be the best human beings they could be. That process involved exactness in personal honesty, a constant assessment of their strengths and weaknesses, and a firm resolve to overcome those weaknesses and recover from whatever failures they produced.

Being examples of honesty, sacrifice, service, faith, and love is the endowment that sun parents pass on to their children. Booker never forgot the lessons his mother had taught him. As a result, his life became a living diorama of their influence on him and subsequently impacted the lives of all those who had the good fortune of having their lives intersect with his.

Avoiding debt and being content to live within our means.

Booker was also grateful to his mother for teaching him a second lesson from the store hat incident. "I have always felt proud," he wrote, "that she refused to go into debt for that which she did not have the money to pay for." Sage advice in today's world of "credit gone wild." When he did borrow money to begin the Tuskegee Institute and to make needed improvements, he worked tirelessly to be sure the debts were paid on time.

Thrift, trustworthiness, reliability, and humility were all hallmarks of the life of Booker T. Washington.

The importance of patience, duty, and enduring to the end.

My parents were part of *The Greatest Generation* that Tom Brokaw wrote about, who endured The Great Depression and World War II. From those experiences they learned the need for patience, dedication to duty, and long-suffering in the face of challenges and opposition. Booker Washington not only faced challenges and opposition in his life, but injustice and prejudice as well. It was his willingness to endure those challenges that made him such a dedicated sun person.

Although a proponent of equal rights and fair treatment for all people, regardless of race, Booker emphasized how important it was for black people to become sufficiently educated and trained in a useful skill that they could use to go out into the world and provide for themselves and their families and become valued members of their communities. He felt that doing so would do much more for the cause of civil rights for blacks than rancorous political debates and court battles. He wrote:

> *It is important and right that all privileges of the law be ours, but it is vastly more important that we be prepared for the exercise of these privileges. The opportunity to earn a dollar in a factory is worth infinitely more than the opportunity to spend a dollar in an opera-house.*

I do not mention this to spark a political debate about civil rights, but to remind parents that we need to prepare our children for the economic and social challenges that lie ahead for them. In the long run, it will be much more helpful to teach them the importance of hard work, dedication to duty, and patience in the face of opposition, than to feed an attitude of entitlement.

How to forgive.

According to Booker Washington, the plantation where he grew up was not unlike many of the other plantations in the South. In describing the reactions of his people to their former masters and owners after the Civil War ended, he wrote:

> *As a rule, not only did the members of my race entertain no feelings of bitterness against the whites before and during the war, but there were many instances of Negroes tenderly caring for their former masters and mistresses who for some reason had become poor and dependent since the war. I know of instances*

where the former masters of slaves have for years been supplied with money by former slaves to keep them from suffering.

Booker also wrote:

In my early life I used to cherish a feeling of ill toward anyone who spoke in bitter terms against the Negro, or who advocated measures that were intended to oppress the black man or take from him opportunities for growth in the most complete manner. Now, whenever I hear anyone advocating measures that are meant to curtail the development of another, I pity the person who would do this. I know that the one who makes this mistake does so because of his own lack of opportunity for the highest level of growth.

It was John D. Long, the Secretary of the Navy during the presidency of William McKinley, who said in tribute to Booker Washington, "God bless the orator, philanthropist, and disciple of the Great Master who, if He were on the earth would be doing the same work."

The greatest happiness and success come from serving others.
Reflecting on his learning experiences at the Hampton Institute, Booker wrote:

The education I received at Hampton out of the textbooks was but a small part of what I learned there. One of the things that impressed itself upon me deeply, the second year, was the unselfishness of the teachers. It was hard for me to understand how any individuals could bring themselves to the point where they could be so happy in working for others. Before the end of the year, I think I began learning that those who are the happiest are those who do the most for others. This lesson I have tried to carry with me ever since.

Similarly, he wrote:

In order to be successful in any kind of undertaking, I think the main thing is for one to grow to the point where he completely forgets himself; that is, to lose himself in a great cause. In proportion as one loses himself in this way, in the same degree does he get the highest happiness out of his work.

And finally, he wrote:

When one takes a broad survey of the country, he will find that the most useful and influential people in it are those who take the deepest interest in the institutions that exist for the purpose of making the world a better place.

The nobility of sacrifice for the benefit of others.

Booker Washington repeatedly demonstrated his willingness to sacrifice his comfort for the benefit of his students and they likewise followed his example on many occasions when fellow students were in need. There were many others on the staff at Tuskegee who shared in that commitment. Among them was Miss Olivia A. Davidson. She came to Tuskegee to teach just six weeks after the school opened and was a model of unselfishness and sacrifice. She would later become Booker's wife.

Olivia put together fund-raising festivals to help raise money to purchase an abandoned one-hundred-acre plantation near the town where construction of the permanent campus of the Tuskegee Institute began. Even the poor wanted to help. On one occasion Booker wrote:

I recall one old colored woman who was about seventy years of age, who came to see me when we were raising money to pay for the farm. She hobbled into the room where I was, leaning on a cane. She was clad in rags; but they were clean. She said: 'Mr. Washin'ton, God knows I spent de bes' days of my life in slavery. God knows I's ignorant and poor; but,' she added. 'I knows what you an' Miss Davidson is tryin' to do. I know you is tryin' to make better men an' better women for de colored race. I ain't got no money, but I wants you to take dese six eggs, what I's been savin' up, an' I wants you to put dese six eggs into the eddication of dese boys an' gals.' Since the work at Tuskegee started, it has been my privilege to receive many gifts for the benefit of the institution, but never any, I think, that touched me so deeply as this one.

This was truly an example of the "widow's mite" and I'm sure Booker shared that story with all the students at Tuskegee for many years afterward so they would always remember and be grateful for the many others who had sacrificed so much to give them a chance for an education and a better life.

Another example of noble sacrifice comes from the life of my wife's grandmother, Matia Burk. Her only daughter, Helen Stott, remembered one Christmas when she was a child during the early years of the Great Depression and wrote a newspaper article about it years later:

That particular Christmas was to be, according to my doting parents, a slim one as far as I was concerned. For as they explained to me, there were so many little "poor children" for Santa to care for there might not be much left for those of us who were more fortunate. Certainly, I never considered myself one of the poor kids because our little family had a nice home in the half of the one-room school house or teacherage where my Mama taught the first grade through the second year of high school. I couldn't be poor! We had our own garden, chickens, two ducks, a goose, a cow and a calf! Then there were my two cats, Tiger and Fluffy, along with a pet civet-cat (a cousin to a skunk) that Daddy had de-fumed, a little billy goat which Daddy got as payment for repairing a neighbor's car, and a wild squirrel that lived under the teacherage. Of course, no one but Daddy could get very near to it, but it would climb all over his neck and arms and eat from his hand. My quarter-Cherokee Daddy had a way with animals and wild plants alike.

My parents adored me and each other. They would break out singing at the drop of a hat and mother would put on three shows a year with her school children which the whole area would attend and enjoy. There was always a kettle of soup or chili beans on the big pot-bellied stove in the school room during the cold months for those 'poor kids' who came to school with little or no lunch. No...I was not poor!

Christmas morning came at last and I was still hopeful that Old St. Nick would have some small gift for me. Most of all I wanted a little sister or brother, but Momma had explained that the doctors couldn't fix it so she could have any more babies. She explained that as soon as we could find a child who needed a new home and family, we would adopt him. It was seven more years before that dream came true when my two brothers aged eight and ten came to live with us.

I woke up first, of course, and as I'd promised, I called to Daddy to get up and build a fire so Mama and I could get up too. "Daddy, is there anything in my stocking?" I called. "It looks awful fat for an empty one," he laughingly called back. When I heard Mama's voice calling me, I scrambled from my bed and headed for the door when the cold floor reminded me to grab my shoes. As I raced into the living room and ran to where I had hung my stocking by the fireplace, I was so excited I dropped my shoes and lost any care about the cold floor. After pulling a huge orange and a shiny red apple from the stocking, I reached in and felt something warm and soft. I pulled out my beloved Mary Elizabeth doll who was suddenly more beautiful than ever before. Santa had given her pretty new lips, brighter eyes, pinker cheeks and real hair instead of the painted–on kind she had before. She had on a pretty party dress and a coat with a white fur collar and matching fur muff that was exactly like my Mama's coat! Tears filled my eyes as I hugged my precious friend and gave her a big kiss on her newly painted lips.

As we began opening the other presents under the tree, Daddy took a large gift and, with a twinkling eye, laid it in front of me. With a pounding heart I tore away the paper to find a warm, soft green tweed coat with a fur collar and a fur muff pinned to the sleeve. I had never seen a more beautiful coat in my life and it just fit! How could Santa know?! As I petted the fur and danced around the room in celebration I squealed, "Mama, it's the exact same color as your coat! We can wear them together! Won't that be fun?!" I saw tears in Mama's eyes as she smiled a big smile and hugged me to her. "I'm so glad you like it," she said. After breakfast Daddy asked if we'd like to go for a ride to visit friends, and of course, I couldn't wait to wear my new coat. As we started to leave, I reminded Mama to wear her coat to match mine, but she said she'd prefer to wear her sweater. All that winter Mama was unusually warm and so we never got to wear our look-a-like coats together. As I prepared for bed that night I knelt down and thanked my Heavenly Father for a memorable Christmas and for my great Daddy and Mama who were so good to me. I prayed that Santa had been as good to all the little "poor children" as he had been to me. Drifting off to sleep I seemed to hear a voice somewhere far away whisper, "Christmas is love; a very special kind of love." I slept.

Life provides ample opportunities for sun parents–regardless of their families' circumstances–to perform some small act of sacrifice for the benefit of others, whether inside or outside of the home. For sun parents, family life is a beautifully orchestrated–though occasionally cacophonous–symphony of service, sacrifice, and love.

The importance of associating with good people.
Booker wrote:

The older I grow, the more I am convinced that there is no education which one can get from books and costly apparatus that is equal to that which can be gotten from contact with great men and women. Instead of studying books so constantly, how I wish that our schools and colleges might learn to study men and things.

Booker Washington read every book he could find on the life of Abraham Lincoln and learned much from the words and example set by this great American President. The founder of the Hampton Institute, General Samuel C. Armstrong, was another of the great men who influenced Booker. He described Armstrong as "the noblest, rarest human being that it has ever been my privilege to meet," who became a close friend and mentor to Booker throughout his life. Sun parents will do all they can to introduce their children to the great men and women of history through books as well as through personal contact with the "better angels" among us.

No fear.

Booker wrote about his fundraising efforts on behalf of the Tuskegee Institute and that it was always his rule to do his duty to the best of his ability and then not to worry about the results. Not worrying can be the hard part, but he concluded:

> *Worrying simply consumes, and to no purpose, just so much physical and mental strength that might otherwise be given to effective work. I have observed that those who have accomplished the greatest results are those who 'keep under the body;' are those who never grow excited or lose self-control, but are always calm, self-possessed, patient and polite."*

The importance of delegating responsibility to others and then trusting them with it.

Booker wrote:

> *Few things help an individual more than to place responsibility upon him, and to let him know that you trust him. When I have*

*read of labor troubles between employers and employees, I have
often thought that many strikes and similar disturbances might
be avoided if the employers would cultivate the habit of getting
nearer to their employees, of consulting and advising with them,
and letting them feel that the interests of the two are the same.
Every individual responds to confidence.*

The same is certainly true of children as well.

"Give them an idea for every word."

When Booker T. Washington began his public speaking career, he sought advice from his life-long mentor and friend, General Armstrong. The advice the General offered was simple, yet profoundly important. He told Booker, "Give them an idea for every word." Sun parents recognize that every interaction they have with their children is a teaching opportunity. As I referred to earlier, something will be *caught* or *taught* in every one of those interactions. For anyone who attended a speech given by Booker T. Washington, they always came away with several ideas that would help them become better people–if they were truly listening and willing to apply them.

The importance of a balanced education that included academic subjects and moral training.

At Tuskegee, the spiritual side of life was never overlooked in favor of the secular side. When Booker lectured his students on the art of right living, the wisdom he imparted did not come from textbooks, but straight out of his life. Then he would send them out into the world to seek more. He wrote that "education is not a thing apart from life; not a system, nor a philosophy. It is direct teaching of how to live and how to work."

To Booker, character and integrity were the foundations upon which all other successes were built. One of his admirers wrote of the Tuskegee Institute that the institution "not only made a carpenter of a man; it made a man of a carpenter."

The Maker of Men

A more recent example of these qualities comes from the life of my wife's childhood "bff" from Chico, California where she grew up.

Her name is Conee and she has faced more challenges and opposition in her life than I could ever have endured as graciously as she has, and she has deserved none of them.

In her first year of elementary school her class was given an IQ test and Conee scored 124. IQ scores are expected to increase as children age, so it is safe to say that Conee had above-average intelligence. For some misguided reason, her teacher told only her parents about her giftedness and told them to discourage it. They were told that if they made it known to their daughter that she was smart, she would get lazy and not work as hard at school. So, throughout Conee's childhood and into adulthood she was told repeatedly by her parents that she was not very smart and was expected to fail.

Her siblings soon joined them in this chorus of criticism. Her parents even discouraged her from going to college because they were convinced she would fail and explained that they were just trying to save her from the heartbreak of failure. She was told that she had been "lucky so far" in school, but that she couldn't expect that luck to continue. Apparently, her parents had begun to believe their own lies and were on the verge of creating a self-defeating prophecy for their daughter.

But she did go to college. It was at that time that she discovered the results of the IQ test while reviewing her high school records and realized how her teacher and her family had betrayed her. Yet, despite ongoing parental discouragement, an emotionally abusive husband, serious health problems of her own, and more severe medical and mental health problems with her only daughter (who eventually died from those difficulties), she persisted.

While working on a master's degree in International Relations with an emphasis in Middle Eastern Relations, she taught at the local community college and was repeatedly recognized by her students as one of the best teachers in the department. She even had students who had not been able to enroll in the course but who would attend her class and hand in the assignments, knowing they would not receive credit for the course.

Conee also worked for the California State University in Chico where she was doing her graduate studies, assisting international students to navigate through the confusion and complexity of college life in America. She was particularly appreciated by the many Arab and Palestinian students whom she mentored and helped to succeed in school. Since she specialized in Arab culture, she would go through their coursework with them and help them to understand the idioms and euphemisms of the American version of the English language and other cultural differences so they could successfully complete their class assignments. But of equal importance for both her and her students was the fact that she understood their religious beliefs and encouraged them to be true to their values and not be negatively influenced by much of what they were being exposed to on the college campus.

When I interviewed her for this book, I asked her how she would describe her role with the many students she has mentored over the last thirty-plus years. She meekly replied, "I was being a mom."

She earned far more than the minimum number of credits necessary for the master's degree, but because of increasing health problems, Conee was never able to complete her thesis so she never received the degree, nor the teaching position she had been promised upon completion of her degree. She has lived as a single mom on the edge of poverty for many years, but she has always maintained a positive attitude and still feels she has been blessed in her life.

She continues to mentor Arab students on an independent basis since she was not able to continue working for the University. Recently, a young male Palestinian student came to her with a problem that he said he needed help with. After hearing his description of the situation, Conee said, "You don't need my help with this. Why did you come to see me?" The young man sheepishly replied, "Because, I knew I had to meet the woman that all of my friends call 'The Maker of Men.'"

> *"I knew I had to meet the woman that all of my friends call 'The Maker of Men.'"*

Conee is a sun parent; a maker of sun children, most of whom are not her own. But to sun parents, everyone's child is their child. After all these years and all her struggles to prove herself to her detractors, on December 29, 2013 she was told by one of her younger son's best friends–who is himself a very intelligent man–"You are the smartest person I know." At that moment, for the first time in her then sixty-one years of living, she suddenly realized that she believed him.

Read the Book

I could easily go on for many more pages describing Booker T. Washington, his exemplary life, and how the qualities he possessed apply directly to our roles as parents. But I would prefer that you read the book yourself. *Up From Slavery* is only one hundred and twenty-three pages, but it will be some of the best reading you and your children will ever do. And to high school and college English literature teachers everywhere, may I recommend that your students study it as well. They will gain infinitely more from reading about the adolescent challenges of Booker T. Washington, than they will from reading about the adolescent challenges of Holden Caulfield, the confused and cynical main character in *Catcher in the Rye.*

The key to becoming sun parents is to first become sun individuals and then sun spouses. (It has been said that the best thing a father can do for his children is to love their mother.) There are millions of sun parents who for thousands of years may never have read a book on the subject, but who have followed the examples of their own sun parents and other sun parents in their communities. For those who are committed to becoming sun parents, there must be a deeply-rooted commitment to the betterment of others and a desire to gain ever increasing levels of light and truth in their lives, so they can pass them on to their posterity.

Sun parents play an active role in the education of their children both in the home and in the schools. This critically important parental role as educator is becoming increasingly important given the confusion of ideas and the conflict of values that are occurring in the nation's schools today. It was film producer Michael Flaherty who commented during an interview about his film *The Giver,* "We need to take seriously the responsibility we have as parents and teachers of being architects of souls and of instilling hope into the lives of children." Only sun architects can do that. If moral values are not included in the education process, parents and teachers may unwittingly do their students more harm than good. Or as C.S Lewis warned, "Education without values, as useful as it is, seems rather to make man a more clever devil."

Are You the People Who Give Out Hugs?

I knew a man who exemplifies the qualities of a sun educator and who effectively prepared youth for the challenges of adulthood. Vincent Keele was a school psychologist for many years in Northern Nevada and worked closely with struggling children and their families. He regularly counseled parents on ways to not only help their children survive childhood and adolescence, but also become healthier and happier adults at the same time.

He had developed a simple formula that any parent could apply and that he felt would help any child to do better in life. He asked parents to spend fifteen to thirty minutes, individually, with each of their children, several times a month, in undisturbed, one-on-one interactions outside of the home. He promised that the experience would transform both of their lives.

The parents were to be the ones who invited and initiated the activity and they were to select a time when they and their child would not be disturbed. They were to *fully* engage with their child during their time together. No distractions. No interruptions. The message the parents should be sending to each child is that "I need to be with you and I don't want anyone else around who might destroy this special time together." If the child was ever made to feel that he or she was just a tag-along on an activity that was not intended just for them, the formula would not work.

For many years during his career and after retiring from his job, Vincent would regularly hear from grateful parents who thanked him profusely for this simple formula that had changed their lives and the lives of their children.

A few years after retiring, he and his equally inspiring wife spent eighteen months in one of the most dangerous neighborhoods in Detroit, Michigan on a voluntary service mission for their church, gathering information about the needs of these inner-city families and what could be done to help them. Applying the same concepts he had taught to the parents of struggling students, the couple reached out to anyone in the community who would accept their friendship. Word got around about this remarkable couple in their late sixties who fearlessly offered love to their affection-starved neighbors. They would often be awakened from sleep at eleven or twelve o'clock at night by a knock on their apartment door. Against all sane advice from their neighbors, they would open their front door and be greeted by a stranger standing in the doorway.

"Are you the people who give out hugs?" a towering, mountain-of-a-man once gently asked.

"Yes" the diminutive grandmother said. "We are. Would you like a hug?"

"Yes ma'am...please." And this tiny grandmother would wrap her little arms around those men-children looking for a brief but unforgettable moment of unconditional love and affection. Sun parents carry that light with them and will invite those solar moments with others wherever they go.

Sun parents are aware of how important it is that they teach sun principles and model a clear and consistent example of sun living for their children to follow. We live in a world where a life based on sun values is routinely dismissed as archaic and children are constantly bombarded with invitations to choose less enlightened alternatives. But sun parents understand all too well what educator Neal Maxwell explained when he wrote, "Small equivocations in parents, can produce large deviations in their children."

Sun parents understand that when they decide to marry and create a family, they are committing to the creation of an environment where their children can "Enter to Learn" and "Go Forth to Serve." This is a motto that embodies the spirit of the Prime Directive of Parenting and will help direct the choices sun parents make throughout their lives.

And the Winner Is...

Once upon a time in a kingdom far away, there was a talent competition to determine the best singer in the land–the one who clearly displayed all the essential talents and skills that the great vocalists of the past possessed. The field of contestants included a wide array of singers, each confident that they deserved a place in the competition. There were country singers and pop singers, folk singers and jazz singers, classical singers and rock singers, even some rappers showed up. (Although the judges acknowledged rap as a form of musical expression and those contestants aggressively lobbied for inclusion, the judges decided it was not really singing.)

Each possessed certain abilities that made them eligible to compete in the contest and each of them also displayed certain flaws–except one. To the vocally experienced judges as well as to most people in the audience, it quickly became apparent that one contestant was superior to all the others. She clearly demonstrated all the skills, talents, and unique qualities that the great singers possessed.

While the country singers were good at their favorite style of music, they faltered when asked to sing other styles. Not her. Her voice was so adaptable and her understanding of different styles so broad that she could sing virtually anything with skill and authenticity. The rock singers could belt out selections from the *Led Zeppelin* and *Van Halen* song books with expertise, but they struggled with sensitive ballads and found it extremely hard to blend in and harmonize with others. Not her. She could keep up with Ann Wilson of *Heart* note for note and yet she could also whisper a lyric so gently and softly that Barbara Streisand and Celine Dion would be impressed. When singing with others she neither under-sang nor over-sang. She had years of backup singing experience under her belt and she was an expert at blending with the voices around her.

The pop singers were perky and cute, but many lacked the mature vocal skills of a seasoned veteran. Under the pressure of the competition, their voices faltered, and they were eliminated. Not her. She displayed the confidence of a seasoned craftsman who performed well under pressure.

The jazz singers were skilled and confident, but they improvised the songs so much that the melodies seemed lost in a flurry of vocal gymnastics. Not her. She interpreted each song in a unique way that made it her own without losing the real message of the music.

The classical singers and the folk singers seemed distant. Something seemed to be missing in their ability to connect with the audience, so the audience felt little attachment to them. Not her. There was joy on her face and a light in her countenance as she performed. She possessed a humble attitude that endeared her to the audience. She was more than just a singer; she was an artist.

When the TV audience cast their votes I'm sure there were those at home who voted for the contestant who sang their favorite style of music. But for the clear majority watching the show and for the judges who were able to recognize the strengths and weaknesses of each contestant, there was no doubt who merited the title.

Was winning the contest a guarantee of a successful career? No. If she chose to, the winner could stop developing her talents; she could abuse drugs or alcohol and let the addiction control her life; she could develop an entitled attitude and walk around like a petulant prima donna who felt she deserved success without any effort; or she could develop stage fright and become a recluse, singing only for her pet cats. If she chose to, she could fail to use all the natural abilities and advantages she had over her fellow contestants and sabotage her opportunities for success. Or, she could be grateful for those advantages, and wisely utilize them to the best of her ability.

This isn't about a singing contest. This is an allegory. I would also ask you to ponder this opening line from the Leo Tolstoy novel *Anna Karenina:* "All happy families are alike; every unhappy family is unhappy in its own way." Please keep both in mind as we examine a vitally important, and a very sensitive subject.

The Challenges for Children in Today's Families

At last count there are eight designs of human families: the blended family, the single parent family, the adoptive family, the polyamorous family, the same-sex family, the surrogate family, the cohabitating family, and the natural family. For decades, organizations like the American Academy of Pediatrics, The National Institute of Child Health and Human Development, The Institute for Social and Economic Research that conducted the British Household Panel Survey, and scores of scholars from universities and governmental organizations around the world have been studying the pros and cons of the various family designs. Of the eight, one design has been proven repeatedly to be clearly superior to all others in reducing risks, providing greater benefits, and producing more positive outcomes for children and parents alike. Let me explain why.

Blended Families

The first design we will consider is the blended or "step" family. This is created when someone with a child (or children) marries someone who is not the birth parent of that child. This could be the result of a divorce, the death of a birth parent, or an out-of-wedlock birth. The potential challenges stepfamilies face are many:

- A stepparent was not there to welcome that new life into the world and to feel the overwhelming sense of responsibility and commitment that comes with that experience.
- They most likely did not share in all of those growing-up experiences with that child and have not had the opportunities to form the same level of emotional bonding that those experiences produce. That would include things like sitting up at night with that child when they were sick, helping them to navigate through the trials of sibling rivalry, counseling them on how to make more friends at school, consoling them when they experience rejection, or savoring the memories of the "best family vacation ever."
- They do not share the same blood; meaning similar genetically-determined physical features, personality type, habits, interests, talents, appetites, or any of the long list of other inherited "mini-me" traits that we pass on to our progeny.
- The child has been raised previously under different parental expectations and rules.
- The stepparent must share the child's time and/or loyalty with a divorced or deceased birth parent and with an additional set of grandparents.
- The stepparent may find themselves competing with the stepchildren for their spouse's loyalty and attention. That is especially common when both spouses bring children into the marriage and the stepsiblings do not get along. Research indicates that second

marriages tend to fail at a higher rate than first marriages, and this kind of stepfamily rivalry is often the cause.

All of these challenges have resulted in a growing body of research that indicate that the children of divorced parents–even when those parents remarry each other–do poorer in a wide range of areas than those raised by their biological parents in a loving, low-conflict marriage.

Does that mean that stepfamilies are doomed to failure? Not at all. But is *does* mean that a successful blended family is often more difficult to achieve. A lesson from sewing applies here: patching up a broken family reminds us that a patch is never as strong as the original material. Blended families are intrinsically more vulnerable to another tear in the family fabric. It is clearly not the preferred option if your intention is to select the design with the greatest potential for success.

However, when sun parents are involved, even a more vulnerable family design can sometimes be turned into a sun system. Let me describe one example with which I am personally familiar.

Her husband died from cancer. His wife died in a car accident. They were introduced by mutual friends and felt very quickly that they belonged together. They were both committed to sun principles and had lived them previously in their lives both as spouses and as parents. They both had adult children from their previous marriages and both were committed to parent each other's children as if they were their own. With that intention, they chose not to create shrines in their home dedicated to their children's deceased parent as some others do, but instead decided that they were creating a new and considerably larger family by blending the two. Each parent was constantly looking for opportunities to develop relationships with the other spouse's children without creating any sense that they were competing with the deceased parent for the children's love and loyalty. They were determined to build on the foundation that both sets of parents had established over the years in raising their children and to make any improvements that they could.

They decided on a weekend father-stepson outing at a mountain cabin in the woods a couple of hours from their home. All of the wife's adult sons and their families were invited. Her oldest son and his young family were late arriving at the cabin. They were tired and not in the best of moods. After corralling the kids into one room of the cabin and trying to get them settled into bed, the frustrated young father resorted to a method of discipline that he had received as a child from his deceased father, who had received the same from his father. The newlywed grandparents were saddened as they heard three sharp "snaps" coming from the room next to theirs and immediately recognized the sound of a belt striking a child's behind.

The next day they discussed how they could approach the son and who should be the one to offer counsel on his discipline methods. As the last day of the weekend arrived and the son began the drive home with his family, his minivan developed mechanical problems and broke down not far from the cabin. Stepdad was called upon to tow the car back to the cabin and he spent the rest of the day helping with repairs. Throughout the day he pondered about how to approach his stepson with his concerns. After several trips to the auto parts store, the problem was diagnosed and a new fan belt and alternator were purchased and installed. The grateful stepson turned to his new stepfather and asked, "What do I owe you for the fan belt?"

The opportunity this concerned stepfather had hoped for had just been gift-wrapped and presented to him and he knew exactly what to say. "I'll trade you the fan belt for the belt you used the other night," he said. The new stepson was taken aback at first by his stepfather's boldness, but he understood the message clearly and that it came from a place of love and concern. "And how about the alternator?" he asked. His stepfather replied, "I'll trade you the alternator for an alternate way to discipline your kids." The perfect answers to demonstrate and teach sun parenting without reproach. That day a bond was formed between that stepfather and stepson; a son who understood that although his birth father would no longer be there to offer him counsel, he now had a second father who would be, and who was equally committed to his welfare and happiness.

Single Parent Families

Being raised by a single parent means a child is more likely to grow up in poverty. That's especially true for those raised by single parent moms. The child will likely grow up without a stable relationship with both parents, is more likely to have problems with school, use drugs, develop psychological and behavioral problem, become sexually active at a young age, become an adolescent parent, and get into trouble with the law. Current statistics indicate that as high as seventy percent of births in inner-city and low-income neighborhoods and forty percent nationally, are to single mothers.

Even with the additional involvement of grandfathers or uncles, having a "drop-in" dad is insufficient for children. Overall, children generally do not do as well in single parent families, but this is especially true for adolescent boys raised without fathers. The additional burden on the single parent to try to fill both parental roles is often overwhelming. And while there are some laudable sun single-parent exceptions, for most children raised in single parent households the outcomes for parents and children alike are alarming. They are similar to the problems faced by blended families, but usually worse.

Becoming a single parent is a decision that most divorcing couples would rather not have to make. But when there are seriously destructive behaviors occurring in the marriage, there may not be another choice. Yet, why do so many unmarried women and girls intentionally choose single parenthood when they don't have to? Having a child out of wedlock so a girl can meet her human need to love and be loved denies the needs of the child to be loved and cared for by both parents. But for far too many people, it has become so familiar in their communities that they don't see the multiple disadvantages anymore.

Adoptive Families

In the past, adoption was a necessity to provide for children whose parents had died, who were incapacitated and unable to care for them, who were suffering abject poverty and couldn't provide for them, or who conceived them out-of-wedlock and gave them up to avoid ostracism. Currently, it has also become a solution to two opposite but related problems:

1. A *surplus* of unattached children resulting from out-of-wedlock pregnancies, poverty, disease, child abuse, addictions, or war and political upheaval; and

2. A *deficit* of children who are dearly wanted by couples who, because of fertility problems, are unable to produce their own.

While some would see adoption as a win-win for both the children and the couples who desire to be parents, it also comes with its share of challenges. One of the primary challenges for any child raised by anyone other than their biological parents is what some refer to as "genealogical bewilderment."

Genealogical bewilderment is exactly what the name suggests—a sense of confusion and emotional disconnection caused by removing a child from the companionship and care of their natural parents. It affects their sense of identity and their ability to form attachment bonds with others. It can lead to problems with emotional and social development in the form of increased levels of aggression, rebellion, depression, anxiety, substance abuse, sexual acting out, suicide attempts, and other behavioral and psychological problems.

And the problems don't just occur with the children. Many birth parents who relinquished children earlier in their lives reported that doing so impacted their parenting practices with subsequent children. They reported being overprotective, compulsively worrying about the children in their homes, and of having difficulty accepting their growing children's autonomy and independence. They also reported that relinquishing a child to adoption as teens had a negative impact on their later marital relationships.

During the last century there have been several examples of well-intentioned groups and governments that thought they were doing children a favor by removing them from their single-parent adolescent mothers or from poverty-stricken and under-educated aboriginal families and placing them for adoption in what they considered to be a healthier family environment. The negative outcomes for many of those children were just as I described above.

Then there are the biological concerns. In most cases of adoption the child shares no DNA connection with either adoptive parent. Because of that there is no way to determine exactly what traits the child may have inherited. Sometimes they may be carrying a genetic "time-bomb" of physical or psychological vulnerabilities that suddenly goes off around the time the child hits puberty. I have worked with several adoptive families and met scores more at the annual conference of the Association for Training on Trauma and Attachment in Children (ATTACh) who have dealt with serious emotional and behavioral problems in their adoptive children that seemed to surface suddenly and unexpectedly.

The child may have lived in an abusive or dysfunctional environment prior to adoption that left psychological scarring. Even if the child is placed with the adoptive parents at birth, what they may have inherited genetically or been exposed to in the womb can also impact the child in the future, regardless of how much sun parenting they have received after adoption.

Also, there's the missing oxytocin experience that occurs when a woman gives birth that helps bind a mother and child together emotionally. That is not to say that an adoptive parent cannot bond with an adoptive child. I have spoken to several women who described their experience when they saw their adoptive child for the first time and felt, in every way, that this child was meant to be theirs, even if they hadn't given birth to them. But complete and exclusive participation in the birth process is just another advantage that birth parents get to experience that adoptive parents do not.

As many adopted children grow up, they often experience the desire to seek out and establish a relationship with their birth parents. That can be a good thing or a bad thing. It may result in the child dividing their attachment and loyalty between the two sets of parents and can create emotional distress for the child and both sets of parents.

For adopted children, expectations can be unrealistically high when meeting birth parents. Their imaginations may fill in the historical blank spots with idealized images. If the child discovers that the birth parents are great people, they will wonder why they were placed for adoption in the first place. They may see themselves as damaged goods. If they discover that their birth parents are not particularly pleasant folk but are instead uncouth, uncaring, or addicted individuals who do not want any involvement in their birth children's lives, the children may wonder if they have inherited the same nasty genes. Rejection is a hard thing for a child, even if it comes from someone they've never met.

I have seen the occasional adoption situation that involves sun people on both sides of this equation–the birth parents and the adoptive parents. I have some close friends whose seventeen-year-old daughter got pregnant out of wedlock and she decided to place her child for adoption with a wonderful couple in another state. As I mentioned, among the challenges for a birth mother who places a child for adoption is that she may find herself worrying excessively about her child's welfare or feeling great guilt for relinquishing custody of the child.

A year later the adoptive couple moved into the same state where my friends live. Actually, into the same community and only a few miles away from their home. The adoptive couple welcomed the birth mother's involvement in their child's life as well as her parents'. They have an open adoption where everyone involved understands the situation, is committed to living by sun principles, and supports each other in raising this child.

But knowing too much about what is going on in an adoptive child's life can be as difficult as knowing too little. The birth mother struggled at first to respect the boundaries that needed to be in place so she wouldn't be intruding into the adoptive parents' family. She has been able to do that successfully and the adoptive parents have been very understanding and supportive. No jealousy. No competition. No fear. The child is now a teenager and has known since he was two who his birth mother is; though his birth father is not involved. These sun families are making the best out of what can often become a very unpleasant situation.

I especially admire couples who are willing to adopt because they see millions of children who grow up in orphanages around the world or who have been passed around from foster home to foster home and who may never experience sincere love nor form healthy attachment bonds with their caregivers. Those couples take on huge challenges when they adopt these children and often find it difficult to understand why the children don't respond to a safe, loving home the way my three-legged cat did. As a result, discussing the challenges adoptive families face can be a difficult conversation for some adoptive parents. One such conversation occurred with a class of adoptive parents that I was presenting a lecture to about this:

Them: *Are you saying that adoptive parents can't love their children as much as birth parents?*

Me: *No.*

Them: *Are you saying that adopted children can't love their adoptive parents as much as they might love their birth parents?*

Me: *No.*

Them: *Then what ARE you saying? Why do so many of these children struggle so much?*

Me: *What I'm saying is that there are biological, psychological, and sociological reasons that favor the natural family as the healthiest environment for both children and parents. That is true especially for natural families who are living by sun standards. Children who experience love and authoritative parenting develop a sense of core value that will help them throughout their lives, even if circumstances make it necessary for them to be raised by someone other than their birth parents. Many of you have adopted children who did not come from sun circumstances and you are realizing the kinds of problems those children will face. The problem is not with the institution of adoption. It's with a world that makes adoption necessary for so many children. What it all comes down to is this: what the world's children need most, are more responsible teens and adults who choose to live by sun standards, and more leaders of governments who do the same.*

Polyamorous Families

Polyamory means being in a marriage or intimate relationship with more than one person. Currently, there are three forms that I am aware of:

1. Polygamy (or polygyny) where there is one husband and more than one wife.
2. Polyandry where there is one wife and more than one husband.
3. A third form of polyamory where there are three or more members of the same sex.

The obvious challenge with multiple intimate relationships is managing the psychosocial and sexual aspects of the relationships. Sex is a bedroom level activity that involves the highest levels of vulnerability for partners and can produce the highest levels of intimacy and trust–when it is used properly. As I indicated previously, when it is not, it can do the opposite.

Polygamy has been around since ancient times and according to the Biblical record, God has apparently approved the practice on occasion, though under specific guidelines and with clear restrictions.

From the divine perspective, the purpose of polygamy anciently was to bring more children into families where the principles of light and truth would be taught to them. Polyandry does not increase the number of children that can be born into a family. In fact, research indicates it can *reduce* fertility rates among women who practice it. It also creates another significant problem. With polygamy we know who both the mother and the father are. With polyandry, we don't. Until blood tests to determine paternity were developed, there was no way to be certain who the father of a child was if the mother had multiple sexual partners.

Knowing who both parents are was what determined a child's legal and moral legitimacy in the past. Keeping accurate genealogical records was essential for that to happen. For a child to grow up not knowing who their father is would also deny that child the legal and emotional benefits of that deeply important father-child relationship. A vitally important kitchen level relationship would be missing, and that could create a heavy emotional burden for a child to carry.

With no identified father, who takes the paternal responsibility for the welfare of that child? The same problem would exist in polygamist families. Whether we are dealing with multiple mothers or fathers, when several people are responsible for something, no one takes full responsibility. Social psychologists refer to this phenomenon as the "bystander problem."

In a polygamist family the women would be competing for the man's attention and in a polyandrous family the opposite would be true. The husband-wife relationship would likely never be as deeply connected as it could be when you are totally and exclusively committed–emotionally and sexually–to each other and to no one else.

Spreading out the parental responsibilities for a child between too many additional caregivers weakens the connection between the birth parents and the child. Those many diapers you change, the playful interactions you engage in, the times you spend with an ill or emotionally discouraged child, and all the other everyday sacrifices you make as a parent are essential to the process of becoming a sun parent and of cementing the attachment bonds within families.

In polygamist families there might be a benefit to having more siblings to interact with, but that will invite more competition as well. The wives are likely to feel more like a mother to their own natural children and a nanny to the rest. For some women, they might prefer not having to be the only provider of childcare or to be solely responsible to meet the sexual needs of their husband. But most women would find it very difficult to share that marital responsibility with another woman. That level of selflessness would be a lot to expect of anyone. So, maybe we shouldn't.

Certainly, it would take a special group of people to make a polygamist family function in healthy ways. It was difficult for one of the Bible's most righteous couples–Abraham and Sarah. And it certainly created challenges for Sarah's handmaid Hagar and her son Ishmael. The rivalry between Leah and her sister Rachel for Jacob's approval also affected the relationships between their sons. It produced some major problems for Rachel's first-born son, Joseph–the one with the coat of many colors who was sold into slavery by his half-brothers.

With the divided loyalties in polygamist relationships, I think it would be nearly impossible for a husband to achieve a bedroom level of intimacy and trust with multiple wives. I realize that some polygamist husbands would describe it as multiplying rather than dividing their love among spouses, but there is no way to avoid having to divide your time, energy, and sexual interest among them.

The children raised in polygamist homes would likely recognize any differences between Dad's relationship with their mom compared to his relationships will all the other moms. If Dad does not seem to be as close to that child's mother as he is to the others, the child is likely to feel insecure about the strength of his parent's relationship and therefore, their own status with Dad. Again, think of "Jacob and Sons" or *Big Love*.

This design is fraught with challenges for everyone involved in it. I don't think I could make it work, and my wife thinks I'm the perfect husband! (lol)

Same-Sex Families

Whether a same-sex relationship involves just two people or a polyamorous relationship, the most obvious disadvantage here is that a child will have to grow up without the presence of at least one of the two most important people in his or her life. Either the birth father or the birth mother (or both) will regularly, if not entirely, be missing from the scene. What will also be missing are the qualities, talents, traits, and life perspectives that make mothers and fathers uniquely different and equally important in a child's life.

On the surface one could say that same-sex parenting relationships are gender discriminatory by design because they assume that having both genders present in the child's life in unnecessary and that either two men or two women is equal to having one of each. But sun parents know better, including the gay ones.

In a heartfelt piece written for the New York Times by gay adoptive father Frank Ligtvoet, he acknowledged that sometimes when he cuddles up to his seven-year-old adopted daughter as she snuggles into her bed at night, she calls him "Mommy." She uses a different voice that he called her "stuffed animal voice." "She can role-play the mother-daughter relationship," he wrote, "but she cannot use her real voice, nor have the real thing." "We could fill our home with nannies, sisters, grandmothers, female friends, but no mothers." Mr. Ligtvoet concluded that his daughter's mother, while not physically present in her life is "still present in dreams, fantasies, longings, and worries." But regardless of his valiant parenting efforts, his daughter's behaviors are clear indicators that just having a loving father is not enough to meet the full set of biopsychosocial needs of a child, male or female.

I doubt that most fathers can adequately comprehend the significant impact on a child's life of having a real-life mother present, not just during childhood, but throughout that child's life. That is something I have repeatedly observed personally as I watch how my wife continues to have a unique and profoundly important impact on the lives of our children as adults and on our grandchildren. The same can be said for the involvement of fathers.

Dads Make A Difference

I saw an example recently of one couple who are in denial of this fact. The documentary film *Romeo Romeo* chronicles the journey of a lesbian couple from New York City who got married and then wanted to get pregnant and raise a child together. It was Lexy's lifelong dream to give birth and be a mom; for Jessica, not so much—at least the birthing part. Initially she had no burning desire to have children, but after they got married, she began to warm up to the idea. They started out with the plan to use donor sperm from a friend in New York but decided against it when he made it clear he would expect to be involved in his child's life. They decided it was safer to go with an anonymous donor.

After several failed attempts at expensive in vitro fertilization using purchased sperm from an anonymous donor, the financially-strapped women decided the best alternative was to accept sperm from a gay friend in San Francisco who volunteered what he promised would be a "clean specimen." ("Clean" meaning free of HIV, Hepatitis, or other STDs.) Ignoring all the mandated and doctor-recommended safety protocols, they flew to San Francisco and met with the donor and his partner. Jessica then implanted the donor sperm into Lexy using the "turkey baster" method. (Actually, they used a syringe.) After several anxious weeks of waiting, the test came back positive. They were pregnant!

At several points during their quest for parenthood, the two prospective moms discussed how they would address the issue of fatherhood. In a somewhat heated debate with some friends prior to their trip to San Francisco, they discussed how they would explain to their longed-for child "where babies come from" and who his biological father was. (I say "his" because the couple later discovered that the baby Lexy was about to be carrying was a boy.)

Lexy admitted that, obviously, they would have to tell their son that he has a biological father. In response, Jessica adamantly declared, "Are you out of your mind?! The answer *always* is, 'You don't *have* a father! *We* are your *only* family!'" She also stated that just because her male friend would be the biological father, "that doesn't make him blood!" Seriously?

The statement about it being "safer" to keep the father's identity unknown suddenly made perfidious sense to me. Safer for Jessica. Safer for the fantasy world she wanted to create where children don't have fathers and a sperm donor who provides half of the genetic material that forms a human body is not considered a blood relative, but somehow an adoptive second mother is.

The lesbian couple was assured by the gay donor and his partner that the two men would take a back seat with regards to any involvement in the child's life because "this is all about you two." No, it's not. First and foremost, parenthood is about the welfare of children. Remember the Prime Directive. Parenthood is not about providing some well-intentioned adults with a variety of emotional-growth-enhancing social experiences.

Their son is very likely going to grow up in a family where fatherhood is considered superfluous and being male is neither understood nor honored. Or from Jessica's perspective, even acknowledged.

Who is going to be there 24/7 to help teach this boy how to grow into a healthy, happy, and mature man? Who is going to provide the masculine version of the virtues men need to develop, like (1) strength in the face of opposition; (2) courage in the face of danger; (3) diligence to duty; and (4) loyalty, compassion, and a commitment to provide for and protect his family? Psychiatrist Dr. Richard B. Corradi explains:

> *While mothers continue to model for daughters what it means to be a woman, boys learn from their fathers how to be men. To help their sons master their strong and potentially unruly sexual drives and tendencies toward physical aggression, fathers need to model self-control and mature coping skills. In particular, sons identify with how their fathers handle emotions and control impulses—how they express anger, how they control their temper, and how they express and control their sexuality. Sons need to learn from their fathers that enduring and loving relationships depend on a reciprocal and empathic regard for another person and not simply on sexuality. Just as girls identify with their*

3 KINDS OF PARENTS | 211

mother's role in marriage, boys identify with their father's marital role. While sex is biologically determined, how men and women treat each other is modeled, for better or worse, by their parents, usually leaving an indelible mark.

Finally, children develop a conscience by identification with both parents. Normally, parents impose constraints on their children's behavior as soon as they become toddlers. Children develop a conscience as concepts of right and wrong are progressively internalized, become part of the self, and automatically govern their behavior. This process of developing a self-governing system of standards of belief and conduct, another element of one's personal identity, is crucially determined by parental models. That is, to a significant extent, children form their conscience by incorporating the consciences of their parents, particularly the same-sex parent.

And what if Romeo (the name they decided to give their son) had turned out to be a Juliet instead? Daughters need a positive relationship with their fathers too. From their fathers' examples they learn what healthy dating and romantic relationships should look like and what reasonable male/female roles and expectations should be in marriage. They learn about emotional regulation, conflict resolution, and the development of loyalty and trust between the sexes from watching their parents' interactions. Dads make an important difference in the lives of children.

So, is the word *father* going to become the word that can't be spoken in this family? Will Romeo come home from his middle school health class confused about the details of his conception? And what happens when he hits puberty?

When a friend of the couple proposed to Jessica a hypothetical future scenario about her someday fourteen-year-old son feeling rebellious and wanting to go live with his father, the friend asked how she would handle the situation. Jessica shouted, "I would kill him! Not the father, the baby!" Certainly, she was not serious, but her authoritarian approach to parenting a teenage boy will unknowingly invite the very rebelliousness her friend was describing.

How quickly a child becomes a possession–a possession that these two women are likely to fight for control of. Like the two women brought before King Solomon to determine who was the real mother of the contested infant, my money is on the birth mother as the one who will make Romeo's best interests the highest priority.

While I have tremendous respect and admiration for any parent–gay or straight–who is willing to take on the demanding role of parent, there are important differences between being raised by a biological father and mother and being raised by same-sex parents. Mothers and fathers are not interchangeable cogs in the family machine. A second mother is not the same as a father, nor is a second father a replacement for a mother. Decades of scientific research supports the importance of the role of both fathers and mothers in the lives of children. It may be hard for social scientists to accurately define and measure exactly what unique and important qualities are missing when a child is raised without a mother or father, but that discrepancy will become more apparent as time goes by and more children experience legally and socially sanctioned motherlessness and fatherlessness. Again, this is not to say that same-sex relationship families are never successful. It means that these parents, and especially the children in these families, face unique challenges and often experience significant difficulties as a result. And the issue of surrogacy adds another dimension to those challenges.

Surrogate Families

Surrogate-produced families are a new form of family that has gained increased popularity in recent years. The practice has a troubling history and an even more alarming future that is creating a whole new set of potential problems for parents and children alike.

Surrogacy involves conceiving and delivering a child and involving one or more third parties in the process. When the surrogate mother is not the biological provider of the egg but a fertilized egg from another woman is implanted, it is referred to as a gestational surrogacy. When the surrogate mother contributes her own egg, it is called a traditional surrogacy.

Sometimes the intended parents will use their own sperm and/or eggs and sometimes they will use only donor sperm and eggs. (Is it starting to get confusing yet?).

In any case, the woman who gives birth is not one of the people who intend to raise the child. Therein lies the problem. This has also created a whole new set of legal issues that further complicate the question of who has custodial rights to the resulting child.

The first court case in America to address the legality of surrogacy occurred in New Jersey in 1986 with the "Baby M" case. The Supreme Court of New Jersey ruled that surrogacy violated public policy and was not in the best interests of children. They raised concerns that the process of recruiting surrogate mothers could result in the exploitation of poor women. They discouraged surrogacy of any kind. While several states outlawed paid surrogacy as a result of this case, many others left the issue unresolved.

In a California case of gestational surrogacy, the intended parents were given custodial rights and considered to be the natural and legal parents because they provided both the sperm and the egg. In one traditional surrogacy case in California the intended father and the surrogate mother were given rights but the intended mother was left out entirely. (Because the couple broke up prior to the delivery and the intended mother had not provided the egg.) In three companion cases involving lesbian couples who produced a child through surrogacy using donor sperm, the California Supreme Court ruled that the lesbian couples had legal rights to the child and the sperm donors had none. It is presumed that the same ruling would also apply to gay male couples using donor eggs. And to make matters even more complicated and confusing, in another California case of gestational surrogacy there were six potential candidates for custodial rights to the child: the egg donor, the sperm donor, the intended mother, the intended father, the surrogate mother, and her husband. The Appeals Court decided in favor of the intended parents even though there was no genetic link to the child, reversing the lower court's ruling that the child had *no* legal parents, effectively making it an orphan. According to the existing statutes in nine other states at that time, there could have been four different outcomes in this same case. In only a few states are the best interests of the child the determining factor when the court must decide who receives custody in disputed cases involving surrogacy.

It gets worse. My home state of California now allows birth certificates for surrogate births to contain only the names of the intended parents. For same-sex parents, birth certificates will list two men or two women as both parents. The term "parent" is now used as a gender-neutral term instead of father and mother. For single men or single women obtaining a child through surrogacy, only one parent is listed on the birth certificate under the category of "mother/parent." Suddenly, the source of the reproductive materials that generate human life has nothing to do with whom the courts define as parents.

The laws vary significantly from state to state and country to country. Some have intentionally avoided addressing the issue because of the controversy surrounding it. In other countries there is also a lack of consensus. Commercial surrogacy has been rejected by voters in Finland, Sweden, Spain, France, Germany, and several other countries around the globe. In France commercial surrogacy was banned in 1991 when its highest court ruled that "the human body is not lent out, is not rented out, and is not sold." In some countries where surrogacy is permitted–including South Africa, the U.K., and Argentina–independent ethics committees are required to evaluate all surrogacy requests on a case-by-case basis. In Ukraine, where commercial surrogacy is a huge business, hiring a commercial surrogate costs an average of $50,000. In some other countries there are no regulations, which means that impoverished surrogate mothers have no legal protection from exploitation. Their bodies have now become vending machines.

What happens if something goes wrong during the pregnancy? What if the child has a birth defect? What if the intended parent(s) are clearly psychologically unfit? Who has the legal right and responsibility to care for the child? The moral implications are huge for society. We are inviting biopsychosocial chaos into the family system and society in general with no legal mechanisms to deal with these kinds of questions and concerns.

Then there are the concerns about the creation of designer children that occurs via the selection of donor eggs and sperm. Do we want a child with blonde hair or black hair? Caucasian or Asian? Blue eyes or brown? Athletic ability or intellectual prowess? And what about the donor-created children who are trying to figure out where they fit in with their parents and siblings? I recently heard an account of a young woman whose story reflects what many children like her are experiencing. But it appears that the children are not the only ones facing some unexpected consequences of the adults' decision to donate or use someone else's eggs or sperm. Here's an overview of the story as told on the National Public Radio (NPR) program, *Radiolab*:

> *She was told by her mother beginning when she was eight years old that there was something special about her. After repeatedly hearing that comment from her mother, Kate (not her real name) finally asked what it was that made her special. Her mother explained to her that the man whom Kate knew as her father was not actually her biological father. Because Mom and Dad were not able to conceive a child between them, they had gone to a sperm bank at Baylor Medical College where "a nice man volunteered" to let them use his sperm so Kate could be born. Kate remembers seeking out her father that day and giving him a big hug, though he was unaware that his wife had told Kate about the special circumstances of her conception and birth. What at first seemed magical to her because it made her feel unique, eventually became problematic as she grew older. She began to notice all of the many ways that she was not like her other family members: (1) She was 5'2" and all of her cousins, aunts, uncles, etc. were between 5'10" and 6' 5". (2) She had blue eyes and most of them had brown eyes. (3) She had talent in drawing and art while her mother could barely draw stick figures. (4) She was the only vegetarian in the family. Kate then began to wonder if her unique traits and talents came from her biological father. All of this fueled her desire to know more about him, but all she knew was that he was a student at the Baylor College of Medicine in Houston in 1981 when she was conceived.*
>
> *When she contacted the school, she learned that any sperm donation records had long since been destroyed. Then she saw*

an episode of the news program 60 Minutes and learned that 30,000 children are conceived each year using anonymous sperm donations and that she might be able to locate possible half-siblings through a national registry of donor-conceived children. She contacted the registry and was able to locate another girl with whom she shared nearly 100 similarities. Hopes were high that she had found a sibling, but those hopes were dashed when the DNA test results came back indicating that there was only a .01% possibility of them being sisters.

Still, Kate wasn't discouraged. She obtained copies of the Baylor College of Medicine annual yearbooks from 1979 through 1984 and copied all six hundred pictures of the students enrolled during those years hoping to find someone who strongly resembled her among the photos. She narrowed the field down to twenty-five "most likelys" and fifty more "possibles" and sent them all a letter explaining who she was, why she was contacting them, that she was not mentally unstable or financially destitute, and invited a response. She got several responses—mostly polite, and some critical of her efforts to contact them. Among the favorable responses was a man who acknowledged he had donated sperm, had placed his career ahead of building a family and as a result, had no children of his own. Both he and his mother were excited about the possibility of having a child/grandchild out there somewhere. Through their many conversations he too began to recognize many similarities between himself and his possible daughter and he began to believe that this was truly his daughter and that fate had brought them together. But again, their hopes were shattered by the DNA test results and everyone experienced a significant grief reaction to the news. Undaunted, Kate decided to write to all the remaining five hundred and twenty-five names on her list, receiving two hundred and fifty total responses out of the six hundred names. (That's a lot of medical students donating sperm.) Sixteen more DNA tests later, there were no positive results. Now, whenever she hears the song "Somewhere, Out There" from the animated movie An American Tail, she is sadly reminded of those unknown family members who are "sleeping underneath the same big sky."

Since the first known incident of conception using donor sperm that occurred in 1884, this procedure has become more frequent and gained greater social acceptance. But in researching this issue I have come across several web sites that invite donor-conceived children, donor parents, and adoptive parents (the ones who raised them) to share their stories. There are also additional web sites like the Donor Sibling Registry where donor children can search for possible siblings. And programs like *MyHeritageDNA, AncestryDNA,* and *23andMe* are often being used to locate lost or unknown relatives.

While just over half of donor-conceived children reportedly express no concerns about being conceived this way, I have read about many others who feel they were lied to by their parents or denied a relationship with both of their biological parents and that it is unfair and unjust. Some see the sperm or egg donor parent in very negative terms while others see the parents who raised them as acting selfishly by their decision to use an anonymous donor, thereby denying the child any hope of access to both biological parents. A study published in 2010 entitled "My Daddy's Name Is Donor" found that forty-five percent of young adult children conceived by anonymous sperm donors were bothered by the fact that an exchange of money was involved in their conception.

Some donor parents have reported concerns about how the children conceived using their donor egg or sperm are doing in life. Some others seem to get a thrill out of the idea that they have produced a bunch of children without having to take any responsibility for their welfare. And in a few cases, narcissistic fertility doctors have secretly substituted their own sperm in the place of dozens of male donors' sperm.

Some parents feel betrayed when the children they have loved and sacrificed to raise, suddenly want to develop a relationship with donor parents who have never been a part of their lives.

Some children and adults have adjusted relatively well to the situation, but for others it has been very difficult for non-biological parents to bond with their donor-conceived children. One case in Belgium involved fraternal triplets conceived with an anonymous sperm donor. It wasn't until they were twenty-five years old that they discovered this fact and began to understand why their father had treated them so badly growing up and differently from their younger brother, who was the "surprise" natural child of both parents. Then, to make matters much worse, they discovered a decade later that one of the three triplets had a different biological father than the other two. Someone had mixed two different sperm samples together.

It appears that no one involved in this process for conceiving children comes out of the experience without some kind of mark on their hearts. And with broader acceptance, the potential misuse of this technology is increasingly and frighteningly likely.

As I have said repeatedly, it's not impossible to make this family design work, but why do we seem to keep inviting more difficulties for children and parents alike, unnecessarily? With each new alternative family design that comes along, the problems only seem to multiply. Society seems to repeatedly allow the desires of adults who want to experience parenthood to take precedence over the best interests of the children involved.

Some use surrogates because they are unable to conceive or carry a pregnancy on their own. Most people seem to be OK with that if it only involves immediate family members, all of whom are available and encouraged to create supportive relationships with the child. But many others are using hired surrogates to avoid the nausea, pain, stretch marks, episiotomies, and other anatomical unpleasantries associated with pregnancy and childbirth, or because a pregnancy might disrupt their career plans.

With the commercialization of surrogacy and the increasing demand for this service, more poor women are being recruited to lease out their wombs. Parents have now become consumers and a human child has now become chattel—a commodity that is being bought and sold.

What will we do about the prospective parents who get cold feet and walk out of their contractual agreement to assume financial responsibility and take legal custody of the surrogate-produced child? Or the dissatisfied customers who will inevitably complain from time to time that they did not get what they paid for? (There have already been cases where the intended parents who commissioned the surrogate pregnancy have walked away and abandoned a handicapped child as damaged goods.)

At one point during the COVID-19 pandemic it was estimated that approximately one thousand surrogate-produced newborns were stuck in hotels, clinics, and foster homes in Ukraine and other countries where commercial surrogacy is legal because their parents couldn't enter those countries to pick them up. When it comes to diversifying our definition of family, we are now treading on very thin ice.

Another related aspect of donor-conceived children has arisen recently with the decision by the British Parliament to legalize what some have termed "3-parent babies." This involves allowing women who are at risk for passing mitochondrial diseases to their children to replace their diseased mitochondria with the healthy mitochondria from another woman's donor egg. Using the father's sperm in the in vitro fertilization (IVF) process, the result is a child with DNA material from three people—one man and two women. The U.K government sees this procedure as a benevolent way to correct a disorder that affects thousands of children born each year to women with this problem. But this raises ethical and safety concerns for many others. How might this ability to manipulate reproductive material be used in the future?

An influential group of scientists known as the Hinxton Group that advises policymakers on various scientific concerns, issued a statement regarding the genetic modification of human genomes saying, "Policymakers should be circumspect when regulating science. When enacted, policies governing science nationally and internationally ought to be flexible, so as to accommodate the rapidity of scientific advance and changes in social values." What changes in social values are they referring to? Sun, moon, or star social values? Could this technology lead to the routine production of GMO children some day? The U.K government dismissed such concerns, but the fact remains that there is a big difference between using this technology to correct a malevolent disorder and using it to "enhance" the human species generally, as the twenty-first century transhumanism movement seeks to do. That was also the intention of the twentieth century eugenics movement.

I fully understand the human drive to improve upon what the Creator has provided us in this world, but this could easily become scientific overreach and an effort to usurp creative and governing authority from the legitimate architect of our mortal lives.

Many people have suggested that technological advancement has outpaced the moral development of mankind. This concern brings us back to the theme of this book: what kind of people are we choosing to be? The same technology that sun people would use to correct the debilitating effects of certain diseases, injuries, or harmful genetic anomalies would be used by star people to promote ableism. It would likely increase competition among people for the additional power and prestige that comes with having a child with superior athletic abilities or intelligence. The results would be a less humane humanity; a society created by a level of social engineering only previously conceived of in futuristic fiction. Depending on the levels of light and truth in societies, what initially appears to be a gentle and progressive societal incline, can quickly turn into a steep and icy downhill slope.

Cohabitating Families

Cohabitating couples are those who live together without getting married. Some choose not to have children, while others do. Still others may choose to blend or adopt. Beginning in the 1960s we began to see increasing numbers of couples living together without getting married. This was considered socially unacceptable by most societies for centuries, but the sexual revolution that kicked into high gear in the 1960s changed all of that. Currently, about sixty percent of couples cohabitate prior to marriage and about half of those never marry at all. Many people tend to believe that living together is a logical and practical way to decide whether a relationship has a good chance of succeeding and that cohabitation is a stepping stone to a more secure marriage. But a growing body of scientific research indicates that cohabitating couples break up or divorce at a much *higher* rate than those who married without cohabitating prior to engagement or marriage.

Cohabitating couples experience poorer communication skills and therefore, greater conflict, higher rates of infidelity, increased levels of domestic violence, higher rates of alcohol abuse, and lower marital satisfaction for those who eventually do choose to marry. Even after allowing for differences in age, ethnicity, education, income, length of relationship, religiosity, and duration of premarital cohabitation, the results are the same.

The HOUSE model reminds us why this happens. Cohabitating couples may say they want the bedroom levels of intimacy and trust in their relationships, but at the same time they are trying to protect themselves from the vulnerability of divorce or separation. As I mentioned previously, **you can't have one (intimacy/trust) without the other (vulnerability).** Cohabitation without the commitment of marriage creates an imbalance between these two necessary components of good relationships. When you lower your vulnerability by avoiding the commitment of marriage, you also lower your potential for achieving higher levels of intimacy and trust.

Research by Dr. William Axinn and colleagues Arland Thornton and Jennifer Barber at the University of Michigan has demonstrated that individuals who cohabit prior to marriage, especially with multiple partners over long periods of time, experienced lower self-esteem as well as a devaluing of marriage and childrearing. Cohabitation appears to erode the motivation to marry and the commitment to make it last, making divorce a more acceptable option when problems occur.

As scholars Howard Markman, Galena Kline Rhoades, and Scott Stanley at the University of Denver described it, couples who cohabitate are *sliding* into a relationship rather than *deciding* on a relationship. These are relationships of convenience rather than of commitment. As decades of research have clearly determined, the more unstable the couple's relationship, the more problems the children in those families will develop. For the children of cohabitating parents, the grim outcomes include being at an increased risk of losing a parent to divorce or separation, increased poverty, and higher incidences of criminal behaviors, substance abuse, and school failure. And for women with children from previous relationships who are living with an unmarried partner, the children are far more likely to experience sexual abuse and maltreatment.

Whatever the perceived advantages over traditional marriage, the real outcomes of cohabitation do not measure up to the fantasy images the media present and do not work in the long run. Even children have figured this out.

For years prior to the marriage of Brad Pitt and Angelina Jolie, it was often reported that their adopted children were pleading with their parents to get married. While marriage may not always fit into the plans of some parents, it most certainly holds a very prominent place on the family agendas of their children. And I'm not talking about going through the motions of a wedding ceremony. That's *sliding*, not *deciding*. Children know the difference between cohabitation and marriage, regardless of how grownups choose to define them. Marriage means commitment. Marriage means fidelity. Marriage means love. Marriage means security. Out of the mouths of babes.

The Natural Family

The final contestant…I mean family design, is the natural family composed of both birth parents who are married to each other, conceive the children within the bonds of matrimony, raise the children together within a loving marriage, and stay married throughout their lives. The natural family has all the advantages and none of the design flaws of the others. Here are just a few of those advantages.

"The blood of the covenant is thicker than the water of the womb." This phrase is often abbreviated as "blood is thicker than water." However, both versions have application here. The phrase "blood is thicker than water" implies that those who are related by blood share a stronger connection than those who are not. Attachment bonds form more quickly, more easily, and more firmly when parents and children share important things in common. It is easier to bond and stay connected with someone who shares your genes, your funny way of laughing, your athletic abilities, your level of intelligence, your quirky personality traits, your dislike for broccoli, or your passion for gardening. And stronger attachment bonds equals better care.

We may have unexpectedly learned something about those who share similar bloodlines from those who have shared the use of the same bodily organs. Some of those receiving organ transplants have reported suddenly recalling memories of events that did not occur in their lives, but in the lives of the organ donor. One heart transplant recipient who had never taken much interest in football before the surgery, suddenly became an instant diehard fan afterward. Guess who was a passionate football fan prior to his untimely death? The donor. Cellular memory occurs in the bodies of every human being during life and apparently, some of that information can be passed on to future generations—referred to as genetic memory—or even to others who share the use of the same organs.

According to Jewish leader R' Richard Pustelniak, the original phrase I quoted reminds us that "my relationship with those to whom I am joined in covenant is to be considered of more value than the relationship with a brother with whom I may have shared the womb."

Not only does the covenant relationship we have with God come before our relationships with family and friends, but the marriage relationship with our spouse is also considered to be a higher priority than the relationships with others. In most religions, marriage is seen as a three-participant promise that involves husband, wife, and God. The Biblical phrase "What therefore God hath joined together, let not man put asunder" reminds us of that triangular relationship. Couples who share that covenant marriage relationship are more committed, more resilient, more passionate, enjoy better health, are more economically secure, and are able to avoid many of the problems that frequently occur within the other family designs. Dr. Phil McGraw cited a statistic in his book *Relationship Rescue* that "the reported divorce rate among couples who pray together is about one in ten thousand. Pretty impressive statistic, even if you reduce it a thousand-fold."

Biological and developmental health advantages for children. Ground-breaking research conducted by Dr. Katie Hinde at Arizona State University has uncovered some remarkable discoveries about the organic connection between birth mothers and their babies. The breast milk produced by birth mothers is the perfect food for their newborn babies during the first year of life. It contains the perfect combination of proteins, fat, carbohydrates, vitamins, minerals, fatty acids, hormones, and the many complex sugars unique to human milk that are essential for the baby's digestive system to function properly. But the most amazing part is that the composition of the mother's milk changes on a daily—even hourly—basis to meet the changing needs of the child.

During breastfeeding, saliva from the baby's body enters the mother's body through the mother's nipples. The mother's body reads the chemical content of this "baby spit backwash" and adjusts the nutritional content of the milk to meet the child's changing needs, especially if the child is undernourished or sick. If pathogens are detected, the mother's body will add specific antibodies to her milk that will help the child's immune system fight the illness. In addition to improved immune systems, Dr. Hinde's research also indicates that children breastfed by their mothers often have increased IQs and lower risks of developing type-2 diabetes, high cholesterol, or obesity later in life.

While some single, blended, cohabitating, polyamorous, or same-sex birth-mothers may also have the ability to offer this health advantage to their children, surrogate and adoptive mothers do not. And according to Dr. Hinde, it is the natural family that faces fewer of the economic, cultural, or political obstacles to breastfeeding that exist, and who are more likely to accommodate the inconvenience of breastfeeding to provide their children with the best nutritional option.

Improved intergenerational connection. Natural families enjoy greater levels of intergenerational connection because everyone knows who the birth parents, grandparents, great-grandparents, aunts, uncles, and cousins are. This not only makes family interactions more likely, but much more impactful to children.

With the natural family, those intergenerational relationships are less likely to break down than in blended families. They involve none of the uncertainty of adoptive families, the confusion of polygamist families, and the entirely absent family lines in many single-parent and surrogate families. With cohabitating families there is also a lack of legal connection, which may also contribute to less of an emotional connection between the children and their caregivers or extended family members.

A higher level of dedication and commitment. Partners who share a high level of connection also share higher levels of dedication to each other and commitment to the marriage relationship. They tend to have a stronger sense of couple identity, or the "we" relationship that I described earlier. That paradigm influences how they approach life. It includes a long-term view of their relationship and a desire for a future together. Dedicated couples display a willingness to sacrifice for one another and to place the needs of their partner ahead of their own. Because of this willingness to serve others they are more likely to invite children into their lives. Less committed couples face less-optimistic outcomes. Case in point.

Relationship Rumspringa

I was listening to an episode of the NPR program hosted by Ira Glass called *This American Life* one Saturday just before Valentine's Day and heard a story that alarmed me. It was about a couple who met the third day of their freshman year of college at the age of seventeen and had been together for the next thirteen years. They had a great relationship, could talk about anything, had a satisfying sex life, and were "each other's worlds" as Ken (not his real name) described their relationship. They were the envy of all their less-securely attached friends.

Though they had been together for so long and were virtually inseparably attached to each other, they had never seriously discussed the possibility of marriage. When friends asked, they would just say that they would probably get married when they had kids. But when Ken approached Barbara (not her real name either) one day about the marriage question, she suggested that they needed to sleep with other people before they got married–you know, to make sure about the relationship before they tied the knot. For some strange reason this seemed reasonable to Ken as well.

He said that they had some sort of arrogant confidence that their relationship was so strong that it could survive *anything*. Barbara felt that they had been together for all of their adult life to that point and she didn't want to feel that she had missed out on what so many of their friends had done throughout their twenties. So, they decided to take a one-month Rumspringa from their relationship.

Rumspringa is a Pennsylvania German word meaning "running around" and is used to describe a two-year period of time when Amish teens turn sixteen and they can choose to run around and smoke, drink, have sex, and live a worldly lifestyle until age eighteen. At that time, they can decide to return to the Amish community and lifestyle and become baptized, committed members of the religion, or leave permanently.

So, Ken and Barbara spent a final romantic weekend together and met at their apartment afterward to discuss their planned relationship hiatus. They talked. They cried. And Ken moved out. Then the contest began.

Being competitive people, the race began to see who could sleep with the most people during the Rumspringa sex-fest. Ken was under the impression that they would both sleep around for thirty days and get this *sex* thing out of their systems. Then he would return to their apartment and they would get married.

Ken was committed to being honest with the women he met and told them exactly what the Rumspringa arrangement with Barbara was. You would think that that would discourage any would-be suitors, but strangely, it did not seem to deter them. When I asked my wife why any woman would choose to get involved sexually under those circumstances, I was a little surprised by her answer. She suggested that either the other women didn't care about the arrangement and just wanted non-committal sex with Ken, or they were competing with Barbara to try and lure him away from her. Either that, or they thought they could give him a sexual experience that would surpass anything he had ever experienced (or ever would experience) with his supposed soul mate of a girlfriend. His naïve openness about the whole situation probably just made him that much more appealing to the other women. Barbara had no such problem keeping their secret from every man she met.

One of the rules the couple had agreed upon for the Rumspringa was that they would not get emotionally involved with any sex-partners. But Ken had trouble with this and found himself struggling to keep himself from saying "I love you" to the women he was sleeping with because that was what he was so used to saying to Barbara. His emotions would fluctuate between feelings of elation at one moment and sudden crying spells the next. Barbara didn't seem to have the same problems at all. But the strangest thing was, the person they both most wanted to talk to about their various experiences was each other. Unfortunately, their rules did not allow for any contact during the thirty days.

In time Ken was able to adjust a little more to participating in these front-gate-level sexual experiences. He would act like an interested boyfriend and not hold back his feelings, but would then break off any relationships he established after a maximum of three dates. Obviously, being used by a man trying to hone his Casanova skills did not go over well with some of these women. While Ken did feel remorse for his actions, the experiment continued nonetheless. In fact, Ken and Barbara both agree that thirty days was not enough time and decided to extend the terms of the agreement to three months.

By now Ken was hooked. He compared his situation to something his pet toy poodle had experienced one day years before when the family cat knocked a five-pound bag of sugar off the kitchen counter and onto the floor. The nine-pound dog consumed the entire five-pound bag of sugar that day and was sick for three days afterward. Ken envisioned the dog eating copious amounts of the sugar and then trying to walk away, but then feeling compelled to return and eat more, thinking "I can't stop! I know this is bad, but when is this *ever* going to happen *again*?!"

When the three months were over, the couple got together again. By that time Ken had begun to develop feelings for another woman and no longer felt the same way about Barbara. They discussed the Rumspringa experience over their usual Saturday brunch in the park and decided to break up.

For Ken, commitment was not a problem. It seemed to be the natural response for him. For Barbara, not so much. They realized that they had decided to test the dedication and commitment in their relationship at the one place where so many relationships are most vulnerable, and sure enough, theirs was too. And it broke.

Neither of them saw anything bad about their prior relationship. Ken said that maybe their relationship had just exceeded its freshness and utility, like something from the grocery store that had suddenly reached an expiration date that neither of them knew existed.

As Ken and the program host Ira Glass discussed the couple's experience together, Ken suggested that relationships need to be evaluated regularly and that marriages should have an escape clause in the agreement. He suggested that marriages should only last for seven years. At that time the commitment ends and the couple has to get remarried again if the marriage is to continue. "That way," he said, "you get to choose." (It would be hard to image the children being OK with that arrangement.)

Ira Glass disagreed with Ken's idea and responded:

> *I think that one of the things that's a comfort in marriage is that there isn't a door at seven years, and so if something is messed up in the short term, there's the comfort of knowing that we made this commitment and we're just going to work this out. So even if tonight we're not getting along and things just don't feel right, you have the comfort of knowing that we've got time, and we are just going to figure this out. That makes it so much easier. You do have times when you hate each other's guts, and the "no-escape" clause is, weirdly, a really greater comfort to being married than I would have ever thought before I got married.*

Ken said he had never thought of it that way. And though he seemed to like Ira's perspective, he said "you just see *so* many examples where people don't think that way." It was at that point that the story suddenly became scary to me.

Scary because we seem to be forgetting as a society about something that throughout human history has been the norm: that the order and strength we see in society is a reflection of the order and strength we see in families. The degree to which we lose our dedication and commitment to one another and to sun values in our homes will be the degree to which we lose our dedication and commitment to one another and to sun values as a society. Dedication and commitment should be expected in a marriage relationship and in society in general. We need them to survive and prosper. Unfortunately, "you just see *so* many examples where people don't think that way."

Promoting the Cause of Sun Families

We are again reminded that there are three kinds of people in the world and therefore, there are three kinds of spouses and three kinds of parents. I realize that parenting is not a contest and many parents are struggling to do the best they can under less-than-ideal circumstances. But think back to the singing contest.

The natural family is like the winning contestant. It possesses all the fundamental qualities that give it the greatest potential for success. Some of the other contestants had difficulty adapting, establishing emotional connection, handling the pressure of the competition, or even accepting the fact that they weren't singers at all. Each of the alternative family designs contain similar weaknesses.

The common denominator in many of these alternate family designs is that children suffer due to a lack of stability, altruism, and commitment on the part of parents. Not only are children becoming less of a priority in our society, we have effectively declared war on them with many of the judicial rulings and policy decisions that have been made in recent decades. And the body count continues to rise.

Sun parents will love their children regardless of which of the eight circumstances formed that parental relationship, and I believe that sun parents can be found in each of these categories. There are moon and star people in each of them as well. But when we have the choice—which we all do—there is clearly a best option. The option that has all the advantages and provides the best circumstances for both parents and children to experience the greatest happiness and the least sorrow.

Decades of scientific research have repeatedly come to the same conclusion. This was eloquently summarized by author Carolyn Moynihan when she wrote, "Children are safest in the care of their own, married, loving parents. The further we are from that ideal the more likely they are to be in harm's way."

It goes without saying that giving life to children and nurturing them through the mounting difficulties and challenges of life is hard work. It takes a toll on every parent, especially sun parents. One theologian drew an inspired comparison between Godhood and parenthood when he wrote, "Giving life costs God something, as it costs us something." Sun parents understand that and wouldn't have it any other way. They understand that sun parenting requires sacrifice, it requires adjustments in our priorities, and it requires a commitment to making sun choices and setting a sun example for our children to follow.

Our Lives Are Our Legacy

In a radio interview shortly after the release of her record-breaking album *25,* British singer Adele spoke passionately about the importance of her role as a mother, how the experience has transformed her life, and that she would never let her career cause her to compromise on the priority of her parental responsibilities. She said that the choices she is making today will be the legacy she passes on to her son. "Careers have an end," she said, "but I'll always be a mum."

Yes, I realize that we do not live in an ideal world and that many believe we should not expect every child to have the advantages of being raised by their own loving, married parents. But we should certainly not abandon the effort to promote the ideal family option among the rising generation of future adults.

So, the contest is over and the winner has been announced. But if the winner is so obvious to everyone, then why am I bothering to bring this up at all?

The Most Important Word in the English Language

Several years ago, a wise man was asked, "What is the most important word in the English language?" After a thoughtful pause he replied, "The word is... *remember.*" The reason so many people are choosing less promising family design options when the winner is so clearly indicated is because we have forgotten the lessons of history and the counsel of history's greatest thinkers and inspired leaders.

As part of their ongoing effort to remind the citizens of the world of the importance of the natural family, The World Congress of Families meeting in Geneva, Switzerland in 1999 issued a declaration that included these statements:

> *We assemble in this World Congress, from many national, ethnic, cultural, social and religious communities, to affirm that*

the natural human family is established by the Creator and is essential to good society. The natural family is the foundational social unit, inscribed in human nature, and centered on the voluntary union of a man and a woman in the lifelong covenant of marriage. The natural family provides the optimal environment for the healthy development of children.

But there are many around the world, including many who are involved with the United Nations, who believe that the natural family is a male-dominated institution that abuses women and children and should be abandoned in favor of something more egalitarian. Rather than defending the natural family and supporting efforts to protect and sustain it, these moon-oriented thinkers believe the solution for men behaving badly toward women and children is to encourage–or even mandate–more women in the workforce, contraception, abortion, and the legalization of prostitution. They misguidedly see these policies as solutions to domestic violence, the under-appreciation of the roles of women in society, and the collapse of the family structure. This approach does nothing to invite more light and truth into those problematic cultures around the globe, nor does it encourage men to change the ways they see their roles as husbands and fathers. Instead, it encourages bad behavior and will only guarantee that weak men become weaker men, and good men find it even harder to remain good men. In recent years a sun solution to these problems has come from a very unlikely source– the poverty-stricken shanty-towns known as "favelas" of Rio de Janeiro.

In 1997 Dr. Gary Barker started an organization called *Promundo* in male-dominated and violence-prone Rio de Janeiro, Brazil to help teach men and boys how to be better husbands and fathers by joining with their wives in the care-giving responsibilities in their homes. The campaign is called *Men-care* and teaches men to value their wives as equals and to join with them in sharing the responsibilities of caring for their children. They also learn to value their roles as husbands and fathers, to develop stronger attachment bonds with their children, and in the process of caring for their children, they learn to take better care of themselves as well.

As PBS personality Bonnie Erbe said when referring to this program, "The final chapter in feminism is to bring men into the gender parody process." For sun men that has never been an issue. They have always been there. They understand the sun vision of the family.

Strengthening marriages and families by applying sun principles in our homes is what will solve the world's problems, not empowering governments to usurp the rights and responsibilities of parents. To paraphrase a line from a poem by William Ross Wallace, "The hands that rock the cradle are the hands we want ruling the world." We must remember what has been proven repeatedly throughout human history: that the application of sun principles as individuals, spouses, and parents is what produces a sun society.

Protect the Family

Noah built a ship designed by God to be both strong and flexible. He designed the natural family the same way. Some of the alternative designs are so frequently portrayed in the media that many have begun to accept them as equals to the natural family design, even though mounting scientific evidence clearly indicates otherwise. According to Allan C. Carlson, editor of *The Natural Family* and co-founder of the World Congress of Families, the result of that blurring of values is that we are now living in the latter years of a dying, sensate culture. Carlson wrote:

> *The term is Pitirim Sorokin's. It refers to a cycle of civilizational change, recurring over the centuries, where the truths of the natural family—just as other great truths behind a healthy culture—give way to an aggressive campaign to normalize and celebrate "chronically excessive, illicit, and disorderly sex activities." The signs of a late sensate culture, Sorokin explains, include low birth rates and diminished parental commitments; vastly increased erotic content in literature, film, and other media outlets; and high levels of divorce, abortion, pornography, promiscuity, homosexuality, and out-of-wedlock births. All this sounds too familiar.*

Sorokin argues that any significant change in the time-honored patterns of courtship, marriage, sexual relationships, and the care of children would have significant consequences for society. He asserts that "societies tend to blossom, be creative, and grow when the sexual mores favour exclusivity, monogamy, fidelity, responsibility, and family stability. Conversely, when mores encourage permissiveness, sexual exploration, serial monogamy, easy divorce, and brief and changeable family relationships (particularly with children), then societies become unstable and alienating, and they decline."

The Gold Standard

This chapter should in no way be considered a criticism of parents who are doing the best they can to raise their families under less-than-ideal circumstances. It is, however, intended to be a comparison of the various family designs and an unapologetic acknowledgement of the supremacy of the natural family and a promotion of it as the Gold Standard for mankind and clearly, the best option for children. If we as adults fail to teach our children the superiority of the natural family and to encourage the next generation to do everything within their power to pursue it as a goal and a model for their lives, we will find ourselves inching closer to an unstable and dysfunctional society; made that way because it is comprised of unstable and dysfunctional families.

Aldous Huxley's *Brave New World* describes a society without families at all; where children are conceived in laboratories, their fetal development is chemically manipulated, and they are psychologically conditioned from birth and raised to maturity without fathers or mothers. Even the terms *father* and *mother* are considered to be virtual obscenities in this seventh century A.F (After Ford) fantasy society.

Within a mere fifteen years after the publication of his book, Huxley was shocked to see how much closer the world had moved during that time toward his fantasy world becoming a reality. And shortly before his death on November 22, 1963 he was even more alarmed that his warnings about the direction the human race was taking had gone completely unheeded.

Brave New World envisions a civilization where the sexual act has been entirely separated from the process of procreation and from the expression of committed and bonded love. A world where the Prime Directive of Parenting has been replaced with the gospel of hedonism, self-importance, and instant gratification. A world where all of life's discomforts and challenges are ameliorated by a daily dose of *soma*–the bigger the challenge, the bigger the dose. I fear that many members of the Baby Boom generation who read *Brave New World* in the 1960s have mistakenly decided that Huxley's world is a desirable one and have not passed on to their children and grandchildren the values of the Greatest Generation that preceded them. We must correct that mistake if we are to prevent those sun values and beliefs from being forgotten. That is my request for your next activity.

Discuss the Prime Directive of Parenting and the Parental Oath of Office with your spouse and children. Ask those who know you best and whose opinions you trust to evaluate your parenting style and how it influences your role as quarterback, coach, cheerleader, and consultant in your children's lives. If it is not authoritative, study the lives of people like Booker Washington to learn how to make it more so.

> Captain's log: Star date 2021.9.
> *To the families of this world, we respectfully offer this time-tested and inspired advice. If you want to become a sun parent, raise a sun family, and create a sun society, these are the steps:*
> 1. *Become a sun person.*
> 2. *Marry a sun person.*
> 3. *Raise sun children by following the Prime Directive of Parenting.*
> *We shall return at an undisclosed time in your future to see how well it has been received. For now, live long and prosper.*
> *Kirk out.*

The next step on the journey to sunhood is creating a sun society where sun families can benefit from the companionship of other sun families. For sun principles to survive in a star-leaning world there must be communities where sun-seeking families can congregate and associate with others who are like-minded. For sun communities to thrive they must be founded on a sun system of government.

CHAPTER 6 Preview

Some believe the role of government is to maintain order in society–by whatever means necessary. Others believe the role of government is to protect freedom and that free people will voluntarily establish order. As one political scientist pointed out, freedom allows people to choose either order or chaos. If they choose chaos, governments will impose order. When the people tire of imposed order, they will desire freedom again. And when they cease to value freedom and begin to exercise it inappropriately, that society will return to chaos. And so it goes.

Some believe that freedom is a gift from God while others believe it is merely a human creation. Maybe that's why conversations about religion and politics tend to be so volatile–because both subjects reflect many of our most deeply held beliefs about our value, identity, and responsibilities as human beings. That also suggests a correlation between the two. That is, religion provides a set of beliefs and expectations that guide and govern our life choices, and governments decide whether people will be free to express those beliefs and make those choices.

The physical, emotional, social, and spiritual advancement of individuals and societies is only possible in an environment that allows this exercise of moral agency and promotes personal and collective responsibility. Both as individuals and as societies, freedom + responsibility = happiness. The opposite is also true. Where there is no personal freedom, few people are willing to accept responsibility for their actions. The result is conflict and misery. Every time. For that reason the system of government a nation adopts is critically important to the way its people will live their lives and shape their destinies.

There are multiple examples from history of how sun, moon, and star principles and values have shaped the cultures and destinies of communities and nations and I will explore just a few of them. While it is not my intention to add to the cacophony of strident voices extolling the virtues of liberal, conservative, libertarian, collectivist, or capitalistic political philosophies and policies, it *is* my intention to inform you about what sun, moon, and star values look like in the political realm, the kinds of governments those values typically produce, and to alert you to the past, present, and potential future consequences that will result from our political choices.

Multiple scriptural references indicate that divine judgement is not limited to individuals but that we are also held accountable for our actions as families, communities, and nations. Names like Babylon, Sodom, Nineveh, and Capernaum are a few that come to mind. So, if we want to establish a sun society we should be mindful that how we structure our government will have a significant impact on the outcome.

CHAPTER 6

3 KINDS OF CITIZENS

● ● ◑ ◖ ◖ ◖ ◖ ◖ ◖

Centuries ago, a group of committed sun people felt the deep desire to create a society based on sun principles where other like-minded people could gather. They built a city on a swampy piece of land that no one else wanted and within five years had created a sizable community that soon became the envy of the land. On one occasion, a curious member of government paid a visit to the community hoping to find out the secret to its success. During a meeting with its leader, the official asked how it was that he was able to govern such a diverse group of people and to preserve such perfect order and harmony, remarking that it was impossible for the government to do it anywhere else. The leader remarked that it was very easy to do that. "How?" responded the visitor, "To us it is very difficult." The leader replied, **"I teach them correct principles, and they govern themselves."**

Moral Agency and Self Government

I share this account to illustrate what I believe to be the single most important factor in defining the three kinds of governments that exist. Sun, moon, and star governments are determined by the degree to which a group of people and those in positions of leadership over them recognize and honor the freedom and moral agency of mankind and the responsibility of people to determine their own destinies. Moral agency is the freedom to choose our beliefs and our actions. With moral agency comes responsibility and accountability for those actions.

At the heart of a sun system of government is the belief in the ability, the right, and the responsibility of human beings to govern themselves. In 1854 Abraham Lincoln stated his support for this belief when he emphatically stated, "The doctrine of self-government is right–absolutely and eternally right." Sun people recognize that within *every* human being is the potential for growth and improvement–seeds of greatness–and that freedom and self-determination are necessary if those seeds are to take root and produce good fruit in our lives.

Sun people believe in the motto of the E.W. Scripps Company: "Give light, and the people will find their own way." Regardless of the contentions and propaganda that surround the question of which system of government is best, I believe that shedding a little light on the differences among sun, moon, and star systems of government will make the best choice obvious.

THE QUALITIES OF SUN GOVERNMENTS

The Fundamental Unit in a Sun Society
In 1831 Alexis de Tocqueville and a colleague were commissioned by the French government to study the American prison system in the hopes of improving the prison system in France. But Tocqueville was much more interested in what made the American people unique and their version of a democratic system of government so successful. For nine months he traveled through the developed areas of America studying the political, religious, and economic character of the American people. One of the most impressive things he noticed was the strength of American families and how they impacted American society in general. He wrote:

> *There is certainly no country in the world where the tie of marriage is so much respected as in America, or where conjugal*

happiness is more highly or worthily appreciated. In Europe almost all the disturbances of society arise from the irregularities of domestic life. To despise the natural bonds and legitimate pleasures of home is to contract a taste for excesses, a restlessness of heart, and the evil of fluctuating desires. Agitated by the tumultuous passions which frequently disturb his dwelling, the European is galled by the obedience which the legislative powers of the state exact. But when the American retires from the turmoil of public life to the bosom of his family, he finds in it the image of order and of peace. There his pleasures are simple and natural, his joys are innocent and calm, and he finds that an orderly life is the surest path to happiness. He accustoms himself without difficulty to moderate his opinions as well as his tastes. Whilst the European endeavors to forget his domestic troubles by agitating society, the American derives from his own home that love of order which he afterwards carries with him into public affairs.

Winston Churchill wrote, "There is no doubt that it is around the family and the home that all of the greatest virtues, the most dominating virtues of human society, are created, strengthened, and maintained." It is in sun families that we learn the merits of cooperation rather than competition, where we learn to serve and sacrifice for the welfare of others, and where we learn to appreciate the value of teamwork. Not because the government requires it, but because sun people are committed to it.

During his extensive travels Tocqueville learned that democracy was more than just a political system for Americans; it was a deeply-rooted culture, with religion at its foundation. He concluded that religion was the distinguishing influence that most strengthened and supported the family, and in turn, strengthened society. He wrote, "In the United States religion exercises but little influence upon the laws and upon the details of public opinion, but it directs the manners of the community, and by regulating domestic life, it regulates the State." Tocqueville observed that it was in American homes that religious principles were taught, where children learned to understand and practice those principles, and from whence they journeyed to share the efficacy of those principles with others.

The family is the fundamental unit in a sun society and a sun system of government fosters and protects the family. Pope John Paul II said, "As the family goes, so goes the nation, and so goes the whole world in which we live."

Education

> "A people who mean to be their own governors must arm themselves with the power that knowledge gives"–James Madison.

Sun governments do not just suddenly appear over night. They are the results of centuries of enlightened thinking and the application of sun principles among a group of people who pass a legacy of sun values on to future generations through the education process.

In America, many of the Founding Fathers realized how important education is to establish and maintain a sun system of government. Maintaining freedom requires an informed electorate. An informed electorate means a population of active citizens who take the privilege and responsibility of self-government seriously. They pay attention in civics classes. They not only learn the language and structure of the Declaration of Independence and the U. S. Constitution but ask probing questions about how and why our system of government came into existence. As students of history, an informed electorate can put the brilliance and inspiration of the Founding Fathers into historical perspective. They not only recognize the threats to freedom that existed in the past, they also recognize the threats that exist in the present, and will continue to exist in the future.

The Founding Fathers understood all too well how important active, informed citizens are to maintaining a free country because they also understood how quickly political power corrupts the morals and judgment of those who wield it. This need for attentive citizens was emphasized by Thomas Jefferson when he said in 1787 to Continental Congressman Edward Carrington, "If once the people become inattentive to the public affairs, you and I and Congress and assemblies, judges, and governors, shall all become wolves. It seems to be the law of our general nature, in spite of individual exceptions." For this reason, a sun government will work to make a good quality education available and attainable for all of its citizens.

Moral Values Are Essential to Create and Sustain A Sun Government

Understanding and committing to abide by sun principles is what makes sun governments possible. President John Adams offered an often-quoted warning to the American people when he wrote, "We have no government armed with power capable of contending with human passions unbridled by morality and religion…. Our constitution was made only for a moral and religious people. It is wholly inadequate to the government of any other." In a letter to his friend Mercy Warren, he wrote:

Public virtue cannot exist in a nation without private [virtue], and public virtue is the only foundation of Republics. But I have seen all along my life such selfishness and littleness even in New England, that I sometimes tremble to think that, although we are engaged in the best cause that ever employed the human heart, yet the prospect of success is doubtful; not for want of power or of wisdom, but of virtue.

In George Washington's farewell address upon leaving office, he counseled the American people, "Of all the habits and dispositions which lead to political prosperity, religion and morality are indispensable supports." John Quincy Adams likewise wrote about the basic religious tenets that are necessary to create moral values:

There are three points of doctrine which form the foundation of all morality. The first is the existence of God; the second is the immortality of the human soul; and the third is a future state of rewards and punishments. Suppose it possible for a man to disbelieve either of these three articles of faith and that man will have no conscience, he will have no other law than that of the tiger or the shark. The laws of man may bind him in chains or may put him to death, but they never can make him wise, virtuous, or happy.

It wasn't just the Founding Fathers who understood this important principle two hundred and fifty years ago. In 2010 political scientists Robert Putnam and David Campbell wrote:

> *By many different measures, religiously observant Americans are better neighbors and better citizens than secular Americans. They are more generous with their time and money, especially in helping the needy, and they are more active in community life.*

It is important to understand that there are differences between political freedom and moral agency. Sun people understand, as did Abraham Lincoln, that political freedom does not include a license to violate moral principles. Lincoln was often heard to say, "Some legal rights are moral wrongs." Similarly, Thomas Jefferson wrote in 1819 that "the people…are inherently independent of all but moral law."

> "Some legal rights are moral wrongs."-Abraham Lincoln

It is only when nations adopt laws and policies that are in harmony with moral principles and natural law that they can expect to be prosperous and happy. The truthfulness of that statement has been demonstrated repeatedly throughout history as we have observed the rise and fall of many great civilizations whose citizens have failed to recognize the connection between personal goodness and national greatness.

The Use of Power

Sun people are fearless leaders. They are willing to courageously face opposition in order to defend sun principles. They recognize that the war between good and evil must be fought, but they also understand that there are sun, moon, and star ways to wage it. Like the character Ender Wiggins from the movie *Ender's Game,* they are committed to the belief that "the *way* we win, matters."

Sun people use their knowledge and influence for the betterment of others, not for self-aggrandizement. They do honorable things without seeking for honor. And while sun leaders do not elevate themselves above the people they serve, they also do not allow themselves to become subjected to emotional contagion by the masses or to be coerced or flattered into making decisions that violate their consciences. They are the embodiment of the slogan, "Only those who do not seek for power are fit to hold it."

Sun leaders are also makers of men…and women. Their goal is to elevate, not subjugate. Much of their time is spent preparing future leaders by instilling the knowledge, values, and sense of commitment those leaders will need to maintain a sun society long after the first generation of leaders have gone. You could say that sun leaders make excellent relay runners. They always run the first leg of the race. Then, through years of practice and preparation with their team members, they are able to pass the baton with precision and confidence onto the next generation of leaders, who in turn pass it on to their successors.

Selecting sun leaders who will model sun principles is essential for the establishment and survival of sun governments. James Madison—the primary architect of the U.S. Constitution—understood this and cautioned American voters to keep in mind that there are three kinds of people with three reasons for seeking public office: (1) to serve the public good, (2) to pursue personal interests, or (3) to feed their ambition to gain power and prominence. Sun, moon, and star.

Bonds of Affection Hold Sun Societies Together

But just having sun leaders is not enough. Sun societies exist because there is a mutual commitment on the part of those who govern and those who are governed, to sun principles.

In 1856 Abraham Lincoln said, "Every nation has a central idea from which all minor thoughts radiate." For him, the central idea that made America so exceptional was the belief in human equality. And he believed that a nation's commitment to the principle of equality is best demonstrated by practicing the principle of charity.

The importance of charity in establishing a free, equal, and harmonious society was emphasized by John Winthrop, the first governor of the Massachusetts Bay Colony. He brought a group of Puritans to America in

1630 and wrote a sermon entitled, "A Model of Christian Charity" aboard the ship *Arbella* during the voyage. He built a strong case for why a mutual commitment to this Christian principle was essential to the colony's success and to accomplishing America's destiny as a "city upon a hill" and a bastion of freedom.

Political science scholar Matthew Holland described charity as "a single principle with a dual dimension: a clear *vertical* axis–humans in a loving relationship to God–and a clear *horizontal* axis–humans in a loving relationship to other humans."

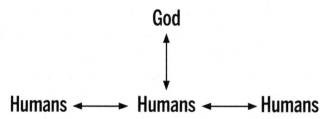

It was Abraham Lincoln who expanded upon Winthrop's expressly Christian view of charity to describe a slightly more secular *civic* charity. Matthew Holland defined Lincoln's view of civic charity as a "generous and forgiving affection among citizens at the same time that it recognizes and vigorously protects the individual as an inherently free being." In his first inaugural address, Lincoln promoted the practice of this civic charity, believing that doing so would strengthen the bonds of affection among U.S citizens; bonds that unite and protect a sun society from the moon and star forces he could see were trying to divide it.

The Law

One of the most outstanding proponents of sun philosophies of government in the last three centuries was nineteenth century French economist and political theorist Claude Frederic Bastiat. His legendary composition *The Parable of the Broken Window* is a brilliantly simple example of freedom-inspired economic policies. But his most significant contribution to the cause of liberty was his brief treatise entitled *The Law*.

Bastiat loved liberty and he understood that government can be the best friend of liberty, or its worst enemy. It all depends on how the law is used.

He believed, as did the Founding Fathers, that each person possesses a God-given right to defend life, liberty, and property–by force if necessary–and that governments are authorized by the consent of the governed to pass laws that are intended to do that. American Founding Father James Madison reminded us, "If men were angels, they would not need governments." But since the "better angels among us" continue to be in the minority, governments are a necessity.

The problems begin when those in positions of leadership in the government begin to think that their authority extends beyond what has been delegated to them by the people and that their accumulated wisdom exceeds the combined wisdom of the rest of society. Then they start concocting ways to "improve" the lives of citizens. They do that by usurping some of those God-given rights and responsibilities that the people possess and using the law to bestow those rights and responsibilities upon themselves. The laws in sun societies are there to promote freedom and self-reliance among their citizens, not dependence on government. They exist to encourage the people to embrace sun principles and practices, not compel them to.

To summarize, sun governments honor and protect freedom of conscience and freedom of choice, but those choices are subject to certain moral limitations in a sun society. A sun system of government requires a *voluntary* commitment to sun principles by its leaders and citizens or it is no longer a sun system of government. In 1863, pioneer leader Brigham Young said, "The government of heaven, if wickedly administered, would become one of the worst governments upon the face of the earth. No matter how good a government is, unless it is administered by righteous people, an evil government will be made of it." To paraphrase T.S Eliot, there is no system of government so perfect that the people do not need to be good. Even the best forms of government cannot protect moon and star people from themselves.

THE QUALITIES OF MOON GOVERNMENTS

> *"From those according to their abilities, to those according to their needs"*
> -The Communist Manifesto

The Fundamental Unit in a Moon Society

Since the family is the primary unit of society, a system of government that makes any other entity the fundamental unit is not going to produce a sun society. Those other entities include the individual, the corporation, the church, or the state.

The Individual

An individualistic society is founded on the principles of moral relativism and social Darwinism which assert that: (1) right and wrong are fluid concepts that each person is free to define; and (2) stronger members of society have nature's permission to dominate–and eliminate, if need be–the weaker members. This is not conducive to a peaceful, thriving, or orderly community. It discourages conformity to morally appropriate social norms, values, and standards. It promotes isolation and competition rather than interdependency and it makes self-interest the primary interest. In their book *The Natural Family: A Manifesto*, authors Allan Carlson and Paul Mero point out, "Such a community of self-interest cannot preserve freedom over the long haul." A free society requires a shared vision, shared values, and shared goals if it is to succeed.

Moon governments tend to mistakenly believe that just providing for the temporal needs of the people is all that is necessary to create a harmonious society. But focusing on temporal needs alone can quickly create competition among individuals–between *my* needs vs. *your* needs. That breaks down the attachment bonds within families and communities, which in turn is destabilizing to society in general. This can eventually lead to anarchy where the individual becomes a law unto himself and society splinters into smaller tribes and factions. Anarchy is usually followed by dictatorship and tyranny because a fractured society will soon look for a strong leader to restore order and economic stability. Carlson and Mero explained, "What those societies come to understand is that the individual is incomplete. And a society of individuals is just as incomplete."

The Corporation

The corporation is an artificial, immortal "person." A Frankenstein-ish creation of the state that exists primarily for two purposes: (1) to conduct business transactions and thereby (2) make money. It is a soulless creation that has no conscience or moral standards of its own, but only those that are imposed upon it by its creators. Economist Milton Friedman declared, "The business of business, is business." He emphasized that the role of business is to maximize profits, not promote social welfare, maintain families, or even advance the well-being of employees and administrators.

From this perspective, the only thing that would prevent corporations from doing harm to people would be the consciences of those who regulate them. That puts a tremendous amount of power in the hands of very few people. Carlson and Mero stated:

> Were we to place the corporation at the center of our society, we would find ourselves in a world lacking in order, beauty, and grace. We would find ourselves competing with other family members and neighbors in a setting of social Darwinism that would divide rather than unify. Our culture, too, would be fiercely competitive, creating a portrait of "haves" and "have nots" painted not only on an economic canvas, but everywhere. An environment in which money alone made something right, or its lack made something wrong.

This is not to suggest that everything about corporations is bad. They create jobs for working people and returns for investors. It's just that building a society that is founded primarily on making money is a moon society that is likely to degenerate very quickly into a star one. This is especially likely when corporate leviathans conspire with politicians and bureaucrats to create deep state situations where the real political power is wielded behind the scenes by a wealthy oligarchy, outside of the view of the voting public and the checks and balances that governments are intended to provide.

The Church

Most people would say that the purpose of religion is to bring out the best in people, or at least, to invite them to become better. The church encourages people to aspire to higher standards of moral living that include generosity, sacrifice, and service by caring for the needs of others who are less fortunate. It teaches its adherents the principles of long-suffering and patience. It also teaches self-discipline, self-restraint, healthy living, and self-reliance. Regarding the church's perspectives on economics, Carlson and Mero wrote:

> The church transcends the narrow and selfish demeanor of homo economicus. The divine economy has a different purpose and structure in which the marketplace is irrelevant and money holds no value. Instead, the church relies on altruism, or selfless giving based on love and duty. Rejecting raw materialism, the church focuses instead on matters of the spirit. In place of money, the church delivers compassion, charity, and personal care.

That is not to say that churches should take no interest in material things. Adequate food, clothing, shelter, and the employment opportunities needed to afford those things are necessary for a thriving spiritual community, and churches would want to see that all of those basic human needs are met.

But with three kinds of people in the world, you will find that there are also three kinds of religions—or at least, three kinds of people practicing the world's religions. In moon religions, truth and error are intertwined. One example is the tendency for some churches to focus on prosperity theology more than on the gospel principles of faith, hope, and charity. For others, freedom of conscience is compromised by an authoritarian demand for conformity, which can lead to discrimination and exclusion.

If one religion was selected to become the governing force in a country, its doctrines might leave little room for diversity of thought or variation in application. That would lead to religious conflicts and even wars within that society, which has occurred repeatedly throughout history. In 1787 James Madison recognized the risks involved in making the church the fundamental unit in society when he wrote, "Who does not see that the same authority which can establish Christianity, in exclusion of all other religions, may establish with the same ease, any particular sect of Christians in exclusion of all other sects?" Madison understood the problem because that is exactly what had already happened in eight of the original thirteen colonies where discrimination and persecution were practiced by various religious sects against other religious sects–groups who had originally come to America to escape religious persecution in Europe.

In star religions like those practiced at Jonestown in Guyana or in radical Islamic states, membership means exploitation, and dissent equals death. A star religion would extinguish both freedom of thought and variety of religious expression. Instead of shepherding their flock, in a star society, the church would be policing them.

Unless sun principles are the basis for the religious doctrine, a government with the church as the fundamental unit of society is not likely to allow its citizens the free exercise of moral agency. Neither does a government where the state is the fundamental unit of society.

The State

In societies where the state is the fundamental unit of society, those who govern believe that all rights come from the state rather than from a higher power. Because of this, they will inevitably begin to usurp the authority of both the church and the family. Loyalty to God is mocked and replaced by loyalty to the fatherland, the motherland, *der Führer*, the Supreme Council of Elders, the Grand Pooh Bah, or whatever other political entity has power. The divinely appointed rights of parents to decide what is best for their children are soon abrogated by the secular power of the state-sponsored "village."

In an effort to make society more efficient, secure, and productive, the all-powerful state begins to exercise more restrictions on personal and parental rights and to intervene into business, industry, education, agriculture, social services, natural resources, and virtually every area of economic, political, and personal life. Like a camel poking its nose into the family tent, eventually the whole camel is standing in the living room. And once it gets inside, it's hard to get it out.

It was this situation that Supreme Court Justice William Brandeis warned about in 1928 when he wrote:

> *Experience should teach us to be most on our guard to protect liberty when the government's purposes are beneficial. Men born to freedom are naturally alert to repel invasion of their liberty by evil-minded rulers. The greater dangers to liberty lurk in insidious encroachment by men of zeal, well meaning, but without understanding.*

As the Chief Elder of the utopian society depicted in the movie *The Giver* stated, "People are weak. People are selfish. When people have the freedom to choose, they choose wrong, every time." That is typically the assumption when the state is in charge. That statement is from a fictional account of a futuristic world that doesn't exist. However, the next statement I will quote is not. It occurred during a meeting that took place in Washington, D.C. in the summer of 2013.

Three is Plenty

A group of senior executives from companies involved in the financial services industry and representatives from the government agencies that regulate them, meet annually for a conference in Washington, D.C. to discuss the future of the pre-paid bank card industry. Several companies were represented who have either already been in that business for some time, or who were looking to get a foothold in it. Some were offering some new and innovative prepaid bank card products that they explained would significantly benefit the public as well as make a profit for their company and create jobs in the process.

During the meeting, representatives from the federal government agencies spoke to the assembled group and said, in effect, "The American people don't understand this product and there are just too many options to choose from. Since we don't believe the American people can make good choices, we're going to limit their choices. We are limiting the number of companies that will be allowed to offer these products and the kinds of products they can introduce." One shocked audience member shouted, "THIS IS FACISM!" Even the companies who stood to benefit from the government restrictions sat in stunned silence at the announcement.

The Bureau of Financial Consumer Protection (BFCP) was established as part of the Dodd-Frank Wall Street Reform and Consumer Protection Act of 2010 to "stop unfair, deceptive, and fraudulent business practices by collecting complaints, conducting investigations, suing companies and people that break the law, developing rules to maintain a fair marketplace, and educating consumers and businesses about their rights and responsibilities." It is an independent bureau within the Federal Reserve System and is funded by the Federal Reserve, not by the federal government. It is therefore, not under the government's control. It has the authority to not only create its own rules, but to enforce them as well.

This has become a common occurrence with federal agencies in recent decades. If there is nothing "unfair, deceptive, or fraudulent" going on with pre-paid bank cards, why is the Bureau allowed to restrict this industry? Because, in the name of consumer protection, order, and efficiency, a moon government can easily justify actions that most people would consider to be a violation of the free enterprise system, democratic principles, and our constitutionally-protected rights–a concrete example of what Justice Brandeis was warning us about.

A friend who attended the conference described it this way: "It's like the government deciding that the people have too many choices of cereal. We're going to limit the choices of cereals to Cheerios, Kellogg's Corn Flakes, and Grape-Nuts. Ten cereals are too many. People will be happier not having to deal with so many choices. Three is plenty."

This kind of government control stifles innovation and competition and eventually results in the production of only three varieties of "cereal"–cereal that gradually begins to taste less and less palatable, is made with increasingly inferior quality ingredients, has ever-diminishing food value, and from time to time is subject to limited availability.

Given the savings and loan debacle of the 1980s and the banking abuses that led to the 2008 recession, I can see why people would see the need for government to step in and increase their regulation of the banking industry.

But as author Peter Whybrow pointed out in his book *The Well-Tuned Brain*, the real source of the problem is this: "**As personal moral regulation by individual members of society declines, more social control falls into the hands of federal, state, and municipal government agencies.**" In other words, the more irresponsible people become and the more self-indulgent "marshmallows" we eat, the more governments will begin to regulate "marshmallow" production and distribution, along with everything else.

Whybrow's statement reminds us that the choices we make as individuals, spouses, and parents will determine the kind of governments we create and the amount of control those governments will exercise over their citizens.

The problem with giving more power to government agencies and unelected bureaucrats is that it takes power away from the people and their elected representatives. Giving anyone more power and less accountability invites the likelihood of corruption. And as Whybrow's comment implies, the more corruption increases among the general public, the faster it will increase among those who seek power. This contributes to an exponential increase in the general pace of moral decline.

Trust Us. It's All for the Best

When the state becomes the fundamental unit of society it is hoping that the people will eventually begin to believe that the state really *does* offer solutions to all their problems and that politicians should be the ones making the decisions rather than the people. As Carlson and Mero point out:

> *The state sees need and want. It sees unhappiness and disease. It sees starvation and poverty, classes and conscience, waste and destruction, greed and envy. It sees the crushing burden of tradition. And it asks why such things must exist? Surely it can be called upon to intercede, to fix what is broken. After all, it has the power to fix everything!*

If that happens, the people will begin to increasingly rely on the state to take care of their needs rather than relying on themselves and their families. They will soon forget that liberty requires sacrifice, hard work, and self-reliance. The people will voluntarily begin to surrender their freedom, their property, and their opportunities for tomorrow, in exchange for the promise of efficiency and economic security, today. Slavery–even when entered into voluntarily–is still slavery. And who wants to live in that state?

Nikita Khrushchev's Son Lives in Rhode Island

Karl Marx advocated for a gradual societal shift from capitalism to socialism to communism–sun to moon to star. It was Soviet Premier Nikita Khrushchev who provided a description of how this process can occur in a society. It happened during a visit to the United States in 1959 at the invitation of President Dwight D. Eisenhower. The President asked Secretary of Agriculture Ezra T. Benson to meet with Khrushchev to discuss agricultural issues. Despite disagreeing with the President's decision to invite Khrushchev to see democracy at work in the U.S., Benson respectfully agreed to Eisenhower's request.

During a conversation with Benson, Khrushchev gloatingly remarked, "Your grandchildren will one day live under communism." Benson replied that he would do everything in his power to see to it that his grandchildren– and Khrushchev's grandchildren–would live under freedom. In an address given by Secretary Benson on October 25, 1966, he said Khrushchev's response was, in substance, "You Americans are so gullible. No, you won't accept communism outright, but we will keep feeding you small doses of socialism until you finally wake up and find you already have communism. We won't have to fight you. We'll so weaken your economy until you fall like over-ripe fruit into our hands." However, the truth is that the citizens of every communist nation have always dreamed of living under the kind of freedom that Americans have enjoyed for over two centuries. We hear that sentiment expressed repeatedly today among the people in totalitarian-governed countries throughout the world. And speaking of fruit, the triumphant outcomes prophesied by various socialist philosophers and communist leaders over the last century have never come to fruition. That's why Nikita Khrushchev's son Sergei moved to Rhode Island. Touché Mr. Benson.

The Reign of Virtue?

In retrospect, we can see how America's sun system of republican government emerged out of the darkness of the centuries that preceded it. In 1776, the Declaration of Independence outlined the principles upon which a sun system of government would be founded and a revolutionary war was fought to defend them. But it was the Constitution of the United States that endeavored to put those principles into practice. Americans could hold up their new constitution to the world as proof that freedom need not be an enemy to order and that human beings were truly capable of self-government. Hoping to duplicate the successful initiative of the American colonies, the politically and economically beleaguered French followed with a declaration of their own.

Drawing heavily from the writings of Thomas Jefferson, George Mason, and James Madison, the French National Constituent Assembly issued the Declaration of the Rights of Man and of the Citizen in 1789. It likewise identified "the natural and imprescriptible rights of man" to life, liberty, property, and security. It protected freedom of opinion, speech, and religious expression.

But what the French Declaration contained in form, French society very much lacked in substance—especially some of its leaders. One of the primary figures in the revolution was Maximilien Robespierre, who wrote, "The principle of the republican government is virtue, and the means required to establish virtue, is terror."

Terror? How could any supposedly "enlightened" person associate the terms *virtue* and *terror* in the same sentence? But between the spring of 1793 and the fall of 1794—a time known as The Terror—thousands of French leaders, dignitaries, intellectuals, priests, and average citizens were rounded up under suspicion of committing "crimes against liberty." Anyone who was perceived as a potential enemy of the revolution and its over-zealous leaders, was rushed through the Revolutionary Tribunal's mock version of a trial and sent off to a speedy appointment with "Madame Guillotine."

For those revolutionaries who didn't want to waste time with the slow pace of a trial and individual executions, whole villages of men, women, and children were eliminated by means of mass shootings and drownings.

One French scholar later remarked that if this radical revolutionary group known as the Jacobins had possessed the gas chamber, "there is no reason to doubt that they would have used it." The inalienable natural rights of all mankind and the rule of law to which the French Declaration professed such allegiance were ignored and trampled underfoot.

In speaking of the French Revolution, political theorist Edmund Burke said that rather than building a new and better French society, "all it accomplished was a cart load of headless corpses and a tyrant,"–that tyrant being Napoleon Bonaparte.

The Difference That Makes All the Difference

How could two revolutions that were supposedly based on similar principles, conducted by people who supposedly espoused similar values, and that were supposedly intended to protect the natural rights of all people and regenerate human society with a new and improved system of government, produce such different results?

Political science scholar Ralph Hancock wrote, "The most fundamental difference between the American Declaration of Independence of 1776 and the French Declaration of 1789 is the willingness of the former to ground human rights in the laws of nature and nature's God."

The Founding Fathers–Alexander Hamilton in particular–wrote extensively about Natural Law. They believed it to be higher than human law, and the standard for evaluating the correctness of all human laws. The French revolutionaries rejected Natural Law because they had rejected nature's God.

They were not just indifferent to religion; they were openly antagonistic toward it. Many French revolutionaries insisted that Catholic priests swear an oath of allegiance to the revolution that was intended to supersede their vows of obedience to God. Hundreds of priests were murdered in their monasteries and cathedrals were desecrated and destroyed. In 1793, radical members of the state-sponsored atheistic Cult of Reason dismantled the altar in the Cathedral of Notre Dame in Paris and replaced it with an altar dedicated to the Goddess of Reason.

Compare the beliefs of the French leaders to those of the Founding Fathers in America who repeatedly acknowledged their dependence on divine intervention and direction if they were to successfully create and preserve a sun system of government. They believed divine intervention was not only desirable, but possible. And not only possible, but readily accessible, given the examples of it they had personally witnessed during the Revolutionary War.

The French leaders believed that human wisdom, unaided by divine direction, was sufficient for France to duplicate what America had done. They believed the Wise Mind application of reason alone would produce the same results. They quickly learned that reason fails in the face of fanaticism.

The doctrines of the Judeo-Christian God had been rejected in the minds of many European philosophers who now called for devotion to a new deity–The People. In their minds, it was the nation that deserved allegiance, not the monarch, the law, or God. Virtually any action could be justified if this all-powerful and infallible new deity willed it.

But the doctrines of this newly minted religion were merely the social constructions of flawed human reasoning and were subject to the whims of this fickle new deity and its self-appointed prophets. As a result, many of the people who started the French Revolution and employed the "National Razor" as its instrument of enforcement, soon became victims of it themselves.

The French Revolution was a critical turning point in European social and political history. It was an opportunity for Europe to join America in correcting the long-established problems that monarchial rule, feudalism, and religious intolerance had generated for centuries. If they had gotten it right, Europe might have avoided the two world wars that engulfed it in the twentieth century and claimed the lives of over sixty-five million of its people. Sadly, that didn't happen.

Sun Talking, Moon Walking

Instead, nineteenth-century political theorists Karl Marx and Friedrich Engels offered socialism and communism as solutions to the injustice and economic inequality that the poor working-class people were experiencing in much of the world.

Socialism grew out of evolutionary theory and the claim that human beings–and therefore, human societies–are evolving, and that the autonomy of individual human beings is less important than the functionality of the societies they compose.

The Oxford English Dictionary defines socialism as: "A political and economic theory of social organization which advocates that the means of production, distribution, and exchange should be owned or regulated by the community as a whole." The new deity–The People–with its ambiguous doctrines and fickle disposition, would control everything. How ironic that a political philosophy that adamantly rejected the existence of any higher power in the universe, would forcefully dethrone one deity, only to substitute a clearly inferior one in its place.

Like all moon systems of government, there is a combination of truth and error in the design and implementation of this form of government. Wanting to correct the inequality, injustice, greed, and abuse of power that have existed throughout human history is a good thing. But designing moon and star systems of government and employing moon and star methods to implement them will never produce what was intended. It's like Michael Jackson doing the Moonwalk: there is the illusion of walking forward, but in reality, he is walking backward the whole time. Despite their good intentions, it would be a big mistake to follow these "backward walking" leaders.

Brilliant nineteenth century American trial lawyer and two-time Secretary of State Daniel Webster warned about trusting misguided leaders when he wrote:

> *Good intentions will always be pleaded for every assumption of authority. It is hardly too strong to say that the Constitution was made to guard the people against the dangers of good intentions. There are men in all ages who mean to govern well, but they mean to govern. They promise to be good masters, but they mean to be masters.*

Impassioned utopian speeches were made about a collectivist system of government that promised to recognize the equality of all its citizens, protect workers from exploitation by greedy landowners and businessmen, and promote the general welfare of all its people. The disciples of Marx believed that allowing the state the power to implement these changes would cause a change of heart among the leaders and the people, promoting less egoism and more harmony among them. They were convinced that it would free the human heart of greed and selfishness; bring hope, peace, and prosperity to countries globally; eliminate idleness; and promote hard work, thrift, and self-respect. If all people were sun people, they might have a point. But if all people were sun people, there would have been no need for a new system of government. Sun people would have already solved the problems of social injustice and inequality long before. Regrettably, the nineteenth-century world had not yet experienced the real consequences of socialism that the twentieth-century world was about to.

Suddenly or Gradually

The two options for implementing socialism are revolutionary socialism or evolutionary socialism. Revolutionary socialism involves the taking of power by means of a sudden and violent revolution and is usually followed by mass executions of those who oppose the new regime. Communism fits that description. Definitely a star option. Evolutionary socialism involves a more gradual transition as political leaders and citizens become convinced that socialism will solve their social problems and they begin to pass laws that implement socialistic principles. That would be a moon option, and I'll explain why.

Sewer Socialism

Support for socialism was mounting in several countries in the early twentieth century, including the United States. The country had begun to shift from an agrarian society to an urban, industrial, and modernized one. Wealth–and the power that comes with it–was becoming concentrated in the hands of fewer people. With those social changes came worsening social problems:

economic insecurity, corruption, and racial and ethnic discrimination. Another issue of concern was sewage.

For years, all of Milwaukee, Wisconsin's raw sewage and chemical waste from manufacturing was being dumped into the nearby rivers that emptied into Lake Michigan, polluting the water and creating significant health hazards. In 1910, the nation's first socialist mayor and city council were elected to solve the problem. The leaders proposed and implemented plans for a community-owned sewage and water treatment system—something that had never been done previously.

Sewage wasn't the only thing that smelled bad in Milwaukee. The police department was rotten too. Corrupt police officials and officers were fired and better-trained, more community-conscious officers were put in their place. Crime rates dropped significantly. Milwaukee was on a roll.

Since nearly all of the beachfront properties were owned by wealthy families, city leaders decided to dredge Lake Michigan and create new publicly-owned parks and beaches that working-class families could enjoy. By applying frugal economic policies, they reduced the cost of garbage collection for the community. They promoted civil rights for minorities, public housing, unemployment insurance, workman's compensation for injured workers, minimum wage laws, an eight-hour work day, and old age pensions for the elderly. They cooperated with industry leaders and business owners rather than competing with them. The entire community worked together with a shared commitment to making changes that benefitted everyone—rich and poor alike. As a result, Milwaukee soon became known as the healthiest, safest, and best-managed city in the country.

But the members of the Socialist Party of America weren't satisfied with what they mockingly referred to as "sewer socialism" as practiced in Milwaukee. They wanted the state to have more control over everything associated with the nation's economy. Even the occupants of The White House couldn't agree on what was best for America. Progressive President Woodrow Wilson openly attacked the separation of powers provision of the U.S. Constitution and maligned The Declaration of Independence, telling members of the Thomas Jefferson Club of Los Angeles in 1911, "If you want to understand the real Declaration of Independence, do not repeat

262 | SHINE Brighter

the preface." (He seemed to be unappreciative of the fact that it is in these opening sentences that the founders enumerated the fundamental principles upon which the nation was founded: the equality of mankind, that all human beings are endowed by their Creator with certain unalienable rights, and of the limited role of government in protecting those rights.)

Fifteen years later, President Calvin Coolidge responded to Wilson's comments when he remarked:

> *About the Declaration, there is a finality that is exceedingly restful. It is often asserted that the world has made a great deal of progress since 1776 and that we have had new thoughts and new experiences which have given us a great advance over the people of that day and that we may therefore very well discard their conclusions for something more modern. But that reasoning cannot be applied to this great charter. If all men are created equal, that is final. If they are endowed with unalienable rights, that is final. If governments derive their just powers from the consent of the governed, that is final. No advance, no progress can be made beyond these propositions. If anyone wishes to deny their truth or their soundness, the only direction he can proceed historically is not forward, but backward toward the time when there was no equality, no rights of the individual, no rule of the people. Those who wish to proceed in that direction cannot lay claim to progress. They are reactionary. Their ideas are not more modern, but more ancient than those of the Revolutionary fathers.*

But during the politically-turbulent and economically-depressed 1930s, more Americans were willing to consider what many forward-thinking Milwaukeeans had recommended decades before. When Franklin D. Roosevelt introduced his New Deal for America, there was very little in it that was new. It primarily contained ideas and policies that had been proposed by the "sewer socialists" of Milwaukee years before–many of which were supported by Republican and Democrats alike and were eventually implemented into federal law. The difference was that local Milwaukee leaders recognized the limits of socialistic principles that many leaders at the federal level did not.

While Progressives believed that the role of government was to do for the people what they were unable to do for themselves, socialists believed that the role of government was to do for the people what they were *unwilling* to do for themselves—a very different and much more repressive political ideology.

Roosevelt's intention was to have government assume greater control of business, industry, agriculture, and many other aspects of the country's economic life. He believed that doing so would provide greater economic stability and security for the masses. His plan included giving some of the law-making authority of Congress to a cadre of executive agencies run by unelected bureaucrats, outside of the disciplinary reach of the people and their elected officials.

In FDR's mind, the three branches of government were like three horses harnessed together which he believed should be pulling in unison to implement the wishes of the people. However, determining what those wishes *were* would be the job of the person holding the reigns and driving the team—FDR, and his successors in the White House.

He went so far as to suggest that the Bill of Rights the founders included in the Constitution was insufficient and offered his "Second Bill of Rights" that included rights to a comfortable home, a profitable job, and recreation. I appreciate the sentiment and his genuine concern for the welfare of the working class, but government officials have neither the responsibility, the authority, nor the ability to fulfill such promises, and it's misleading to suggest that they can. (Another example of what William Brandeis and Daniel Webster both warned about.)

United States Senator Huey Long's *Share Our Wealth* movement wanted to give the state virtually unlimited power to guarantee a more equitable distribution of the nation's wealth, believing that individual property rights must yield to the needs of social justice. (On January 15, 1964 President Lyndon Johnson voiced a similar intention when he initiated his plans for the Great Society and the War on Poverty and said, "We are going to try to take all the money that we think is unnecessarily being spent and take it from the 'haves' and give it to the 'have nots' that need it so much.")

Even well-respected American Protestant theologian Reinhold Niebuhr joined the Socialist Party of America in the 1930s and began expressing his concerns that religious faith was not a sufficient influence in American society to eliminate injustice and inequality. He wrote:

> *It is therefore revealed that no inner checks are powerful enough to bring them [the people] under complete control. Social control must consequently be attempted; and it cannot be established without social conflict.... The inequality within and between nations will require desperate devices to preserve any sense of national unity and prevent global conflict and destruction from occurring.... But political strategy without religious morality may therefore substitute new forms of injustice for old ones and enthrone a new tyranny on the throne of the old.*

Niebuhr struggled to find a way to honor individual freedom while achieving social justice. But he had lost confidence in the wisdom of the Founding Fathers who emphasized that the key to social order and justice in a society is for each citizen to maintain an active, educated, and spiritually-informed personal conscience–an Inspired Mind, sun conscience. He may also have forgotten a basic tenant of the Christian faith he espoused–a tenant expressed in a hymn written in 1805 by an unknown author that proclaims:

> *Know this that every soul is free to choose his life and what he'll be;*
> *For this eternal truth is given, that God will force no man to heaven.*
> *He'll call, persuade, direct aright and bless with wisdom, love, and light.*
> *In nameless ways be good and kind, but never force the human mind.*

While Niebuhr may have acknowledged that living by sun principles must be a voluntary choice and that "God will force no man to heaven," he apparently believed that governments should be allowed to try. But you don't convert people to sun living through the use of force. The Crusades and the Spanish Inquisition demonstrated that.

While he felt that non-violence was to be preferred, he feared that it was not always effective, leaving coercion and violence as justifiable alternatives to achieve social justice. But what kind of justice? Niebuhr himself acknowledged, "Justice achieved through the use of unjust methods soon becomes injustice in time. Any justice which is *only* justice, soon degenerates into something *less* than justice."

Socialist leaders defended their behaviors by invoking the philosophy of Niccolò Machiavelli who argued in his classic novel *The Prince*, "A leader cannot observe all those things for which men are held good, since he is under a necessity, to maintain his state, of acting against faith, against charity, against humanity, against religion." Matthew Holland wrote, "For Machiavelli, the defining characteristic of a successful modern leader is knowing how to enter into evil when forced by necessity." German sociologist Max Weber went still further by suggesting that violence was a necessary part of *all* political rule. But by definition, justifying the use of evil to accomplish some perceived good would make such a person a moon leader at best, and the public moon people for allowing it to happen.

What transformed the community of Milwaukee was not the political system and ideology called socialism. What transformed Milwaukee was a shared commitment to the sun principle of *stewardship* among the citizens of that community.

In a 1961 newspaper article, editor William Evjue described those early twentieth century Wisconsin legislators as individuals who "never were approached by the lobbyists because the lobbyists knew it was not possible to influence these men. They were incorruptible."

There were enough self-government-loving sun people living in Milwaukee at that time to elect sun people to office who were committed stewards of the common resources of that city. All were committed to the best interests of the entire community. All believed–as did Markel Karamazov–

that "each of us is responsible to all men, for all men, and for everything." They did not punish the wealthy for their success, nor enable helplessness and dependency among the poor. There were high levels of responsibility and accountability among the citizens of Milwaukee.

Nevertheless, the FDR-era developments gave fledgling American socialists some hope that political thinking at the federal level was moving in their direction. But all of that changed after World War II when the Cold War began and the murderous, freedom-crushing regime of Joseph Stalin was exposed by–of all people–his successor, Nikita Khrushchev.

Behind the rhetoric of freedom and equality, the true nature of socialism and communism now became more apparent. Lesson learned, right? Not necessarily.

"Socialism: The Failed Idea That Never Dies"–Kristian Niemietz, PhD

Sun systems of government work because citizens are taught correct principles and they govern themselves through hard work and voluntary participation in the civic process. Freedom and responsibility go hand in hand. As I explained the relationship between vulnerability and intimacy/trust in chapter four with the HOUSE model, so it is with freedom and responsibility: you cannot have one without the other.

But with each successive generation there seem to be more people who have forgotten–or never been taught–these important lessons from the past as outlined by political commentator Daniel Mitchell:

1. You cannot legislate the poor into prosperity by legislating the wealthy out of prosperity.
2. What one person receives without working for, another person must work for without receiving.
3. The government cannot give to anybody anything that the government does not first take from somebody else.
4. You cannot multiply wealth by dividing it.

Moon governments employ what some have referred to as "compulsory benevolence" and "false philanthropy." Bastiat called it "legal plunder" when the government authorizes itself to take the possessions of one person and give them to another, regardless of whatever good intentions may be cited to justify it. Benjamin Franklin warned the American people against this practice in the formative years of the new republic. Reasonable and limited taxation is one thing, he explained. Ever-increasing legal plunder is another. Bastiat and Franklin clearly understood the difference, and so should we.

The result of legal plunder is not equality or prosperity, but a phenomenon known as "leveling down." Rather than improving the standard of living for all the people, it worsens it. Everyone suffers, except the elite group of people in power.

100% Responsibility 0% Excuses

The conflict between twenty-first century "haves" and "have nots" is escalating. Politicians who promise universal health care, a free college education, and state-sponsored free childcare that "the rich" will be forced to pay for are attracting more support from a rising generation who weren't around during the Cold War. They have no personal experience with the consequences of socialism and may have been fed misinformation about the ideology and its historical application. They may also be uncomfortable with a concept promoted by business leadership guru Dr. John Izzo who teaches that the key to economic success is for everyone to accept "100% responsibility 0% excuses" for themselves and their futures.

I realize that many in the millennial generation are comfortable with the idea of owning little and sharing everything, so I can understand why, in principle, socialism might sound attractive to them. They share houses, vehicles, clothing, textbooks, and lots of other things. Some of them want to believe that socialism offers a guarantee of success for everyone, without the possibility of failure, for anyone. History indicates otherwise.

But in order to make socialism more palatable to the general public, some of its adherents are trying to repackage it. They call themselves "democratic socialists" and insist that they do not support state ownership of property and the means of production, but instead want government to redistribute the nation's wealth through intensive regulation of business and industry, high taxation, and a bevy of new taxpayer-funded welfare programs. Socialismlite. The result would be a weakened economy, increasing debt, and a welfare state with more people developing an ever-increasing dependency on government.

In spite of this, they are encouraged by people whom economist Kristian Niemietz refers to as "socialist pilgrims." These are people who continue to ignore the repeated failures of socialism and maintain what Niemietz calls the "self-manipulating, reality-filtering, selective seeing, not-seeing, and un-seeing" opinion that socialism has never been tried. They believe that what occurred in the Soviet Union, China, North Korea, Cuba, North Vietnam, Cambodia, Venezuela and over a dozen other countries was not *real* socialism, and that someday a Wise Mind group of people will get it right and experience all of its promised benefits. But they seem to ignore the fact that there are three kinds of people in the world and that moon and star people will always be attracted to power and will misuse it when they get it. The greater the power, the greater the attraction. Catnip for moon people. Catnip-on-steroids for star people.

At the local level—like Milwaukee—the people can use a free press to monitor the actions of their leaders and respond quickly to prevent corruption and the abuse of power. The people hold the power. But at the national level, socialism puts supreme power in the hands of the few. If the all-powerful few become corrupted, they will use that power to intimidate and imprison those who challenge them. Then the press becomes a tool of propaganda; the justice system becomes an instrument of injustice; the military becomes a weapon for punishing free speech rather than protecting it; and government of the people, by the people, and for the people is lost.

For any society, when government no longer requires the consent of the governed and when sharing a nation's collective resources is no longer voluntary, freedom wanes and personal responsibility along with it— responsibility for ourselves as well as for the welfare of others. As novelist Poul Anderson pointed out, that's a government that is "doing more *to* the people, than *for* them." That's a moon government. And if the people are not vigilant, it can quickly turn into a star government.

THE QUALITIES OF STAR GOVERNMENTS

> *"It is not truth that matters, but victory"*-Adolf Hitler

The Fundamental Unit in a Star Society

Since star governments are all about power and control, none of that power is shared with the citizenry. I say citizenry instead of electorate because star governments are rarely the result of fair and open elections. The state is considered the fundamental unit in these societies with a ruling political party in control of the state, and a supreme leader in control of the party. They disavow the sovereign rights of individuals, seek to undermine the bonded attachments within families, seize control of the corporate-owned means of production, and attack the credibility and authority of the church. As political philosopher and author Roger Scruton explains, people living under star governments are not citizens living in a consensual society of sovereign individuals. Rather, they are subjects from whom the state requires unquestioned obedience.

Any governmental regulatory organization exercises some degree of power. But as economics professor Don Matthews wrote, "Power corrupts. But it does more than that. Power attracts the corrupt, then corrupts them further." Because star people crave power they will seek to infiltrate and dominate all levels of government and any professional or social institutions that have power or influence with the people.

Thomas Jefferson understood the powerfully positive influence that religion can have on society. As President, he ordered federal buildings to be made available to religious groups to conduct their services. And although his famous statement in a letter to the Baptist Church in Danbury, Connecticut in 1802 promoted the idea of a wall of separation between church and state, he held that position primarily as a means to protect churches from encroachment by the state, not the other way around. But in many countries that wall only remains in place when the interests of the church do not conflict with the agendas of the state. In a country controlled by star people running a star system of government, churches are among the first organizations that the state must control. That's because churches are one of the few places where people can go and still be reminded that "all men are created equal and are endowed by their Creator with certain inalienable rights"–rights that come from an eternal source, rather than an unreliable and unpredictable temporal one.

When I think about it, star governments remind me of black holes in space. Black holes are caused by suns that are no longer doing what suns are supposed to do and have gone bad. Instead of *producing* light, they *absorb* it. These circles of darkness are surrounded by an area known as an "event horizon"–the theoretical boundary that marks the "point of no return." Once matter passes that boundary, it is sucked into the black hole and can never return.

Star governments can occur even in countries where a sun system of government once existed, but which has been corrupted by greed, immorality, materialism, violence, and the lust for power. The people may have experienced freedom in the past, but they didn't value it. They did nothing to protect and maintain it, so their society inched ever closer to the event horizon between good and evil.

Whether willingly or unwittingly, they have enslaved themselves by their irresponsible and self-destructive choices and they may be too close to ultimate darkness to reverse course and free themselves. And like a black hole whose gravitational power is so strong that even light cannot escape its grasp, star systems of government suck the light, hope, compassion, trust, and joy out of the lives of their people.

Star Methods

As I explained previously, the primary tool-of-the-trade for star people to gain and maintain power is the **Lie**, in all its hues, gradations, fractions, or forms. That includes black lies, white lies, gray lies, propaganda, sophistry, promises they do not intend to keep (as opposed to threats they *fully* intend to keep), half-truths, quarter-truths, micro-truths, exaggerations, minimizations…any variation from things as they are, as they were, and as they are to come.

I realize that some people believe there is such a thing as a "noble lie." Noble lies are literal falsehoods that express some emotional sentiment that artificially unites and motivates the people in a society. They are often used by politicians to manipulate the public into embracing faulty political ideologies and policies. They have also been used by some scientists and philosophers to advance their pet theories and social agendas. Honestly, I don't believe there is anything noble about these lies. And any society that relies on lies to create a shared identity or promote national unity can just as easily have that unity destroyed by another, equally convincing, set of lies.

The second tool is violence and the fear that the threat of violence produces in people. Whether they fear death, injury, confiscation of their property, ostracism, unemployment, or merely the displeasure of the ruling classes–like the story of the emperor's new clothes–fear is a powerful motivator that mutes the voices of dissent and snuffs out the fires of resistance. Concerning fear, author Theodore Dalrymple wrote:

> *In my study of communist societies, I came to the conclusion that the purpose of communist propaganda was not to persuade or convince, nor to inform, but to humiliate; and therefore, the less it corresponded to reality the better. When people are forced to remain silent when they are being told the most obvious lies, or even worse, when they are forced to repeat the lies themselves, they lose once and for all their sense of probity. To assent to obvious lies is to cooperate with evil, and in some small way to become evil oneself. One's standing to resist anything is thus eroded, and even destroyed. A society of emasculated liars is easy to control. I think if you examine political correctness, it has the same effect, and is intended to.*

But sometimes propaganda and humiliation are not enough to control others, and star leaders begin to realize that there will always be a segment of society who will fight to defend truth, even when victory appears doubtful.

This presents a dilemma for star leaders: the realization that they are dealing with people, not sheep. Force then becomes the inevitable, and indeed, the preferred option to address it. Carlson and Mero described the dilemma this way:

Then the real answer emerges. People are the problem. Of course! Perfectibility is not possible so long as people are allowed to choose activities and behaviors that run counter to the quest for efficiency. … It is at this point that the story of the state turns ugly. This is the point of the final option—it must save the people from themselves and it must do it with rapidity and force. A helping hand becomes a backhand. The servant becomes the master. The people are now the problem; all will suffer; some must die. Choosing this path is deceptively easy. After all, the state is only trying to help. And by the way, the people asked for the help. The state is only doing what the people asked it to do. The requests were reasonable enough—work for the common good, for decency, for the common man, for the provision of order and for the unity of the people. We must all live together in peace. This can only be accomplished if the state is allowed to fulfill its purpose, and if the people are not allowed to choose their own existence. The story of the state has been lived and relived, tried over and again with the results always being failure. To place the state as the fundamental unit of society is to dehumanize people. No longer are people the reason for, or the purpose of life. Perfection becomes the end game—a game lost even before it is played.

Along with force, an equally important way star governments control the people is through the controlling of information.

The Power of the Kings to Change History

> "He who controls the past controls the future. He who controls the present controls the past"-George Orwell, 1984.

In ancient Egypt, the pharaohs had enormous power. Not only were they honored and feared as kings, they were also revered as Gods. Some pharaohs exercised one power that you will often see being used today by many moon and star rulers. The Egyptians referred to it as the power of the kings to change history. No, they didn't own a time machine and they couldn't travel into the past and change events that had already happened, but they did have the power to remove the memories of those events from the minds of future generations of their people. I will explain with an example from Egyptian history.

Thutmose I reigned as pharaoh in Egypt from approximately 1511 B.C to 1498 B.C. in the early years of the eighteenth dynasty of the Egyptian kings. He had a daughter named Hatshepsut with his wife Ahmose and a son named Thutmose II with a second wife, Mutnoferet. Thutmose II married his half-sister Hatshepsut and became pharaoh after his father's death. Unable to have a son with his first wife Hatshepsut, Thutmose II had a son named Thutmose III later in life with his second wife, Iset. Since Thutmose III was still a young child when he was made pharaoh, his step-mother Hatshepsut reigned in his stead as co-regent until her death around 1458 B.C. She has been recognized as one of the great female leaders in ancient history and there does not appear to be any record of any major problems between her and her stepson who succeeded her as pharaoh.

Suddenly, after reigning as pharaoh for over twenty years after Hatshepsut's death and establishing his own reputation as Egypt's most accomplished military leader and a gifted historian, architect, botanist, and athlete, Thutmose III set about to erase his stepmother's memory. He ordered statues of her destroyed and obelisks buried or hidden. Anything he could find that had her name or image inscribed on it was defaced and chipped away, leaving Hatshepsut-shaped blank spaces on the walls of several buildings. His second son and successor as pharaoh, Amenhotep II, continued the effort after his father's death. But there were just too many accounts of Hatshepsut's accomplishments and reminders of her existence etched in stone to complete the erasure process.

Why would a legendary king who was raised and groomed for his own successful reign as pharaoh, want to erase the memory of his mentor? Because as the teenage daughter of pharaoh Thutmose I–a man who apparently couldn't say "no" to his favorite (and only surviving) child–she brought into the royal palace an infant son of Hebrew slaves whom she had drawn from the Nile River as he floated by in a basket. She gave him a name derived from the Egyptian verb meaning "to give birth,"–specifically to a son–and raised him as her own. This adopted son would later leave Egypt during the reign of Hatshepsut's husband, Thutmose II, and return again about forty years later during the reign of his son, Thutmose III.

Now a lowly shepherd, this adoptive stepbrother would become the cause of this accomplished general's greatest military defeat and the death of his firstborn son. His name would be a shameful reminder of failure and humiliation that would forever be attached to the name of one of Egypt's most accomplished pharaohs.

It wasn't just Hatshepsut's name he wanted blotted out of Egyptian history, it was also her adopted son's. That vile name that must never again be spoken and must be erased from the collective memories of all future Egyptians. The name of Moses.

Revised history books in various totalitarian states delete any references to military defeats or other embarrassing events in their histories. Or the authors just rewrite history to reflect the stories as the government wants them remembered. It is not just free speech that star leaders fear and want to suppress, it is also free listening.

Through control of Internet communications, television and radio broadcasts, music, art, telephone communications, even the reconstruction of language by redefining or eliminating certain words from the nation's lexicon; there is no end to the efforts of some leaders to keep light and truth out of the minds of their people, especially the minds of the children. As Adolf Hitler was fond of saying, "He alone who owns the youth, gains the future."

But eventually, the truth comes out. Truth will always survive as long as there are sun people willing to search for it, defend it, and share it with others.

> **"Every nation gets the government it deserves"** -Joseph de Maistre, 1811

On June 8, 1978 Russian novelist, historian, and political exile Alexander Solzhenitsyn delivered an address entitled "A World Split Apart" at the 327th commencement ceremony for Harvard University. He reminded the audience that the motto of the university is *Veritas*, which is Latin for *truth*. He said, "Truth eludes us if we do not concentrate our attention totally on its pursuit."

In the past, Solzhenitsyn had been criticized for being a little *too* truthful with his opinions and for holding all nations and peoples accountable to the standard of truth. The casual listener on that June day in 1978 might have found fault with his comments or been offended by his bluntness and critical tone, but with each passing decade more people have come to understand how accurate his comments were then, and are even more so, today.

Solzhenitsyn included a sober warning to the Western world about the misguided direction it is taking socially and politically and what the future would hold for us if we did not take the pursuit of truth and the preservation of freedom more seriously. He noted some significant areas of decline in the Western world when he said:

> *A decline in courage may be the most striking feature which an outside observer notices in the West in our days. The Western world has lost its civil courage, both as a whole and separately, in each country, each government, each political party, and, of course, in the United Nations. Such a decline in courage is particularly noticeable among the ruling groups and the intellectual elite, causing an impression of the loss of courage by the entire society.*

Solzhenitsyn warned that this decline in courage spelled the beginning of the end for society: the end of morality, the end of self-restraint, the end of virtue, the end of responsibility, the end of prosperity, the end of self-reliance, and the end of freedom. He also warned of the efforts of some people at creating convergence between East and West—of combining aspects of both democracy and socialism—and that the results would be a system of government that would likely include defects from both. A moon system at best.

The promise of such a government would be to provide order, security, and the material things necessary to ensure happiness for the people. The real result, he warned, would not be happiness at all, but a morally inferior, "freedom-lite" version of that word.

When a government promises to meet all their needs, the people will expect it to keep that promise. But government doesn't produce wealth; the people do. Government is merely the bureaucratic middleman. Solzhenitsyn understood what the history of socialism has repeatedly demonstrated: that the greater the distance between the true provider of benefits and the receiver, the more the receiver develops a sense of entitlement, and the more empowered and demanding the middleman becomes. That's when true givers decide to stop giving, and middlemen become plunderers.

To Solzhenitsyn, protecting the values of a society from attack is much more important than protecting the nation's borders, economy, or infrastructure. The attack on freedom that we should fear most is the attack from within, caused by the corruption of democratic values. As Abraham Lincoln and many others have warned us, it is national suicide we should be more concerned about than national homicide.

Moral Mediocrity and the Abuse of Freedom

Solzhenitsyn pointed out that a sun society requires more than just a legal system to protect it. He said, "Whenever the tissue of life is woven of legalistic relations, there is an atmosphere of moral mediocrity, paralyzing man's noblest impulses." It is a commitment by individual citizens to lives of moral integrity that creates and protects a sun society and inspires laws that reflect sun principles.

But in a moon society where moral integrity is often compromised for the sake of material gain, governments will always find excuses for more restrictive laws–laws often enacted by less enlightened moon leaders who don't trust the majority of the human race to govern themselves. Rather than creating greater solidarity among the people, these kinds of laws will inevitably spawn more contention.

While sun governments are based on freedom, Solzhenitsyn reminded us that it is the destructive and irresponsible use of freedom that has created so many of the problems in western society. He credited the misuse of liberty as being responsible for the inability of the West to prevent itself from falling into what he referred to as "the abyss of human decadence." He pointed out the proliferation of pornography, crime, and horror in the media as prime examples. (If he thought TV and movies were bad in 1978, he would be shocked by what is happening in the media today.) He lamented the fact that "thus we mix good and evil, right and wrong, and make space for the absolute triumph of absolute evil in the world." A brilliant description of a moon society in decline.

Solzhenitsyn noted that the thin layer of civility that covers a society in decline can easily be broken when natural disasters happen, incidents of racial injustice occur, or simply when the power goes out for a few hours. It doesn't take much for some people to reveal their willingness to exploit a situation and plunder their neighbors. While his conclusions about western culture are accurate for the star people among us, I believe there are still examples of people who step up and come to the rescue of those in need when difficulties occur rather than profiting from their vulnerability and misfortune. These are the heroes that Dr. Philip Zimbardo refers to in his book *The Lucifer Effect*.

Where Have All the Heroes Gone?

Zimbardo also determined that there are three kinds of people in the world: (1) perpetrators of evil; (2) those who look the other way in the presence of evil, tacitly condoning it; and (3) those who act heroically on behalf of others who are the victims of evil.

Sun people are heroes. They move quickly from being passive observers to being heroic actors when circumstances require it. They are the ones who demonstrate the courage that Solzhenitsyn sees as missing from much of western society.

An excellent example of this kind of courage was demonstrated on a subway platform in New York City by construction worker Wesley Autry who risked his life to rescue a young man who had fallen onto the subway tracks during a seizure. When asked why he—out of a group of over seventy-five people standing on the subway platform that day—had been the only one willing to risk his life to save a stranger's, he said, "I did what anyone would do, and what everyone ought to do."

The world needs more heroes. But you don't have to risk your life to be a hero. There are daily opportunities for each of us to perform simple acts of heroism: like demonstrating generosity and compassion for others, or admitting a mistake and taking responsibility for our actions when lying might get us out of trouble, or speaking out in support of sun principles when all of those around you are denigrating them. Solzhenitsyn blamed moral weakness and the preoccupation with materialism and self-interest for preventing more of us from engaging in these kinds of heroic actions.

At the root of this dilemma, "at the very basis of human thinking in past centuries," he said, is our faulty belief in rationalist humanism, which he defined as "the proclaimed and enforced autonomy of man from any higher force above him." He felt that we have untethered ourselves from religion, and with that action we have disconnected ourselves from God and our neighbors. He believed that the West has entered a time of de-spiritualization, self-worship, and materialism and that those vices are now influencing social and political reasoning and policymaking.

Solzhenitsyn was alarmed and saddened by the fact that we have lost touch with the divine influences that used to restrain our passions and our irresponsibility. "We have placed too much hope in political and social reforms" he said, "only to find out that we are being deprived of our most precious possession: our spiritual life." And as is always the case, there is a societal price to pay when that happens. Solzhenitsyn summed it up this way:

> Over a half century ago, while I was still a child, I recall hearing a number of old people offer the following explanation for the great disasters that had befallen Russia: "Men have forgotten God; that's why all this has happened." Since then I have spent well-nigh fifty years working on the history of our revolution; in the process, I have read hundreds of books, collected hundreds of personal testimonies, and have already contributed eight volumes of my own toward the effort of clearing away the rubble left by that upheaval. But if I were asked today to formulate as concisely as possible the main cause of the ruinous revolution that swallowed up some sixty millions of our people, I could not

put it more accurately than to repeat: "Men have forgotten God; that's why all this has happened."

American Founding Father Patrick Henry similarly admonished his fellow eighteenth- century citizens when he said, "Bad men cannot make good citizens. It is when a people forget God that tyrants forge their chains."

Solzhenitsyn warned that the West could face a similar fate if we continue down the same path. He wrote:

We the oppressed people of Russia watch with anguish the tragic enfeeblement of Europe. We offer you the experience of our own suffering. We would like you to accept it, without paying the monstrous price of debt and slavery that we have paid.

There are three kinds of people in the world, experiencing three different levels of light and truth in their lives and living by three different sets of standards. Those standards will determine the kinds of governments they create and the kinds of people they select to govern them. In the end, every nation gets the government its people deserve.

> *"Men have forgotten God; that's why all this has happened."*

What Does the Future Hold?

In 1850 Frederic Bastiat considered the United States to be the greatest friend and protector of liberty in the world. Would he feel the same way today? Is the United States of America still the land of the free, or have we abused our freedom and invited darkness into our midst? Are we closer to becoming what Winthrop believed we were foreordained to be, or of forever remaining "God's almost-chosen people" as Abraham Lincoln often referred to the Americans of his day?

But that reproach begs the same question today: have we fallen from our favored nation status with The Almighty? Many recognize that the United States and its constitution came into existence only because a benevolent God wished it so. For nearly three centuries He gradually led foreordained groups of sun people to the New World. Miraculous events then led to victory in the Revolutionary War and inspiration from The Almighty distilled upon the minds and hearts of the men assembled in Independence Hall during that hot summer of 1787. There they faced the seemingly impossible task of rallying a diverse group of leaders from a diverse group of states, around a common, more enlightened purpose. But they did it. And they did it because Benjamin Franklin reminded the assembled representatives that God rules in the affairs of men and that a freedom-inspired system of government could not be designed without His help. Certainly, Franklin's was an Inspired Mind perspective.

As he walked from Independence Hall on September 18, 1787 at the close of the Constitutional Convention, Franklin was approached by a resident of Philadelphia named Mrs. Powell who asked him, "Well doctor, what have we got, a republic or a monarchy?" "A republic," Franklin replied, "if you can keep it." Where much is given, much is expected.

However, lest Americans forget, this great gift was not intended solely for their benefit. It was a gift to the whole world. It was just that America was the only place on the face of the earth at that critical time that was adequately prepared to receive it. That's why it was delivered here. And with that gift comes the responsibility to protect it and promote its principles.

But we couldn't seem to maintain the "attitude of gratitude" necessary to hold this divinely appointed free system of government together on our own. By 1860 we were on the verge of self-destruction brought on by greed, pride, and the obscenity of slavery. It took a much bloodier war than the American Revolution to uproot from American society this immoral practice that threatened to destroy it. The same benevolent God that brought the U.S. Constitution into existence, now rescued it and its republican system of government from the ashes of the Civil War.

Then we repeated our folly in the 1920s and 1930s, bringing upon ourselves moral decay, economic chaos, and political upheaval that threatened our existence as a free nation. Again, it took the most savage and bloody war in human history to bring us to our senses and to unite us again as a people.

But each new generation seems to forget many of the lessons their parents learned, and today we find ourselves repeating the same mistakes of the past. What will it take to bring us to our senses this time?

While moon people may not promote violent revolution as a means of gaining power, they will often promote contention and division among the people to gain and maintain it. The statement, "Vote, it's the best revenge" may have been spoken by a member of the Democratic Party, but the desire for revenge lies within the hearts of some members of the Republican Party and other parties too. The Founding Fathers expressed their concerns that political parties could create factions among the people that would lead to power struggles and political gridlock. They recognized the potential for these parties to manipulate the voters with sophistry and inflammatory rhetoric. They feared exactly what authors Katherine Gehl and Michael Porter described in their book *Why Competition in the Politics Industry is Failing America* and what we are seeing today—a two-party duopoly, fighting to maintain control of the political system at the expense of what's best for the people. This prevents anyone outside of these two opposing parties from presenting any serious challenge to their power, leaving many sun-minded citizens without an Inspired Mind political alternative.

The Founding Fathers were hopeful that the American people would be able to distinguish between truth and error by staying informed on political issues and maintaining spiritual vigilance. But I fear we may be in danger of forgetting that counsel.

When the national conventions for the two major political parties were held during the presidential campaign of 2012, something startling happened at one of them. It was proposed and approved (by a questionable majority vote) that any references to God be eliminated from the party's political platform. There was a public outcry followed by a hasty public-relations effort to correct the blunder that in reality, only reinforced the appearance of an anti-religious sentiment among many delegates to the convention. This trend was repeated at their 2020 national convention when the leaders of the same party deleted the words "under God" from their recitation of the Pledge of Allegiance.

Do we really believe that this free nation, or a free world, can exist and endure without its Creator's protection? A satirical dialogue between Americans and God as imagined by religious scholar Dr. Hugh Nibley describes our current situation well:

We: Dear Father, whenever the end is scheduled to be, can't you give us an extension of time?

He: Willingly. But tell me first, what will you do with it?

We: Well…uh…we will go on doing pretty much what we have been doing; after all, isn't that why we are asking for an extension?

He: And isn't that exactly why I want to end it soon—because you show no inclination to change? Why should I reverse the order of nature so that you can go on doing the very things I want to put an end to?

We: But is what we are doing so terribly wrong? The economy seems sound enough. Why shouldn't we go on doing the things which have made this country great?

He: Haven't I made it clear enough to you what kind of greatness I expect of my offspring? Forget the statistics; you are capable of better things—your stirring commercials don't impress me in the least.

We: But why should we repent when all we are doing is what each considers to be for the best good for himself and the nation?

He: Because it is not you but I who decide what that shall be, and I have told you a hundred times what is best for you individually and collectively—and that is repentance, no matter who you are.

We: We find your inference objectionable, Sir, quite unacceptable.

He: I know.

George Washington reminded the American people what God expects of the citizens of this favored nation when he said, "The propitious smiles of heaven can never be expected on a nation that disregards the eternal rules of order and right which heaven itself has ordained." Similarly, Alexis de Tocqueville warned:

Despotism may govern without faith, but liberty cannot. How is it possible that society should escape destruction if the moral tie is not strengthened in proportion as the political tie is relaxed? And what can be done with a people who are their own masters if they are not submissive to the Deity?

History has provided multiple examples of the calamities that Tocqueville warned would happen when any society forgets that it is only through obedience to sun principles that free societies are created and maintained. Aristotle warned the Greek people of his day as the Founding Fathers have warned the American people in ours, what happens to democracies in which only selfish desires rule the minds and hearts of the people.

One of the indicators of where a society is on this selfishness continuum is reflected by what happens at the ballot box. But the deeper concern is that the problems in a society lie not just with the leaders they elect, but with the people who elect them. As the saying goes, "Politics are downstream of culture." The values of those we elect, reflect the values of the electorate.

Is American society becoming increasingly void of the virtues espoused by the Founding Fathers? Have we lost our moral compass? Is the U.S.A. a moon society in decline? If so, who is to blame? These accusations apply to people across the political spectrum.

The current political climate suggests that a lot of people are more committed to self-interest than public interest. In the years to come, these contentious events will either be viewed as a clarion wake-up call that brought us to our senses, or another warning gone unheeded. If the latter turns out to be the case, then the best counsel I would have to offer my grandchildren's generation would be, "Cherish the blessing of living in a sun society while you can, because tomorrow…isn't looking very promising."

It's Twilight Time

Abuse freedom and we lose freedom; here a little, there a little. Supreme Court Justice William O. Douglas put it well when he cautioned the American people in the 1950s:

As nightfall does not come at once, neither does oppression. In both instances, there is a twilight when everything remains seemingly unchanged. And it is in such twilight that we all must be most aware of change in the air–however slight–lest we become unwitting victims of the darkness."

As the vocal group The Platters sang in 1958, "It's twilight time." And in the "post-truth" and "fake-news" world in which we are now living, there are a growing number of indicators of approaching darkness.

Your activity for this chapter is to do what you can to inject light into the political conversation. I recommend studying the Declaration of Independence, the Federalist Papers, and the U.S Constitution with your family and discussing the founding principles of this nation. Examine today's contentious social and political issues and their moral as well as legal implications. Consider current events and how they are influencing the cultural values of our society and how they may shape future legislation and court decisions. And most importantly, define, as a family, what you believe are the responsibilities of a sun citizen. Then go and be one.

We've talked about how sun people view power and how they only use it in ways that benefit others. Next, we will look at one of the main sources of power and how sun, moon, and star people differ in their attitudes about it. Let's talk money.

CHAPTER 7 Preview

The Creator designed the earth with enough resources to sustain life, in reasonable comfort, for all of its past, present, and future inhabitants. Yet there continue to be many destitute people in nations around the world who lack adequate food, clothing, shelter, and medical care. It appears that humanity has not done a very good job of sharing the world's resources as intended. There are often huge discrepancies between what all of us *need*, and what some of us *want*.

This chapter will discuss the role of money in our lives as individuals, families, and communities. I'll point out how errant ways of thinking about money may threaten the fiscal and moral stability of the world and offer an example of a sun solution that could make the world a more economically secure and peaceful place for everyone.

3 KINDS OF PEOPLE AND HOW THEY VIEW MONEY

●●●●●◖◖◖◖

On May 16, 1986, Wall Street trader Ivan Boesky spoke at a graduation commencement for the Haas School of Business at the University of California at Berkeley. In his speech he made this infamous statement: "Greed is all right, by the way. I want you to know that. I think greed is healthy. You can be greedy and still feel good about it." Those comments were immortalized a year later in the "greed is good" speech made by the Boesky alter ego Gordon Gekko in the movie *Wall Street*.

The sun students in the Berkeley audience were likely thinking, "Dude!" (We're talking 1986 California, remember.) "He just redefined one of the seven deadly sins as something good! That's totally bogus!" The moon people in the room probably thought, "That's totally tubular!" because for them it meant they had an excuse for allowing the pursuit of personal wealth to become a higher priority than the well-being of others. The star people probably cheered inside and gleefully rubbed their hands together like the villainous Simon Legree. They heard the statement as tacit approval to do the things that sent Boesky to prison a short time later, and potentially, a whole lot worse. (I'm thinking the Bernie Madoff kind of worse. But for some, the villainy doesn't stop at mere theft.) As I quoted earlier, "When plunder becomes a way of life for a group of men, they create for themselves, in the course of time, a legal system that authorizes it and a moral code that glorifies it." And once plunder takes root in one country, it's corruptive influence can quickly spread to others. (As demonstrated by several kleptocrats around the world who have invested much of their ill-gotten gains into American real estate.)

Love or Lust?

Money is not the root of all evil, but as the Apostle Paul cautioned the Christian community of his day, the love of it is—or maybe more accurately, the *lust* for it. I love the good that money can do when used correctly, but great harm can be done when it is not. It can be used to buy education, healthcare, housing, and wholesome recreation, or it can be used to indulge every selfish and destructive desire imaginable. It can be used to build bridges, hospitals, cathedrals, and temples, or it can be used to build the bombs and artillery shells used to destroy them. It can be used to feed the hungry and clothe the naked living in poverty-stricken, third-world countries or by corrupt government officials in those same countries to buy gold-plated bathroom fixtures to inflate their social status.

It can be used to pay for a love-affirming honeymoon for a newlywed couple starting out their lives together, or for a prostitute for the evening by an unfaithful spouse on a Super Bowl junket. Used properly, it can build people. Used inappropriately, it can destroy them. We are reminded of this dual nature of money by comparing the actions of the Good Samaritan and Judas Iscariot. The same coinage that one used to heal injuries and preserve a life, was the incentive for the other to send an innocent man to his death.

Money can be a blessing or a curse for those who have it, as well as for those who don't. It all depends on our attitudes about it. There are three kinds of people in the world, and one of the factors that determines which group we fall into is the way we acquire and use money.

A Brief History of Money

Money is a device for exchanging what we have for what we don't have, but that we need. Anciently, people lived in an agrarian society and were able to produce most of what they needed to live. They grew, raised, or hunted their own food; built their own dwellings; used animal skins or wove cloth for clothing; and made their own tools and pottery. What they lacked they could obtain by trading some of the surplus of what they had produced, for some of the surplus produced by others.

Some historians believe that money was originally devised to facilitate this kind of trading transaction. For example, Abel raised sheep while his brother Cain grew crops. If Cain wanted mutton for dinner or wool to make cloth, he could trade some of his surplus fruits, vegetables, or grain for one of Abel's surplus sheep.

This bartering system worked fine, except for what is called the "coincidence of wants." Abel's need for wheat had to occur at the same time that Cain's wheat crop was harvested and available. And Cain's need for sheep had to occur at the same time Abel had surplus sheep, or there would be no exchange. If Abel wanted wheat and was willing to trade an equal value of sheep but the wheat crop was not going to be harvested for six months, that was a problem.

People had to come up with some system that would allow Cain to trade his produce to other people at the height of its freshness and nutritional value and still allow him to buy Abel's sheep later when they were fully grown and available.

Other historians believe money was first used as a means of keeping track of debt. For example, Moe wants to trade some of his handcrafted tools to Larry for some grain, but the grain harvest is still months away. So, Larry acknowledges his debt to Moe and gives him something that served as a receipt for his tools that he can use later to exchange for the promised grain. If Moe needs food before the grain harvest, he might decide to trade some of his grain credit to Curly (who is OK with waiting for his grain) for a bow and arrow to go hunting.

Either way, our ancestors needed something that would serve as a tool for conducting these kinds of business transactions and as a means of storing value for the times when they had no surplus goods to barter. They needed to use something that was scarce enough to have intrinsic value, was durable, could be measured and divided easily, and was portable so it could be used in the place of animals, grains, clothing, pottery, tools, or whatever else was being traded.

Cowry shells were popular in several ancient Asian and African countries, but pieces of precious metals like gold and silver soon became the most convenient and therefore, the most popular commodities for exchange both locally and internationally. Some historians estimate that minted coins made of gold or silver began to appear around 600 B.C. with various images imprinted on them to indicate different denominations or values. Paper currencies began to appear in some countries around 800 A.D. and by the seventeenth century European banks began issuing their own notes which could be exchanged at the bank for gold or silver coins. This made it easier to conduct commerce so people didn't have to carry around large amounts of heavy coins. Eventually governments took over the issuing of currency and our modern monetary systems were born.

As people became even more diversified and specialized in their professions and more products and service were developed, reliance on money as a method of exchange increased. In today's world, most people are unable to produce for themselves all the commodities and services they need to live. As a result, we have become increasingly dependent on having money to meet our basic human needs.

The questions that arise at this point are:
- How much money is enough to meet our needs?
- What are we willing to do to get it?
- How do we use it when we do get it?

How Much Money Do We Need?

There is a common misunderstanding about the relationship between happiness and money. This point was eloquently illustrated in the Tom Shadyac documentary *I AM* in which he dispels the myth that achieving happiness is dependent upon how much stuff we own. In one segment, author Thom Hartmann described it this way:

These foundational notions of our relationship to stuff are grounded on a truth and a lie in our culture. The truth is, that if you are naked and cold, at night, outdoors, all alone, in the forest, and it's raining, you are unhappy. We can all agree on that! And if somebody opens the door and says, "Come on in, here's a fire you can sit next to, here's clothing you can put on, here's a blanket, here's a warm place to sleep, here's a bowl of soup," suddenly you go from being unhappy to happy with very little stuff, but it's stuff that makes the difference, just like that (snaps fingers). So that's the truth. The lie then is...well...if this amount of stuff will make you that happy, then ten times as much stuff will make you ten times happier, a hundred times as much stuff will make you a hundred times happier, a thousand times as much stuff will make you a thousand times happier, and Bill Gates lives in a state of perpetual bliss!

That is obviously not the case, but many still want to believe that it is. Money not only does not buy happiness, it often creates some significant obstacles to happiness for those who spend too much of their time and energy focused on obtaining it, and retaining it.

Jesus spoke of the "deceitfulness of riches" in the parable of the Sower and the Seed where he reminded his listeners that wealth can be one of the "thorns" that chokes off a person's spiritual growth and prevents him or her from "bearing fruit" and experiencing the happiness that comes from a productive, sun-directed life. I think most people understand what amount of money is sufficient to meet their basic needs and have learned to be content with that. It is failing to find contentment with having enough in life that feeds the addictive desire for more.

Peter Whybrow wrote about this addictive fixation on materialism, consumption, and wealth creation. He described how this cultural shift toward stuff accumulation occurring in America and in virtually all the western world, has failed to produce the promised benefits of security, personal well-being, enjoyment, and happiness. But moon or star thinking never does. It is only through an accurate, Inspired Mind determination of our legitimate temporal needs that we can then determine the right ways to go about meeting them.

What Are We Willing to Do to Get It?

Ralph Waldo Emerson once cautioned his contemporaries that "Money often costs too much."

For star people, money is the way to get what they want, and what they want is ever-increasing levels of power, privilege, prestige, and property–lots of stuff. Because of this fixation on the ability of money to satisfy their every desire, star people begin to believe that everything and everyone has some fixed monetary value–*a price*. For them, it's just a matter of determining what that number is. According to Irish poet and playwright Oscar Wilde, this means that star people know "the price of everything, but the value of nothing." For them, the monetary value is the only value.

A quick scan through the annuls of world history reveals a long list of star people who have resorted to a litany of bad behaviors to get money. And they will readily violate any laws that get in their way. Or, if they are smart enough, they will learn how to manipulate the system to steal the money "legally." (Remember Lincoln: "Some legal rights are moral wrongs.") But as Rumpelstiltskin reminds his ardent but misguided supplicants before sealing his devilish deals with them, "Magic always comes with a price, dearie!" So does the lust for money.

Moon people may let the world get in the way, but they are not necessarily malevolent about it. Many of them are just misguided. In Michael Sandel's book *What Money Can't Buy*, he describes how some people and organizations can mistakenly justify making money in ways that most sun people would find morally questionable and potentially corrupting to society. His list included things like:

- An $82 prison cell upgrade so offenders in some city jails can receive better accommodations than their less-financially-fortunate fellow prisoners.

- Letting solo drivers use the "Lexus lanes" (carpool lanes) during rush hour for an additional fee. (Carpool lanes were not originally intended to generate revenue, but to reduce traffic congestion and air pollution by decreasing the number of cars on the highway.)
- Selling permanent U.S. residency to wealthy foreign immigrants who invest $500,000 in an American business that creates at least ten jobs in areas of high unemployment.
- Individual or corporate investors buying life insurance policies on AIDS patients or the elderly and collecting the death benefit when they die. (A similar use of life insurance is known as "janitor's insurance" where corporations buy life insurance policies on certain employees, often without their knowledge.)
- Parents offering to sell naming rights for their new-born children to corporations to promote their products or services. (I wonder how one of my children would have liked being named Nike or Exxon?)
- Government-sponsored gambling.
- Renting space on your body to display commercial advertising.
- Scalping free tickets to attend a papal mass.
- Poor couples in China selling their right to have a child (procreation permits) to wealthier couples.
- Selling organs from aborted fetuses.

We have created financial markets for things that should not be marketed.

In looking at the list above I'm sure there are many who would see no problem with Lexus lanes or maybe even state-sponsored lotteries and sports betting to raise revenue for financially strapped state budgets. But the ends do not justify the means in these examples, and many of these methods of generating revenue encourage destructive behaviors. They may also contribute to increased feelings of inequality in society and quicken the pace of moral decline in general. Because they let the world get in the way, one of the biggest challenges moon people face in life is recognizing what constitutes good and what constitutes evil when it comes to making and spending money.

For example, encouraging children to read a book, eat healthily, brush their teeth, get better grades, not use illicit drugs, avoid pornography, or abstain from sex before marriage is a good thing. But paying them to do those same things tends to diminish the intrinsic value of those behaviors and will not sustain them over time. For some, financial incentives have replaced moral reasoning and personal commitment as the primary motivation behind some of life's important decisions. But a commitment to sun values and behaviors is not something money can buy.

For all of us, making money matters. But for sun people, *how* they make money matters more. For them, any honest work–white collar, blue collar or no collar–that provides a worthwhile product or service that is marketed ethically and that benefits others, is an appropriate way to make a living. Sun workers give an honest day's work for an honest day's pay, and sun employers give an honest day's pay for an honest day's work. They believe that money is like a taxi: the more it moves around, the better it does its job.

What Do We Do With It When We Get It?

For some people, just making enough money to meet the everyday needs of their families is the best they can do. But there will always be those whose greater levels of intelligence, skill, and determination enable them to produce much more than they need. The question then arises, what do they do with that surplus?

In his film *I AM*, director Tom Shadyac tells the story of an ancient native tribe of people who had lived in peace and harmony for thousands of years. There was no hunger among the tribe, even among the sick or the elderly, because the skilled hunters among them would bring back the bounty of their hunt and share the meat equally with the whole community. Then one day the most successful hunter decided that his greater skills entitled him to a greater share of the food, so he began storing an extra share of the meat in icy-cold, high mountain banks…I mean…*caves*. Other hunters followed suit, and soon the old, the weak, and the sick began to go hungry while others were well-fed. Often, over-fed. This practice became so common among the tribe that no one seemed to be concerned that some people were starving while others had much more than they needed. Even more surprising, the tribal leaders began to embrace the practice, encouraging these hoarding habits among the rising generation of youth. Shadyac goes on to say:

> *Now, that story isn't true because it happened, it's true because it's happening. We are that tribe. I am that tribe. Nature is very clear on this. In fact, there is one fundamental law that all of nature obeys that mankind breaks everyday...and the law is this: nothing in nature takes more than it needs, and when something does, it becomes subject to this law and it dies off. An ocean, a rainforest, the human body, are all cooperatives. A redwood tree doesn't take all of the soil's nutrients, just what it needs to grow. A lion doesn't kill every gazelle, just one. We have a term for something in the body when it takes more than its share—we call it cancer.*

The insatiable desire for greater wealth, power, pleasure, glory, property, natural resources, and whatever else the world offers is indeed a cancer that has grown inside the body-politic of many societies throughout human history. It has led to countless wars, millions of deaths, and the extinction of entire civilizations. And yet, like the tribal elders in the story, we somehow continue to justify it by claiming that it is human nature—survival of the fittest—that drives us toward these self-destructive behaviors when in reality, it is a personal choice.

We have already discussed the advantages of choosing cooperation over competition. Let's look at a sun economic system that is based on the principle of cooperation and how changing our financial paradigm may be the only way to prevent the world from falling off the fiscal cliff that many economists believe we are rapidly approaching.

A Sun Economic System: Beyond Capitalism and State Socialism

In the last century many of the great minds in the fields of politics, law, economics, philosophy, and religion have struggled to identify an economic system that is free of the weaknesses inherent in the two major competing economic philosophies of our day: capitalism and socialism. They envisioned a third way that is both fiscally effective and morally sound. By morally sound I mean a system that reflects what I have discussed in the previous chapter–a system that honors individual agency (freedom) and accountability for the welfare of self and others (responsibility). A system based on sun principles that does not involve coercion. A system that, by design, is less vulnerable to manipulation and adulteration by less-enlightened people espousing less-enlightened principles.

Regarding capitalism, investment advisor Harry Dent has often referred to the relationship between capitalism and democracy as the perfect marriage. I would qualify that statement by adding that it depends on who is performing the ceremony. For sun people, capitalism and the free enterprise system allows people to achieve whatever level of financial success they aspire to, while also encouraging them to share the bounty of their success with others. Those who attack capitalism as a system that promotes greed and selfishness are wrong. Capitalism is not the problem. The problem is with the kind of people who practice it. For sun people it is a system that provides the greatest freedom and incentive to achieve prosperity for themselves and all of society. But democracy and capitalism require greater personal discipline, morality, and altruism on the part of the public if a democratic nation is to avoid creating the divided societies of "haves" and "have nots" that have become so common today. It is the popularity of moon and star thinking that is responsible for that.

For moon people, capitalism presents a challenge. Since their tendency is to let the world get in the way, they often allow the accumulation of wealth and the self-aggrandizing social status that comes with it, to become more important than the welfare of others. The pursuit of wealth can easily insulate us and prevent us from recognizing the challenges others are facing. That separation can lead to class envy and pride–both kinds of pride. Pride from the top looking down, but also from the bottom looking up. Both are equally destructive and result in enmity toward others. We see this moon approach to capitalism occurring more often in American society today as well as the popular "greed is good" star philosophy which had proponents long before Ivan Boesky came along.

The Invisible Hand vs. The Clenched Fist

In 1714 Dutch physician Bernard Mandeville published an essay entitled *The Fable of the Bees* or *Private Vices, Public Benefits* in which he extolled greed and the desire for luxury as virtues. He suggested that these vices were actually the engines that drive economic growth in a society and therefore, are beneficial to the public. He faced some stiff opposition from the clergy of his day who felt that Mandeville was promoting a selfish, hedonistic, and anti-religious ideology. But his ideas soon gained favor with other economists, including America's Adam Smith whose 1776 book *The Wealth of Nations* laid the groundwork for the advancement of free-market economics and laissez-faire capitalism.

Smith promoted the self-interest aspect of a democratic, free-market system because he believed–like many of the Founding Fathers–that Americans were intrinsically altruistic and concerned about the welfare of their neighbors. They assumed that successful American entrepreneurs, while primarily focused on self-improvement, would naturally–and even unknowingly–put their profits to work to increase opportunities and improve conditions for others. In his earlier book *The Theory of Moral Sentiments* written in 1759, Smith referred to an "invisible hand" that somehow guided the rich "to make nearly the same distribution of the necessaries of life, which would have been made had the earth been divided into equal portions among all its inhabitants." He concluded, "When Providence divided the earth among a few lordly masters, it neither forgot nor abandoned those who seemed to have been left out in the partition." Thus, without intending it or even knowing it, the rich would advance the interests of the whole of society.

From Smith's perspective, the eighteenth century was a time when most Americans still acknowledged and revered a providential God whom they believed oversaw the distribution of the planet's resources and seemed to be using a version of trickle-down economics to do it. But in the twenty-first century, the invisible hand is quickly being replaced with the clenched fist of Boesky-inspired corporate capitalists who want to "take it all." This alarming trend is strikingly demonstrated by a more predatory version of capitalism that has gained acceptance among some Silicone Valley tech companies. Many people are concerned that the gathering and selling of massive amounts of customers' personal data is a capitalistic enterprise that is exploitative by design and is putting the public at ever increasing risk.

For star people, capitalism and the wealth it can produce does not represent an opportunity to better serve others, but to gain greater power over them. For that reason, the marriage relationship between capitalism and democracy can quickly become competitive and abusive in a star society. If either partner fails in their duty, they may take the other one down with them. Or as Supreme Court Justice Louis Brandeis once put it, "We must make our choice. We may have democracy, or we may have wealth concentrated in the hands of a few, but we can't have both." Choose incorrectly, and we may lose both freedom and prosperity.

But if both are to survive, sharing the wealth must be voluntary. Economist Milton Friedman said of Adam Smith's invisible hand concept, "it offers the possibility of cooperation without coercion," and cooperation clearly produces better and more sustainable outcomes for society.

The question is, how do we maintain a healthy relationship between democracy and capitalism so we can properly utilize the incentives they both provide for people to achieve financial self-reliance? Peter Whybrow points out that if self-interest is the engine that drives economic growth, then Adam Smith's concept of moral sentiment must serve as the braking system.

What is needed now is a sun-directed *intentional hand* that applies capitalism and free-market economics in a sun-inspired way. We need a system that is designed to maximize the strengths and minimize the weaknesses of traditional corporate capitalism.

It was President Ronald Reagan who said regarding the future of economic policies and practices in the free world, "I can't help but believe that in the future we'll see in the United States and throughout the western world, an increasing trend toward the next logical step: employee ownership. It's a path that befits a free people."

An Economic Model for a Sun Society

As a result of the Spanish Civil War that occurred between 1936 and 1939, the Basque community of Mondragon in northern Spain was in ruins and its economy destroyed. The Basque people were known for being hardworking, self-reliant people who valued independence. So, they set out to try and rebuild their community and provide employment for their people. In 1941 a young, newly-ordained Catholic priest by the name of Jose Maria Arizmendiarrieta was assigned to the village's Catholic parish. In retrospect, this may well have been an example of the intentional hand of Providence at work.

Don Jose Maria, as he was known by the villagers, had studied economics and Catholic social doctrine during his years in the seminary and came to Mondragon with the desire to create an economic system that honored democratic principles while also responding to the economic needs of the entire community. He rejected the Adam Smith approach of laissez-faire capitalism because he felt it favored the welfare of the individual over the welfare of the community. He also rejected Marxist theories of socialism which he knew had not lived up to their pretended promises of social justice and equality. Don Jose Maria understood what I mentioned earlier–that the role of sun leaders is to be shepherds, not policemen. The people must be *invited* to live sun principles, not *forced* to live them.

The priest chose to focus on the work of Robert Owens and the Rochdale Pioneers who organized the first known production cooperative in England in 1854. In 1943 he started a technical college that, unlike previous schools of this kind, was open to anyone to attend. That included women. He knew that education was the key to job creation and economic development in the Mondragon community and that everyone should be given equal access to that opportunity. In 1956 he and five graduates of the technical college started the first worker-owned production cooperative of the twentieth century. They named it ULGOR, which was an acronym made up from the surnames of the five students who began the cooperative company.

What began initially as a single industrial cooperative making a few simple household appliances, soon began to prosper and expand. Several more industrial cooperatives soon followed. Within a few years the founders had created their own cooperative bank to help finance the startup of additional cooperative companies and a research company to help develop new and improved products for the cooperatives to manufacture. Cooperative schools, grocery stores, construction companies, hospitals, an insurance company, a retirement and social services program, and many additional industrial cooperatives were added to the growing list of ULGOR affiliates.

The cooperative structure provides each worker the opportunity to buy into the cooperative business they work for and to own one share of the company. No outside investors are allowed, which eliminates the potential conflict between the best interests of investors (return on investment) and the best interests of the workers (protecting jobs.) The board of directors, general managers, and supervisors are elected from among the rank-and-file workers by a fully democratic, one-worker-one-vote system.

Directors receive no additional pay for their service on the board. Entry-level assembly worker salaries are equal to or above the average for similar positions in privately owned companies. Positions requiring higher levels of education and skill make higher salaries, but the highest paid executive makes no more on average than five times the amount of the lowest paid worker.

Company profits are distributed with ten percent going to the local community for schools and other community improvements, twenty percent going into a reserve account for the co-op to use to grow the business and carry it through difficult financial times, and seventy percent is divided among the workers and added to their share of capital holdings of the company.

When workers retire, their share is bought back by the co-op (remember, no outside investors allowed) and they receive their accumulated capital holdings through the co-op's retirement program where their capital savings have been responsibly managed and conservatively invested.

The workers are self-reliant and proactive. They are not dependent upon a taxpayer-funded retirement program that is overseen by government bureaucrats who fill the fantasy social welfare "trust fund" with IOUs that shift the financial burdens of one generation onto future generations.

Not only do the workers share in the profits of the company, they share in the sacrifices as well. If the business faces hard times, the co-op members voluntarily vote to reduce their salaries when necessary. On rare occasions when a company needs to reduce its workforce, workers are trained to serve in positions in other ULGOR-affiliated co-ops that are doing better. This policy is the embodiment of the ULGOR slogan, "In unity is survival."

But it is about more than just survival. This sun approach to business offers workers dignity, mutual respect, and security. But that's not all.

Multiple studies of residents of the Italian-American community of Roseto, Pennsylvania revealed that there are also health benefits to the members of a community where the welfare of the family and the community is the focus, rather than just the welfare of the individual. This emphasis also reduces stress, improves the quality of life, and extends the duration of life for community members.

Because the cooperative model offers shared ownership and shared decision-making authority, cooperative businesses can also implement needed changes quickly. This means they can compete more effectively in the global marketplace than some of their non-worker-owned neighbors. They are also less likely to be affected by the culture of greed and self-interest that is common among many of today's corporate executives and company stockholders.

The twin sun principles of freedom and responsibility are two of the foundational pillars of successful cooperative businesses. In Mondragon, the people are free to join the cooperative or not. But once they do, they are no longer the average under-involved, wage-earning employee: they are committed partners. They are now responsible for the success or failure of the business. They have "skin in the game." But more importantly, they have heart and soul in the game. This results in a deeper and more personal connection among the business owners/workers rather than the us vs. them mentality that is often the case with the traditional management vs. labor culture of corporate capitalism.

The mission statement for the Mondragon cooperatives is, "To create wealth within the society through entrepreneurial development and job creation." The primary goal is the creation and sustaining of jobs, not just making a profit. And they are invested in the welfare of the whole community, not just their workers. That means that the workers live and work in the communities where the businesses are located. The cooperative businesses engage with and support each other. The workers never have to worry that the business they work for will suddenly shut down and move to another location like other companies commonly do who have used up their tax incentives and are moving on to financially greener pastures.

Over sixty years later, the Mondragon Corporation is the largest cooperative organization in the world. It includes over one hundred and twenty-five independent ULGOR-affiliated companies with facilities located in over twenty-two countries around the world. They employ over 84,000 members, generating over $25 billion dollars annually in revenues.

Fear: One of the Greatest Obstacles to Success

One of the biggest challenges the Mondragon cooperatives are currently facing as they expand globally is the reluctance of some workers to join the cooperative. In countries with histories of corporate and political corruption, it is hard for the people to trust any corporation or government to keep its promises. Rather than contributing part of their salary to purchase a share in the company with the promise of greater job security and future financial benefits, some workers want all of their earnings now. But as I explained previously with the HOUSE model, developing greater intimacy and trust requires a willingness to experience increased vulnerability.

My advice to those reluctant workers is similar to the counsel I have given my children as they began dating and looking for that "someone special" with whom they could create a loving, trusting, and committed family relationship. When you find a "company" that is founded on sun principles, that creates a high-quality product or service that excites and inspires you, that has a clear vision for its future and possesses the knowledge and motivation to achieve it, that is loyal to its people and treats them all as valued equals, and that has a proven track record of making good on its promises—don't let it out of your sight! Don't be afraid to take the plunge, to become an active partner in the relationship, and to work hard to produce the outcomes you are both committed to.

Leaders Worth Following

Several American companies have joined the worker-owned business revolution. They come in all shapes and sizes, including companies like United States Steel Corporation, Isthmus Engineering & Manufacturing in

Wisconsin, Evergreen Cooperative Laundry and Ohio Solar in Ohio, and Arizmendi Bakery in the San Francisco Bay area. These companies attract people who have chosen to stop complaining about the problems with corporate capitalism and socialism and instead are creating a better alternative.

A sun-inspired business provides a supportive work environment, honors the needs of the workers as much as it honors the needs of its investors, and forms collaborative and sustainable relationships with the community and the environment in which it is located. It also contributes to increased levels of oxytocin among all the people involved.

As I mentioned in chapter four, increased levels of oxytocin produce increased levels of trust and trustworthiness among people. Research by economist and neuroscientist Paul Zak has concluded that in countries where there are increased levels of trustworthiness among the people, those in government are also more trusting and trustworthy. Therefore, there are fewer restrictions placed on businesses because they are run in a trustworthy manner. Where there are fewer restrictions, more financial transactions occur. Where more financial transactions occur, greater wealth is created. Where greater wealth is created, poverty is alleviated. Voilà! *That* is the sun way of viewing money, and *that* is how capitalism will be saved and greater income equality achieved. I think Robert Reich would agree.

But it all hinges on whether the belief espoused by Adam Smith and the founders of this nation continues to be true: that the American people (and hopefully all people) still possess a moral sentiment that causes them to be conscious of the needs of others, and to be conscientious in applying sun principles on their behalf.

There is a practical side to this altruistic philosophy as well. Consider it this way: most people pursue the accumulation of wealth to provide economic security against future difficulties, foreseen and unforeseen. What would be a better form of security? Having a million dollars stuffed in a mattress that could disappear at any time, or sharing some of that million dollars with hundreds of struggling families, most of whom would be willing to share whatever they have to help you during your times of trouble? Think of Jimmy Stewart in *It's A Wonderful Life.* True security–temporal and spiritual–can only be found in a sun community.

The Wisdom of Searocket

Like the benevolent nursing plant described in chapter three, the Mondragon cooperative is the Searocket of the economic world. Its altruistic philosophy strengthens families, builds communities, and promotes a culture of compassion, mutual respect, shared sacrifice, and brotherly love around the globalized world of today. Many more people seem to recognize that this approach may be the solution to our global economic woes. We'll see what the future holds.

For sun people, the future is as bright as they choose to make it. I believe that sun people, living sun lives, committed to sun marriages, raising sun families, participating as sun citizens in a sun system of government, and running sun businesses can and will change the world for the better for future generations. It all begins with a commitment to learn, love, and live sun principles.

Your activity is to consider ways that you can participate in this process by introducing sun principles into your socio-economic environment. Discuss with your family the role of money in your lives, how much constitutes "sufficient for your needs," and some simple ways you may be able to help others to more successfully meet their needs as well.

CHAPTER 8 Preview

Many of the world's scientists were unsatisfied recently with the way the exact mass of a kilogram is determined. They were concerned that the platinum-iridium cylinder protected under three layers of glass in a vault in Paris, France which has served as the world's standard for all measurements of mass for one hundred and thirty years, had lost a few atoms–*atoms*–of mass since it was forged in 1889. On November 16, 2018, in Versailles, France, representatives from fifty-seven countries voted to change the way a kilogram is measured in favor of using the Planck Constant: a theoretical number (6.62607015 x 10^{-34}) that is based on natural laws and used in quantum mechanics. Even though there continues to be a tiny degree of uncertainty about the accuracy of this number, scientists consider it to be the most reliable means of determining the exact mass of a kilogram. No longer will the world depend on a physical object that can change over time to determine the exact measurements of smart phone components, pharmaceutical products, and sensitive scientific instruments. Now we will have a permanent, unchangeable method of measurement that will apply for all times and for all people, throughout the universe. Some scientists see this discovery as a pivotal point in human history. Uh…OK?

When I read about this announcement, I couldn't help but think of Cicero and his definition of Natural Law as "one eternal and unchangeable law that will be valid in all nations and at all times." It seems puzzling to me that so many people today are obsessed with knowing–with *absolute* certainty–how the temporal world operates, and at the same time show such little concern for understanding the principles that govern the eternal world that awaits us all. All truth matters, but some much more than others.

Can truth always be identified with empirical accuracy and certainty? What is our responsibility to truth once we find it? How do we recognize untruth? Why is it important to recognize both?

Although many have popularized phrases like "his truth," "her truth," "my truth," or "your truth," truth is not determined by a solipsistic evaluation of the world around us. There is only *the truth*. The nearer we get to God, the closer we get to truth. The reverse is also true: the further we stray from God, the more likely we are to encounter and embrace untruth.

Sun people are committed to the pursuit of truth–the whole truth, and nothing but the truth–in all areas of knowledge. This chapter explains the importance of that pursuit and the dangers that occur for everyone when we allow untruth to infect our thoughts and influence our behaviors.

CHAPTER 8

FINDING TRUTH: LIFE'S GREAT ADVENTURE

● ●❙❙ ❙ ❙ ❙ ❙ ❙

T he challenge that confronts anyone who has decided to pursue the path to sun-hood is knowing how to distinguish between truth and error so we can accurately remove error from the various aspects of our lives. But as Alexander Solzhenitsyn tried to remind a somewhat-indifferent 1978 audience at Harvard, truth can be hard to recognize at times and equally hard to retain once you find it. It can be as elusive and hard to hold onto as a wiggling fish on a hook; as subtle and nuanced as a Mozart symphony; or as simple and obvious as one of Aesop's fables. And like diamonds in a cavernous mine, every bit of it has infinite value and requires dedicated effort to find.

Encountering truth can be exhilarating on some occasions and humiliating on other occasions. Like a telescope, it can allow us to see and understand wonderful things "afar off" that we never before imagined. Like a magnifying glass, it will also expose all of our blemishes and flaws.

Finding truth and applying it in our lives are processes that require honesty, patience, and diligence. Unless we are confident that the principles we each carry with us on our belief windows are true, we will inevitably make wrong choices and act in ways that will produce negative results for ourselves and others.

The Puzzle of Truth

Like pieces of a grand puzzle, all truth fits together perfectly, seamlessly, without disagreement, into a great and complete whole. This includes all areas of life and all fields of knowledge. When free of any particle of untruth, each piece will fit snugly into its position in the truth puzzle.

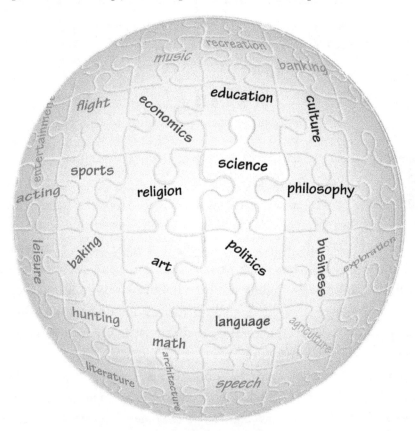

Figure 8.1 The Puzzle of Truth

But since there is opposition in all things in this world, you will find varying degrees of both truth and error in science, religion, business, politics, philosophy, education, agriculture, law, entertainment, art, music...in literally every area of knowledge and every field of endeavor. But if we are paying attention, we should be able to recognize even the subtle differences.

> *All truth fits together perfectly, seamlessly, without disagreement, into one great whole.*

For example, think of some of the art, music, movies, and other forms of entertainment you have seen and heard recently. How did they make you feel? Light-hearted, hopeful, uplifted, inspired…or dark, aggressive, debased, and discouraged?

Consider also the way political campaigns are run. Some candidates address real solutions to our social problems and instill patriotism, cooperation, and hope into the lives of citizens. Others engage in rancorous and ugly debate, employ character assassination, and promote endless contention. Some systems of government promote freedom, equality, community, and responsibility while others promote division, suspicion, competition, and subjugation.

Some business practices are honest and ethical, while others are deceptive and corrupt. Some philosophies inspire people to develop the best of human qualities, while others encourage selfishness, immorality, violence, and fear. Some farmers grow crops in ways that protect the quality of the soil, air, and water and that produce healthy foods for consumers. Others use methods that have been shown to cause harm to plants, animals, and people, or that produce food of questionable nutritional value.

An engineer can design a building with features that will create a stable, safe, and durable structure, or in ways that skimp on structural integrity to increase profit margins, creating a building that will likely collapse under moderate stress. Some lawyers use their knowledge of the law to exact justice and to protect the innocent, while others use it to rob justice by colluding with the guilty.

As we go through life, we will encounter the many competing ideas and practices that represent the varying degrees of truth and error that exist in the world. Like the currency investigator from Scotland Yard, our life experiences will provide opportunities for all of us to become more familiar with truth so we may more successfully spot and reject the many counterfeits that have been introduced repeatedly throughout history. Here's an example of how this may occur.

One generation of people who have lived under favorable conditions brought about by the hard work and integrity of their ancestors, now begin to be less diligent about maintaining those values and practices. They start to get a little proud, greedy, and self-indulgent. Then someone comes along and tells them what they want to hear—that sun people are deluded and boring and star people have lots more fun. So that generation further dilutes the truth in the culture by inviting even more untruth into it—like the ancient Romans did to their currency. Over two centuries they increasingly adulterated and devalued their gold and silver coins by replacing some of the gold and silver with base metals until the coins were eventually worthless.

Each successive generation adds to the accumulation of untruth until many of the people begin to lose the ability to recognize and appreciate even the most basic and obvious truths. Then a bunch of capricious power-seekers come along and mount an impressive propaganda campaign to convince the people that what was obviously wrong for prior generations, is somehow right today. Unless there are enough courageous sun people willing to combat the invasion of untruth, the civilization begins to die.

Parasites provide a good metaphorical example of this process. Once parasites enter a plant, animal, or person they begin to multiply and take over the body. They eventually use up all of the resources and in the end, they kill the host, not realizing that they are also dooming themselves. That's how cancer works.

Sun people take precautions to try and protect the body from this invasion. Moon people sometimes allow cancerous untruths to be introduced because they are not paying very close attention to their general physical, emotional, intellectual, or spiritual health. They don't recognize the warning signs of approaching danger. Or they may want to justify some unhealthy behaviors and to believe that "a little cancer won't hurt" and that their immune system is strong enough to handle it. Or, maybe they just want to believe that life is not worth living if we are not willing to take some self-indulgent risks. Whatever the reasoning, over time, untruth begins to metastasize.

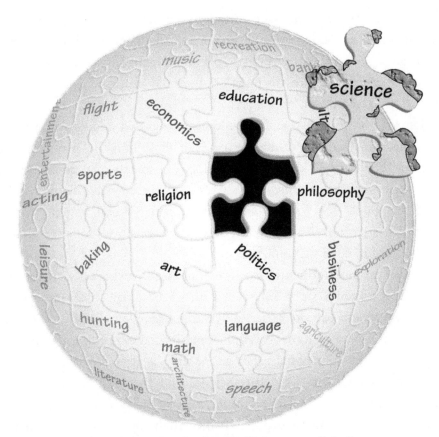

Figure 8.2 The Puzzle of Truth with Cancerous Untruth

Continuing with the puzzle metaphor, if we attempt to return a piece to the puzzle that now has cancerous untruth attached to it, it won't fit. There is only room for pure, unadulterated truth. In order for that piece to fit back into the puzzle there are only two options to solve this puzzle piece problem. We must either:

1. Remove any untruth from the puzzle piece until it fits naturally and comfortably back into its proper position; or
2. Trim off some of the truth from the neighboring pieces in order to accommodate the untruth, and thereby spread the problem.

How many times have past civilizations repeated this destructive cycle of starting out with good intentions, but then allowing greed, violence, sexual immorality, idolatry, corruption in government, pride, the lust for power, and other cancerous untruths to gain a foothold in the culture and spread until they destroy the entire society?

Untruth on some pieces can be easily recognized and removed before it spreads. But for some others, untruths in those domains may be harder to spot. They can quickly multiply and spread to others areas of life. For example, let's consider the pieces of the truth puzzle called *science* and *religion*.

In her book *The White Album*, author Joan Didion wrote, "We tell ourselves stories in order to live." We rely on those stories to make sense of our lives and to cope with uncertainty.

Two of the most influential stories in human history have been the science story and the religion story. The science story is based on observations of the natural world and educated guesses by various people trying to understand and explain what they have observed. Sometimes they're correct, sometimes they're not. What is accepted as fact at one time, is often proven to be fallacy at another. As Oxford University science and theology professor Alister McGrath reminds us, "Science is on a journey, and has not yet reached its final destination." And as experience has taught us, if we are not paying attention to the road signs and making regular course corrections along the way, this journey may take us in the wrong direction.

As more scientists test and retest their conclusions and make more detailed observations, they should be better at separating truth from error. But the opposite can also occur. Faulty conclusions and intentional distortions of information can cause errors to become part of a culture, and scientific truths to be lost over time. What Copernicus and Galileo learned in the sixteenth and seventeenth centuries about Earth's location in the universe was known in ancient Egypt and ancient America many centuries before, but that knowledge was lost to much of the world during the Dark Ages.

Sometimes it happens because moon people are more vulnerable to superstition or are anchored to one particular belief and are slow to change their opinions because of pride or self-interest. And sometimes it happens because star people just make stuff up and want others to believe that it is true. One errant conclusion based on untruth often leads to another and another and so on.

While science focuses on the natural and observable world, religion often focuses on the spiritual and unseen world. For that reason, some religious stories have the potential to include a lot of elements that may be difficult to scientifically test and prove. But that doesn't make them false.

There have been times when religion and science were in total harmony with each other and there have been times when they were not. True religion and true science are always in harmony because *all* truth fits together seamlessly and in perfect accord. The problems arise when one of three things happens to these puzzle pieces:

1. Untruth becomes attached to religion.
2. Untruth becomes attached to science.
3. Untruth becomes attached to both.

At times, religion and science have both been guilty of getting in each other's way because there have been various times when untruth has been present in both. In Galileo's time, it was religion that was somewhat in the dark on some scientific issues. In the days of Immanuel Kant and Charles Darwin there were inaccuracies present in both.

As a result, we now live in a time when some people believe that religion and science are incompatible. That science is about reason, and religion is about faith. That science deals with concrete facts, and religion deals with ethereal concepts. That scientific hypotheses and theories can all be tested and proven or disproven, and that spiritual principles cannot. That science is infallible, and religion is irrational.

But science can be irrational too. I once heard a lecture by scientist Donald W. Patten addressing the debate between evolutionism and creationism. Evolution is said to occur as a result of a long series of spontaneous, unpredictable, and random changes in an organism. Those changes are referred to as mutations. Zoologist Dr. Bolton Davidheiser has estimated that only about one in a thousand mutations is favorable to an organism and that it would take approximately 100,000 favorable mutations in a row, for a new species to develop.

Do the math. In estimating the probability of a new species evolving, the odds of it happening are one in …let me give you Dr. Davidheiser's comparison. The estimated number of electrons in the universe is an unfathomably large number that takes up two lines on a word processor. According to Dr. Davidheiser, the mathematical probability of just one new species evolving is one in a number that takes up every line on an entire page…times *1500 pages*. That's irrational.

The truth is that there are questions that science can answer and questions it can't. Some might say that the same can be said of religion, though in reality, true religion incorporates all other truths. Psychologist Dr. Allen Bergin taught, "Transcendent spiritual truths are real, though they cannot always be empirically observed, replicated, or verified using scientific methods. The Church does not reject empirical ways of knowing, but it does reject the view that empirical knowledge is the *only* valid source of truth, or that data gathering alone can lead to an understanding of humans and the universe."

While science strives to be precise and accurate, it is also provisional, limited, and vulnerable to manipulation. Religion is similarly vulnerable to manipulation and adulteration. But when Richard Dawkins and other members of the New Atheists club declare that science has proven that God does not exist, that there is no life after death, or that Adam and Eve never lived, they are the ones being irrational. Science has proven none of those statements, so scientists have no business making them. Then they compound the error by enlisting the authority of "unerring science" to imply that their opinions are somehow beyond question and are empirically proven.

Far too many scientists routinely violate their own rules when they make statements that are not based on scientifically tested and proven hypotheses and thereby invite error onto the puzzle piece of science. Those errors then conflict with truths found in some surrounding pieces and contend for space in the truth puzzle. People have to be sufficiently educated in many areas of knowledge if they are to discern what constitutes truth and what constitutes error. But since some spiritual knowledge can only be obtained using spiritual methods, sun people understand that both faith *and* reason are essential to the pursuit of truth.

There were no first-century social scientists on the scene to conduct a qualitative study and interview the thousands of eye-witnesses who saw the face, heard the voice, and touched the resurrected body of the Redeemer nearly 2000 years ago. And no one is going to get a DNA sample to examine any time soon. But geneticists have traced the origins of human DNA back to one man and one woman. Over time, science will likely be able to substantiate more of the events chronicled in the Bible.

But can science answer life's biggest questions—where we came from, the purpose of life, and what awaits us after death? No, but religion can. Anyone committed to the pursuit of truth must be willing to include all areas of knowledge in their search and to resolve apparent conflicts when they encounter them. The challenge for sun people is to differentiate between what we know and what we don't know; between truth and sophistry; between revealed knowledge and conjecture; between what invites people to do good, and what entices them to do evil. This requires a commitment to finding and applying truth, regardless of the difficulty or costs.

As the puzzle indicates, the more untruth we allow to attach to one area of knowledge, the more likely it is to spread to the surrounding areas. If that happens, the puzzle of truth can quickly become a cancerous collection of lies and distortions. And people will be making important decisions based on those lies and distortions.

Sun people must be willing to do the hard work of fearlessly examining and, when appropriate, challenging the assertions of the philosophical, scientific, religious, political, and business communities. They must be willing to defend truth and to risk rejection. Moon people will likely bypass the opportunity to engage in such a painstaking effort. Star people will discourage, mock, and harass any people who do accept the challenge. That's OK. Do it anyway. Conflict is inevitable, so prepare for it. But remember that when conflict occurs, the emphasis for sun people is not on attacking star ideologies or maligning star people, but on teaching and defending sun principles and policies. A sun example is the best way to demonstrate the differences and to assist the undecided in choosing for themselves.

A Community of Truth Seekers

What would happen if you assembled a room full of sun people of differing ages, backgrounds, cultures, political affiliations, genders, religions, sexual orientations, shoe sizes, IQs, incomes, eye colors…whatever categories you choose, and gave them a list of various social problems that needed solutions? Would the conversation turn into an acrimonious and fruitless debate that would only increase the likelihood that the problems would never be resolved? No. Because of their shared commitment to finding truth, sun people–despite their differences–would find sufficient consensus to agree on a course of action to address the problems. And because of their differences, they would discover that each person brings additional knowledge and experience into the conversation.

Members of sun groups would quickly recognize those among their ranks who possess the greatest levels of light and truth, and those would be chosen as their leaders. A community based on sun principles with a core of sun leaders could successfully identify true principles in many areas of knowledge and incorporate them into their lives and into their laws. They could sift through the opposing ideologies that exist among even the most conflicted groups of people in today's world and remove the cancerous untruths.

Sun people seek unity amid diversity. The Latin phrase "E Pluribus Unum" that appears on the Great Seal of the United States and on many coins, is one of their mottoes. It means, "Out of many, one." And what is the force that unites and binds diverse communities together? It is a mutual commitment to sun principles and practices.

Sun people will always seek and invite harmony, even in the midst of cacophony. One remarkable example of this commitment occurred on Christmas Eve in 1914 when a few German, French, and British soldiers fighting in World War I were able to bring peace–albeit briefly–to one of history's bloodiest battlefields when they crossed that battlefield and joined together to sing Christmas carols and share their food rations. The peace may have only lasted a couple of days, but the memory of their sun efforts will never be forgotten.

Even the sometimes-contentious dogmas of religion, science, and politics can be reconciled in a sun community. That is because sun people will be able to recognize sun, moon, and star elements within these domains, and integrate the sun components of each.

Justice Louis Brandeis once wrote, "Sunlight is said to be the best of disinfectants." The cancerous growth of untruth that has become attached to many areas of knowledge can only be removed when illuminated by the light of truth. Because of their familiarity with light and truth and their commitment to applying it in all areas of their lives, sun people are the ones best able to do this.

But because they are in the minority and so few of them tend to aggressively pursue positions of power and authority in the world, they are facing increased opposition from other less-enlightened, power-seeking members of society who want to continue the proliferation of error and evil.

The solution is...*we need more sun people!* We need more sun leaders and sun followers at every level of society. Wouldn't it be great to someday see a huge street rally taking place in cities around the world where all of the participants are chanting:

"What do we need?"
"Sun people!"
"When do we need them?"
"NOW!"

Your activity is to promote the pursuit of truth. Choose an area of interest where increased understanding of truth would benefit you and other people in your home, at work, at school, or at church. Do your homework. If you are better informed in that area, you will also be better able to recognize untruths. Then share what you have learned with others. Don't waste time on trivial issues. Focus on something that matters. The world is desperately seeking leaders who possess truth in the areas that matter most.

CHAPTER 9 Preview

I have described the roles, responsibilities, and challenges we face in life and how our choices will shape our destinies in this life, and in the next. An essential part of this process is deciding which groups we will affiliate with. Group selection will significantly influence your personal as well as our societal outcomes. Once you are aware of the outcomes these groups produce, and you have made a commitment to the kind of person you want to become, the next step is to align yourself with other people who share the same commitment.

Time is short. Game time is approaching. Choose the right team. Assemble your teammates. Select the best coaches. Prepare yourself physically, emotionally, and spiritually. The contest will be intense, but be assured, a sun victory awaits all those who are sincerely committed to it.

MAKING THE CHOICE THAT MATTERS MOST

C onfrontation requires a decision. As we go through life we will be constantly confronted with examples of light and darkness, truth and error, good and evil. All of these experiences will require us to decide which direction on the path of light we will take and what kind of person we will become.

As we encounter the competing ideologies and beliefs present in the world today, these questions will repeatedly arise:

- Which ones are true and which ones are false?
- How will I know?
- Who can I trust to help me understand what my choices are and to choose wisely?
- Why is life so hard?!

Dr. Hugh Nibley was considered by his peers to be one of the brightest scholars of the twentieth century. He was most recognized for his vast

322 | SHINE Brighter

knowledge of ancient cultures, languages, and religious texts. In commenting about his life's work, he once wrote:

> *Those who ask, "What is the meaning of life?" and get no reassuring answers have been known to conclude that the whole thing is a cruel joke. "If we are supposed to find the answers," they say, "why are they hidden?" Precisely because we are supposed to find them, which means we must look for them; the treasure is buried to keep us digging; the pearl of great price lies glittering in the depths where we must seek it out. Treasure hunts can be both instructive and fun, provided the clues are not too discouraging, and kind Providence has strewn the most exciting and obvious clues all over the place. It is only when we choose to ignore them, like the pigheaded constable in the English murder mystery, blind to all but his own opinion, that we court frustration and cynicism.*

There will be times when we are faced with challenges and opposition in life. Times when tragedies will occur. Times when we will teeter on the precipice of disaster. Or times when we are just unhappy with life and are finally ready to seriously contemplate the true meaning and purpose of our existence. When that happens, there seems to be a natural tendency for people to look in the same direction…up…into the sky and beyond the thin layer of atmosphere that surrounds our little planet. Something inside each of us seems to know that there is something that lies beyond. Or more importantly, someone. And when we look up, we see the sun, the moon, and the stars and are reminded that God has placed these heavenly bodies in front of us to serve as constant reminders of who we are, where we came from, why we are here, and how our choices will determine our destinies.

Adding to our treasure-trove of light and truth requires optimistic and persistent effort. So, don't be discouraged. Remember, we asked for this opportunity. Seek and you *will* find. But also remember, we *find* what we *seek*. If we seek light, truth, virtue, love, and forgiveness, we will find them. If we seek darkness, violence, immorality, and contention, we will find them too.

The Path of We

I have explained that becoming a sun person is not a solo activity. In fact, reaching the pinnacle of progression, the heights of enlightenment, the summits of happiness and joy, cannot be done alone. It is only through your relationships with others as a child, a spouse, a parent, a family member, a neighbor, and a citizen that you are able to perform and perfect the behaviors that will make you a sun person; that is, sharing light, truth, love, and positive influence with others, while also encouraging them to do the same for you.

The time and effort we invest during our formative years toward becoming a sun individual will prepare us to become a sun spouse. By doing so, we will also attract other people who are looking for a sun relationship. Our experiences as sun spouses will prepare us to become sun parents, and our experiences as sun parents in a family community, will prepare us to become sun citizens of a larger community. It's a linear progression—each stage preparing us for the next.

We Learn and Grow at Each Other's Expense

For me, writing this book has been a very intense reflective process. I have been reminded that we often learn as much from our poor choices as we do from our good ones. That means that we all learn and grow in life at each other's expense. We make choices that affect others—often in negative ways. We are then responsible to correct those mistakes and do better in the future. As simplistic as that may sound, even brilliant minds have come to the same conclusion.

Near the end of his life, Aldous Huxley wrote, "It is a bit embarrassing to have been concerned with the human problem all one's life and find at the end that one has no more to offer by way of advice than, try to be a little kinder."

We are all guilty of making life unpleasant for others at times. We seek their forgiveness for our mistakes, and they in turn, seek our forgiveness for theirs. That is why the two most important qualities we are here to learn and develop, the qualities most associated with God, are the abilities to love and to forgive. These are among the defining qualities of sun people.

Unfortunately, those are not the qualities being promoted by many in the world today.

But we should not let the choices of others determine our own. Sun people may not be able to prevent others from making poor choices that will impact their lives and the lives of many others, but they do have influence. As sixteenth-century English philosopher Thomas More wrote:

> *Don't give up the ship in a storm because you cannot hold back the winds. Instead, by an indirect approach, you must strive and struggle as best you can to handle everything tactfully, and thus what you cannot turn to good, you may at least make as little bad as possible. For it is impossible to make everything good unless all men are good, and that I don't quite expect to see for quite a few years yet.*

Or as others have stated, "We may not be able to change the direction of the wind, but we can trim the sails." If you are not familiar with nautical language, to "trim" means to adjust the number and the angles of the sails. Doing this allows sailors to harness the power of the wind–even though it may be blowing in the wrong direction–to propel a ship forward in the preferred direction. The better world that was centuries away from Thomas More's perspective, may be only decades away for this generation if we learn how to trim the sails in the face of the approaching storms and still move forward. Creating a sun society is the destination, and some specific things will need to occur for that to happen.

Calling All Sun People!

Edmund Burke wrote, "When bad men combine, the good must associate; else they will fall one by one, an unpitied sacrifice in a contemptible struggle." The battle between good and evil continues, and at times it may appear that evil is winning. But as the social, economic, and political ties between nations and peoples continue to break down and conflict escalates, the ties among sun people must get stronger. As much of the world chooses conflict, individualism, and materialism, sun people must choose community and altruism.

Not an *Atlas Shrugged*, John-Galt-version of community where select people gather to a sheltered and secretly sequestered idyllic village hidden away in the recesses of the Rocky Mountains. Nor a utopian Wakanda-like community protected by an impenetrable force field. Instead, it will be something resembling a Bedouin tent–a place of refuge set up in the midst of a spiritually-parched, desert world. This tent will be capable of unlimited expansion. By stitching on more fabric and adding additional stakes that expand the skirts of the tent, it will accommodate greater numbers of people seeking shelter from the encroaching darkness and violence of the world around them. It will be a gathering place for those who have decided to join others in the dedicated pursuit of light and truth.

For a visual of what I am describing, look at the cover of this book. There are eight phases of the moon depicted. The four to the left of center are each progressively increasing in light (waxing), while the four to the right are losing light and increasing in darkness (waning). There will be a time when undecided moon people will need to choose which direction they will take in life–toward the sun, or further away from it. That means the gulf between good and evil will expand and both will become more easily recognizable. As the parable of the wheat and the tares teaches us, good people will get better, and bad people will get worse.

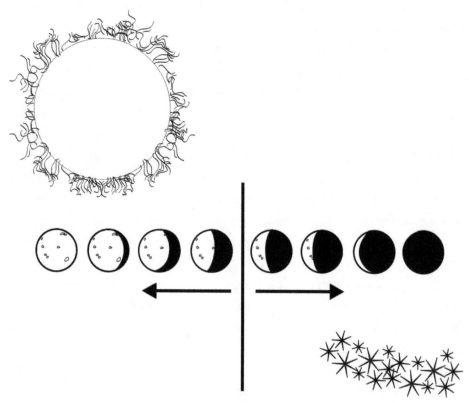

Figure 9.1 The Division of the Wheat and the Tares

As that happens and conditions worsen in the world, sun people will begin to increase their efforts to seek each other out, forming an ecumenical global community based on shared sun values. They will become increasingly adept at discriminating between good and evil and magnifying the practice of sun values. In the face of mounting opposition, they will become stronger, more resolute, and more enlightened in all areas of their lives.

Sun people are willing to stand **out**, so others will recognize what they stand **for**. And if others want in their lives, what sun people have in theirs, they will know where to find it. Sun people will model the principles and practices of sun living by creating a social order based on love, respect, morality, equality, freedom, hard work, and responsibility.

*Sun people are willing to stand **out**, so others will recognize what they stand **for**.*

Inspired Mind sun leaders will create school systems that provide sun-quality educational opportunities. They will create businesses that provide employment for sun people, many of whom will become ostracized because of their sun beliefs. They will create social media platforms that facilitate communication and connection among sun people, and that offer information and inspiration to others who seek to know more about sun principles and practices. They will organize a communications network that provides accurate and reliable information to sun communities, offers sun-quality entertainment for families, and that combats the sophistry and propaganda of the world around them.

As I indicated in chapter six, this social order will not come into existence through the use of force or coercion nor by the mere application of reason and intellect, but by divine invitation and direction, and through a voluntary commitment to sun principles.

These are the "fruit" by which sun people will be recognized; the kernels of wheat described in the parable. Yet, as farmers know all too well, when desirable fruit-bearing plants and weeds grow together in the same space, they begin to compete for the resources in the soil to determine which will thrive and which will die. With each passing day, the time of harvest gets nearer. Which also means, increased opposition is inevitable.

Alexander Solzhenitsyn warned us in 1978 that much of this opposition will come as the result of our continuing to place too much emphasis on individualism and materialism. He said:

> *The defense of individual rights has reached such extremes as to make society as a whole defenseless against certain individuals. It is time in the West to defend not so much human rights, as human obligations...If humanism were right in declaring that man is born to be happy, he would not be born to die. Since his body is doomed to die, his task on earth evidently must be of a more spiritual nature. It cannot be unrestrained enjoyment of everyday life. It cannot be the search for the best ways to obtain material goods and then cheerfully get the most out of them. It has to be the fulfillment of a permanent, earnest duty so that*

one's life journey may become an experience of moral growth, so that one may leave life a better human being than one started it.... **Only voluntary, inspired self-restraint can raise man above the world stream of materialism**.

Self-restraint–not eating the marshmallow–involves a commitment to something other than self-interest. David Brooks teaches his students at Yale University, "You make four great commitments in life: to a spouse and family, to a vocation, to a philosophy or faith, and to a community. How well you make and live out those commitments will determine the quality of your life."

In 2015 Pope Francis warned about the false promises of the present-day world. He said that today's world suggests that unlimited freedom in the pursuit of self-interest is the path to happiness, when it actually produces "world weariness" and a disconnection from the things that matter most.

As much as we would all like to believe that the world will eventually come to its senses on its own and gratefully embrace sun principles and establish a world order based upon them, Inspired Mind thinkers understand why this is not going to be the case. There is no system of government that will eliminate the ideological differences between sun, moon, and star people and create a cohesive community where all three kinds of people will dwell in peace and harmony. A division among the people is inevitable.

Sun people may be in the minority, but they are a powerful minority who have the powers of Heaven behind them. With that power comes a solemn responsibility and obligation–that permanent, earnest duty that Solzhenitsyn spoke of. **It is to pursue the path of light and truth and to light the way for others to follow.**

That does not mean that sun people want to deny others the freedom to choose their own path and their own destinies, even if that choice is self-destruction. But it *is* about protecting the rights of others–especially children–to choose their paths free from the coercion, manipulation, and deception perpetrated by those who hide their star (wolf) intentions under the mantles (sheep's clothing) of the sun principles of freedom and tolerance.

So, if reading this book has caused you to reconsider your current location on the continuum of light and truth and to question the direction in which you are headed, I would suggest the following course of action–the final activity of this book.

Find a quiet place where you will not be disturbed and where you can sit and reflect on your life and your commitment to the pursuit of light and truth. Then ask yourself these questions:

- Am I ready to make a sincere and tireless effort to increase the levels of light and truth in my life, to apply those truths in all aspects of my life, and to share them with others?
- Am I willing to face whatever opposition may come as a result and to sacrifice whatever is necessary to protect and defend those truths in the darkening world around me?

If the answer is "no," then get up and move on with your life, doing your best to live by whatever levels of light and truth you are comfortable with. Then, as your circumstances in life change, and if the idea of spending your future in the company of moon or star people begins to sound less desirable, return to that same quiet place and ask yourself the same questions.

If the answer ever changes to "yes," then stand up, and start living the way sun people live. And be patient. The light will come, often when you least expect it.

And don't give up, even if you fail to meet sun standards on occasion. Remember the next time that you read the parable of the sower and the seed that the sower never suggested that hardened waysides could not be plowed and made fertile again, or that rocky ground could not be cleared and good soil added, or that thorns could not be uprooted. What was previously poor soil can be fortified and replanted. You can correct the course of your life if you have the desire to, and are willing to learn and apply sun principles.

But also remember that good soil can be neglected, used as a dumping ground for rusty cars and worn-out mattresses, and taken over by noxious weeds whose seeds have been blown in by the shifting winds of social doctrines. Diligence and vigilance are required to keep the soil both fertile, and protected. Then good seed can be sown and take root.

Regardless of how difficult the journey to sunhood may appear at times, there is hope. In his inspiring oratorio *Lamb of God*, composer Rob Gardner encourages us all to remember "that every sorrow here, is but a moment's tear," and the day is approaching when the tears of all sun people will be joyfully wiped away.

And so, my friend, life presents you with a monumental decision. A decision that will shape your life and determine your destiny. Sun, moon, or star. The choice is yours.

Choose wisely.

Shine brighter.

Choose the SON.

ABOUT THE AUTHOR

D
r. Fred Dodini is a therapist, life coach, and family life educator who resides in Indianapolis, Indiana. He has enjoyed a diversity of life experiences with careers in the entertainment industry, business, and behavioral health. For information regarding workshops, lectures, and podcasts, Dr. Dodini can be contacted at: thereare3kindsofpeople@gmail. com or through Morgan James Publishing, 5 Penn Plaza, 23rd Floor, New York, NY, 10001, (212) 655-5470. For a complimentary list of book references and chapter notes, please contact Dr. Dodini at the same email address.

AFTERWORD

My wife and I are the parents of 10 children. That means, before the end of this century we could feasibly have more than 300 descendants. Maybe even 400. That's a lot of people–people to whom I feel a significant obligation. So, I've been thinking about what counsel I might offer to my posterity that will help them navigate through the turbulent waters of life, especially life in the destiny-shaping and increasingly-troubled 21st century. That's one of the reasons I've written this book.

In addition to my posterity, I also wanted my audience to include the thousands of people I have worked with over the years as a therapist and educator as well as the many millions of other truth pilgrims in the world whom I will never meet. So, if after reading this book you feel it contains insights that you would like to share with the people you love most, please do. If that happens, I will feel that I have accomplished my goal.

"I have tried to assemble a collection of the best books to help my children successfully navigate the complexities and opportunities of life. I am delighted to add Dr. Dodini's book to that list."
–Ryan P., JD, MBA.

A free ebook edition is available with the purchase of this book.

To claim your free ebook edition:

1. Visit MorganJamesBOGO.com
2. Sign your name CLEARLY in the space
3. Complete the form and submit a photo of the entire copyright page
4. You or your friend can download the ebook to your preferred device

Print & Digital Together Forever.

Snap a photo   Free ebook   Read anywhere